Critical Concerns
in Transfer Pricing
and Practice

Wagdy M. Abdallah

Westport, Connecticut
London

Library of Congress Cataloging-in-Publication Data

Abdallah, Wagdy M. (Wagdy Moustafa)
    Critical concerns in transfer pricing and practice / Wagdy M. Abdallah.
        p. cm.
    Includes bibliographical references and index.
    ISBN 1–56720–561–5 (alk. paper)
        1. Transfer pricing. 2. Intangible property—Valuation. 3. International
business—Taxation. I. Title
    HD62.45.A237 2004
    658.8'16—dc22   2004044378

British Library Cataloguing in Publication Data is available.

Library of Congress Catalog Card Number: 2004044378
ISBN: 1–56720–561–5

First published in 2004

Praeger Publishers, 88 Post Road West, Westport, CT 06881
An imprint of Greenwood Publishing Group, Inc.
www.praeger.com

Printed in the United States of America

The paper used in this book complies with the
Permanent Paper Standard issued by the National
Information Standards Organization (Z39.48–1984)

10 9 8 7 6 5 4 3 2 1

To my wife for her love, support, and understanding;
and to the memory and soul of my parents

Contents

Tables and Figures

TABLES

FIGURES

1

Introduction

For the past three decades, all multinational companies (MNCs) have experienced no business function that goes so deeply into nearly all business operations—including manufacturing, marketing, management, and financing—as international transfer pricing. For MNCs, international transfer pricing decisions have great impact on their international operations all over the world, directly affecting their global revenues and profits, and can help or limit an MNC's ability to operate, manage, and utilize its economic resources on a global basis for the purpose of achieving its ultimate goals. Moreover, transfer pricing is considered one of the most important as well as most complicated business issues in the world. This complexity is compounded when transfer pricing is combined with e-commerce and intangible assets' cross-border business transactions.

As globalization and Internet technology expand so quickly, tax authorities worldwide are paying close attention to transfer pricing issues and are trying to change their tax regulations and rules at a fast pace, which can mean headaches for corporate and financial executive officers of MNCs. However, the upside is that many countries are adopting a similar approach to eliminate or reduce tax abuses or tax evasion as a result of using non–arm's-length transfer pricing techniques.

As international business speeds up—accompanied by international profit manipulation—tax authorities worldwide are elevating transfer pricing to a key political priority. In the United States, transfer pricing tax regulations, under Section 482 of Internal Revenue Code, are different from those of foreign countries in many aspects, such as tax rates, tax treaties, tax bases, foreign tax credits, and taxes imposed on any profits resulting from using intercompany transfer pricing policies for goods and services crossing the border of the country. Tax authorities around the world require that prices charged for goods and services transferred between related parties be consistent with the amount that would have been charged if the uncontrolled taxpayers had engaged in the same transaction under the same conditions or circumstances. Recently, most industrialized countries have imposed new regulations that enforce strict transfer pricing requirements. Most of them have followed the lead of the IRS-U.S. as a model, adopting and enforcing similar arm's-length standards for transfer pricing by means of documentation requirements with penalties for noncompliance (Felgran and Yamada 2001).

In June 1998, the Canadian government amended its tax laws to align them with current international business and tax practices. Section 247 of the Income Tax Act describes the new transfer pricing regulations. In 1999, Revenue Canada became the Canada Customs and Revenue Agency and initiated a transformation of its operating environment to more effectively protect Canada's tax base. Section 247 includes several provisions to ensure that MNCs use the appropriate transfer pricing.

In an attempt to eliminate double taxation in connection with profit adjustments between related parties of the same group, the European Union in 1990 adopted a Transfer Pricing Convention that went into effect almost five years later. This convention applies when profits are included in the income of more than one contracting country by reason of allocations among related taxpayers in order to reflect arm's-length conditions. Competent authorities who fail to reach an agreement pursuant to their treaty's mutual agreement procedure must establish an advisory commission to deliver an opinion on elimination of the relevant double taxation. The convention allows tax authorities to ignore the commission's decision. Within six months after the commission's decision has been rendered, the competent authorities may decide to deviate from it. However, the decision is binding only if the competent authorities fail to agree otherwise, because both countries remain free to disregard the arbitrators' decision by deciding to settle the case in a completely different manner than the one stated in the Transfer Pricing Convention (Park 2002).

In light of the transfer pricing trends that have been taking place in several European countries and at the level of the Organization for Economic Cooperation and Development (OECD), since 1996 France has been carrying out a reform process that imposes new obligations on taxpayers and strengthens its tax authorities' power. In general, the

French tax authorities tend to follow the OECD Guidelines when determining in which types of cases the transfer pricing rules are to be applied. In practice, the tax authorities often use comparative methods. However, the main issue is one of justifying the method used by the multinational companies.

Among foreign countries there are great differences in many aspects of their tax regulations and laws. Developed countries such as the United States, the United Kingdom, Canada, Sweden, France, Japan, and Switzerland have different objectives in their tax structure, policies, and regulations than those of less developed countries such as Chile, Mexico, Zaire, Saudi Arabia, Bahrain, Korea, and Kuwait, among others.

Global transfer pricing for competitive advantage must achieve certain objectives for MNCs while adapting to local and international trade policies and tax regulations. Operating in the global environment makes the rules and strategies of the transfer pricing system dynamic. As many governments incorporate new tax rules and more strictly enforce current transfer price regulations, the need to develop a responsive documented transfer pricing system becomes increasingly important. Decision-makers of MNCs must continually refine components of their transfer pricing systems to reflect current and potential environmental influences.

THE CRISIS OF TRANSFER PRICING

MNCs face the dilemma of choosing the right price as they transfer goods and/or services among their own subsidiaries between two different countries with different tax rates, regulations, tariff systems, and many other factors. In general, making pricing decisions for MNCs is an important, complex, flexible, and complicated task because these decisions have a significant effect on other major functions of MNCs. Moreover, MNCs have a global reach, whereas governments—especially tax authorities—are limted by their geographic boundaries to a national border limit.

MNCs may use their own strategies, or manipulation, of transfer pricing to take advantage of differences in tax rates and other factors in different countries to reduce their global tax liability and achieve their other corporate goals. International investors often have at their disposal several alternative methods of structuring and financing their investments, arranging transactions between related parties located in different countries, and returning profits to investors. These alternatives have important tax implications, and there is considerable evidence that tax considerations strongly influence the choices that MNCs make (Hines 1999).

Overwhelming use of the Internet now plays a significant part in global business life. Presently, e-commerce is the driver of present and future developments in cross-border business transactions. However, current international tax regulations were written within the framework of national sovereignty in its tax system before the discovery of e-commerce. The rapid changes thrust upon the global business world through e-commerce are pushing every government, including the United States, to ensure its tax system integrity by closing the loopholes for either tax avoidance or tax evasion through the use of e-commerce transactions. E-commerce is considered, by many tax authorities, as a threat to revenues from traditional income and consumption tax systems (Merrill 2001). The main concern of tax authorities is that the highly mobile nature of e-commerce will lead to the significant increase of tax haven transactions that will further erode their tax base (Maguire 1999). Reports of several tax authorities, including the United States, Canada, the United Kingdom, the OECD, and many other foreign tax authorities, identified the major tax issues of e-commerce as jurisdiction, identification, information, and collection mechanisms (Boyle et al. 1999).

Transfer pricing of e-commerce transactions has not been discussed to the same extent as other important strategic business and tax issues. International transfer pricing is a subject that no MNC, regardless of size or location, can afford to ignore. The complexity of the issue might require MNCs to redefine and update their transfer pricing strategies to go with the new challenge of information technology in the new millennium. Until now, the literature on the impact of e-commerce on international transfer pricing has not been discussed to the same extent as other tax and global issues. Most research efforts of management and accounting scholars have addressed either the issue of international transfer pricing or e-commerce in the United States and different countries around the world (Abdallah 2002; Boyle et al. 1999; Burns 2000; Eccles 1985; OECD 1995 and 1997; and Tang 1997). In recent years, extended research has not been undertaken on international transfer pricing strategies that are founded on e-commerce and international taxation of the United States and foreign countries.

In 1995, the OECD identified several issues affecting transfer pricing of global e-commerce transactions and suggested that the use of the profit-split method (OECD 1995), as currently applied to the global trading of financial instruments, might be appropriate for e-commerce activity (OECD 1995). Difficulties in applying existing transfer pricing guidelines to e-commerce transactions include applying the transactional approach; establishing comparability and carrying out a functional analysis; applying traditional transaction methods; the tax treatment of integrated businesses; and determining and complying with appropriate documentation and information reporting requirements (Ibid.).

Usually associated with large decentralized MNCs and widely discussed in the management accounting and finance literature, transfer pricing issues now occupy center stage in international tax litigation and court cases over tax avoidance and evasion through manipulated transfer prices. In 1999 Ernst & Young conducted a survey of several MNCs. That survey showed that 75 percent of MNCs believed that they would be hit with a transfer-pricing audit within the next two years (Hamilton 2000). On the other hand, in the same year, the U.S Tax Court decided on three major transfer pricing cases, GAC Produce, Inc., Compaq Computer Corp, and H Group Holding (Burns 2000). The IRS won the H Group Holding and GAC cases and lost the case against Compaq (Ibid.). Therefore, MNCs should pay close attention to transfer pricing issues and think wisely about going into an Advance Pricing Agreement program with the IRS.

MNCs, tax authorities, and international organizations are at the crossroads of not being able to solve the complicated problems created by e-commerce and transfer pricing. As MNCs manage their cross-border business transactions, transfer pricing methods and strategies for e-commerce transactions may be more difficult to apply in reducing their tax liabilities and integrating their production and marketing strategies on a worldwide basis.

TRANSFER PRICING CORPORATE GOALS

Nine different corporate goals of establishing an international transfer pricing policy for MNCs' operations have been identified: reduction of income taxes, reduction of tariffs, minimization of foreign exchange risks, avoidance of conflict with host countries' governments, management of cash flows, competitiveness, performance evaluation, motivation, and goal harmonization. For the first two goals combined, as long as the tax rate differential is higher than the net effect of the tariff rate imposed by the country with the higher tax rate, the higher transfer price will always generate net savings for the MNC. However, if the higher transfer price results in showing artificial losses for the buying subsidiary, the net effect will be detrimental for the MNC as a whole.

With the fluctuations in foreign exchange rates, assets in weak currencies can be moved through the use of higher transfer prices. However, host-government intervention with or without price controls will certainly limit the MNC's use of this technique. When performance evaluation systems combine with fluctuations in foreign exchange rates, transfer pricing policies will lead to misleading and imperfect financial measures of performance. A new transfer pricing system (dollar-indexing technique) was suggested, and it is believed to help in evaluating foreign subsidiary managers performance and avoid any distorted financial results for performance evaluation.

Motivation, goal harmonization, and autonomy of foreign subsidiaries and their managers always lead to conflicting results with performance evaluation, reduction of income taxes, reduction of tariffs, and avoidance of foreign exchange risks. However, when different corporate goals lead to conflicting consequences, MNCs have to make trade-offs between achieving different objectives and must be satisfied with lower global profits when one objective has a priority over others, especially for achieving long-term goals.

METHODS OF TRANSFER PRICING

Several transfer-pricing methods that are considered appropriate for MNCs to achieve their internal and external objectives in managing their foreign operations are discussed and analyzed in this book. Section 482 of the U.S. Internal Revenue Code and its impact on foreign activities of MNCs are covered in detail.

The objective of an appropriate ITP technique for either internal reporting, external reporting, or both is determined largely by the objectives of establishing an ITP policy. Transfer pricing methods are divided into two groups: Economic and accounting oriented analysis includes the market price, cost-based, cost-plus, marginal cost-based, and negotiated price; mathematically oriented analysis includes linear, nonlinear, and goal programming models.

The transfer of goods and services between two different countries may be priced at two different prices using two different approaches by the two different tax authorities for the same item. Also different objectives and policies of tax regulations of different countries could lead to conflicting results. When different tax authorities of two countries adjust the appropriate transfer price according to their belief on what is called the appropriate arm's-length price, an MNC may be liable for more than a double tax liability on the same item.

TRANSFER PRICING AND MANAGEMENT ACCOUNTING

Management accountants of MNCs will be hit with transfer pricing audits of either the IRS (United States), Inland Revenue (United Kingdom), Customs and Revenue Agency (Canada), National Tax Administration (Japan), or any other foreign tax authority. Unlike other tax planning issues, transfer pricing is very much linked to day-to-day operational and financial decisions. Traditionally, transfer pricing stimulates the complicated and conflicting objectives of avoidance of foreign exchange risks, tax minimization, cash flow management, and performance evaluation of foreign subsidiary managers. However, transfer pricing is still considered the number one tax issue for financial executive directors of MNCs.

Management accountants are responsible for designing and implementing effective transfer pricing systems based on facts supported by documents to help their companies reduce or eliminate the risk of transfer pricing tax audits. This book provides accountants, and management accountants in particular, with effective, practical, and the most convenient tools of transfer pricing systems.

TRANSFER PRICING AND PERFORMANCE EVALUATION

To date, the literature on the use of transfer pricing as a tool for performance evaluation of foreign subsidiary managers has not been discussed to the same extent as other tools of managment, international accounting, and tax issues. Most research efforts of management accounting scholars have addressed either the issue of international transfer pricing or performance evaluation measurements in the United States and different countries around the world. Moreover, management accounting literature is full of universal remedies that often prove to be impractical solutions (Abdel-Khalik, Rashad, and Lusk 1974; Abdallah and Keller 1985; Eccles 1985; Grabski 1985; Abdallah 1986; Leitch and Barrett 1992; Emmanuel and Mehafdi 1994; Anctil and Dutta 1999; Borkowski 1999; Abdallah 2001 and 2002). Current theory does not address the more global view of the MNC where foreign subsidiaries all act together according to a global decision by top management to maximize profits and therefore can be evaluated in a similar fashion. Borkowski (1999) has found out that there is some evidence, however, that specific performance evaluation criteria do vary in importance by country.

The use of performance evaluation of foreign subsidiaries and their managers as one of the objectives of transfer pricing is discussed and analyzed. First, traditional performance evaluation measures are discussed. For most MNCs, an objective and practical way in which to treat the effects of environmental factors on foreign operations has not been reached. A foreign subsidiary manager's performance should not reflect how well the manager has done, without regard to foreign environmental variables, but how well the manager has performed his or her job within those environmental factors.

Traditional management accounting techniques are inadequate to appropriately solve these problems, and MNCs are unable to achieve satisfactory and desired levels of performance evaluation. Management accounting techniques has not adequately considered the distinct characteristics of the environment within which MNCs operate and manage their businesses.

Second, a suggested performance evaluation system for foreign countries is presented. The proposed system estimates foreign subsidiary managers' relative performance after considering the effects of noncontrollable foreign environmental factors on the measured performance of foreign subsidiaries. Third, the suggested environmental model is applied to one of the foreign subsidiaries of an American MNC to illustrate how MNCs can implement it in practice, some guidelines on the important issues in managment, financial reporting, and taxation of American joint ventures in foreign countries. Countries' rules, regulations, facts, and experiences that uniquely affect management and financial reporting of American-foreign joint ventures is also discussed.

TRANSFER PRICING AND E-COMMERCE

International transfer pricing activities using e-commerce have not been discussed to the same extent as other important strategic business and tax issues. The complexity of the issue might require MNCs to redefine and update their transfer pricing strategies to meet the fast growth of information technology in the new millennium. The traditional framework of transfer pricing strategies and tax regulations may not be appropriate in dealing with global e-commerce activities. However, finding the appropriate transfer pricing method to deal with e-commerce transactions may be difficult with no availability of comparable uncontrolled transactions.

Accountants and CFOs are responsible for designing and implementing effective transfer pricing systems of e-commerce based on facts supported by documents to help their companies reduce or eliminate the risk of transfer pricing tax audits. This book provides accountants and CFOs with effective, practical, and the most convenient tools of developing effective transfer pricing systems of e-commerce.

To choose the best transfer pricing method, the rule requires that the arm's-length result of related party transactions be determined under the method that, given the facts and circumstances, provides the most reliable indicator of an arm's-length result. In the case of lack of available transactional comparables and the existence of intangible property may lead to the use of the profit split method (PSM).

One of the most important issues of e-commerce is whether a traditional permanent establishment concept retains its vitality when business is conducted in cyberspace. To impose tax on e-commerce tangible and intangible transactions, it is important to know whether or not an MNC has created a taxable presence in a country. In deciding what is an indicator of permanent establishment (PE) and determining the taxability of the income generated by e-commerce transactions, three important issues are discussed: the Web server (hardware), the Web site (software), and the Internet service provider (ISP). A Web site should be distinguished from the server that hosts the site. A web-hosting arrangement with an ISP does not create a PE for the Web site owner because an ISP is not considered an agent of the Web site owner (Merrill 2001). The Web server that is located for a sufficient period of time within a country and is used to carry on part or all of a business may constitute a PE even if no personnel are at that location.

TRANSFER PRICING AND INTANGIBLE ASSETS

Five related issues dealing with transfer pricing of intangible assets, e-commerce, and international taxation are introduced, discussed, and analayzed: general understanding of the characteristics and the nature of intangible assets of multinational companies and the related transfer pricing issue; new trends in transfer pricing of intangible assets; MNCs' strategies of intangible assets ownership; transfer pricing methods for intangible assets; and designing the right transfer pricing system of intangible assets.

Understanding the nature and the characteristics of intangible assets of MNCs and the related issues of transfer pricing systems is considered an essential step in designing the right and most appropriate pricing systems for MNCs. Intangible assets require different analysis than what is required for tangible assets, because they are the key to commercial success, especially in the hi-tech industry.

MNCs and tax authorities have been facing great challenges in dealing with transfer pricing of intangible assets. The challenges include: the globalization of MNCs and rapid expansion in the cross-border business transactions of services and technology; the shift from a predominantly manufacturing economy to a service economy spurred by innovative technology; and the increasing importance of intangibles in the production of income. In the twenty-first century, the significant and fast development of e-commerce and service companies' paradigms in proportion to the bricks-and-mortar business activities pushes tax authorities around the world to continue the attack of transfer pricing practices of MNCs by issuing new transfer pricing regulations and adjusting old ones to meet these e-commerce challenges (Levey 2001).

In the strategic planning stage, an MNC may choose one of three approaches for an intangible asset ownership: a centralized intangible asset ownership; a distributed intangible asset ownership; or geographic or regional distributed ownership. Each one of the three approaches is discussed in detail; however, the most important question for an MNC is: Which approach may be the most preferable? Three important variables should be the drivers for an MNC decision: the historical circumstances of how the group or related subsidiaries were created or the way that the intangible asset was developed; the management philosophy of the group; and the tax strategy, including the effect on transfer pricing method used, from the MNC's perspective.

International transfer prices are nonmarket, internal prices at which goods, intellectual property, and services are exchanged between subsidiaries or companies under common ownership and control. In the absence of a corporate tax system, such prices might be set in order to promote efficiency, structure managerial incentives, or accomplish any other corporate goals. However, in the presence of a corporate tax system, transfer prices may also serve to shift profits from one tax jurisdiction to another and thus have important implications for the cross-border allocation of multinational income (Johnson 2001).

To arrive at the arm's-length transfer pricing methods used by tax authorities for intangible assets, six transfer pricing methods are evaluated: the comparable uncontrolled price (CUP) method; the resale price method (RPM); cost-plus method (CPM); comparable profit method (CPrM); transactional net margin method (TNMM); or profit split method (PSM). The first three are viewed as traditional transaction-oriented methods, and the last three are profit-based methods.

ARM'S-LENGTH PRICE AND ADVANCE PRICING AGREEMENT PROGRAMS

Two important issues of transfer pricing are discussed and analyzed: arm's-length standard and advance pricing agreement programs in selected countries. Comparative analysis of selected countries is made. The OECD guidelines on transfer pricing issues are used in the comparative analysis of the selected countries.

With respect to arm's-length standard of transfer pricing, the United States has been the historic leader in establishing the standard as the recognized principle for determining cross-border transfer pricing and the allocation of profits between related subsidiaries of MNCs. Responding to increasing globalization, overwhelming use of e-commerce transactions, and growing international trade in services and intangibles, transfer pricing regulations in the United States have changed several times over the past three decades. In 1994, the United States updated transfer pricing regulations, and they enforce the arm's-length standard as the overreaching principle in setting transfer prices under Section 482 of the Internal Revenue Code. Many foreign tax authorities have followed the lead of the U.S.-IRS as a model, adopting and enforcing similar arm's-length standards.

In 1995, the OECD adopted parallel arm's-length transfer pricing principles in the first major update of its 1979 transfer pricing guidelines. These revised guidelines provide an internationally accepted statement of principles and methods that are broadly similar in scope and standards to the U.S. Tax regulations (Miesel et al. 2002). Even though some differences exist, the guidelines are generally consistent with Section 482 of IRC on transfer pricing regulations.

DOCUMENTATION AND PENALTIES OF TRANSFER PRICING TAX REGULATIONS

An MNC is expected to have sufficient transfer pricing documentation of intracompany transactions including e-commerce to support and prove compliance with the arm's-length standard and to avoid the risk of transfer pricing penalties. In addition, it has to maintain updated and convincing documents about their e-commerce or industry practice and current market conditions of all countries involved. To prove a consistent compliance with multiple jurisdictions, a global transfer pricing documentation system may be the best choice for an MNC (Abdallah 2002).

Documentation requirements are not limited to the United States. All selected eight countries require taxpayers to document related party transfer pricing transactions; however, half of them—Canada, Mexico, the United Kingdom, and the United States—have formal specific documentation regulations for transfer pricing. The other four countries either do not have formal rules for documentation or try to adhere to the OECD guidelines. In France, transfer pricing documentation is required only if the tax authorities have gathered evidence giving rise to a violation of transfer pricing tax rules. Germany has no legal basis for field tax officers to ask for special transfer pricing documentation. Japan has adhered generally to the OECD guidelines of documentation. The Dutch tax authorities require taxpayers to have available sufficient information in their administration to indicate how the transfer prices were established and from which it can be determined whether the prices satisfy the arm's-length standard.

It is critical that an MNC's documentation show compliance with both U.S. and foreign transfer pricing tax rules. Without a well-designed and workable transfer pricing system enabling MNCs to create and receive the right transfer pricing data, there would be no way for a multinational to avoid penalties imposed by tax authorities. It is very important for MNCs to note that transfer pricing tax rules in France, Mexico, the Netherlands, and the United Kingdom may impose penalties up to 100 percent of the amount of tax determined to be underpaid by tax authorities as a result of a tax audit examination or if taxpayers acted fraudulently or negligently. However, for any related party transfer pricing fraud or substantial valuation misstatement, Canada imposes penalties of 10 percent, Japan up to 35 percent, and the United States between 20 percent and 40 percent. Germany is the only one of the eight countries that does not specify penalty rates for violations of transfer pricing tax rules.

At the international level, the United States and the Pacific Association of Tax Administrators (PATA)—including Australia, Canada, and Japan as its members—issued a proposal to harmonize transfer pricing documentation requirements. PATA members have agreed on principles under which taxpayers can create uniform transfer pricing documentation so that one set of documentation can meet their respective transfer pricing documentation provisions (PATA documentation package) and thus eliminate the need to prepare different documentation for each country. The PATA documentation package is a voluntary procedure that, if satisfied, protects taxpayers in each of the four PATA jurisdictions from otherwise applicable transfer pricing documentation penalties. The objectives of the proposal are to reduce transfer pricing compliance costs and burdens; to promote the efficient and equitable operation of the tax systems; to facilitate the efficient preparation and maintenance of transfer pricing documentation thereby enabling the timely production of such information upon request by tax auditors; to develop uniform, multilateral guidance for taxpayers and tax administrators; and to create and maintain a single package of transfer pricing records and documentation in order to satisfy the transfer pricing documentation of all PATA members.

AN OVERVIEW OF THIS BOOK

This book covers five main themes. In Part I, the issue of transfer pricing in general is covered in chapters 2 through 4. Part II focuses on e-commerce, intangible assets and transfer pricing of MNCs, and these are discussed in chapters 5 and 6. Part III stresses management accounting and transfer pricing, covered in chapters 7 and 8. In Part IV, I explain and discuss transfer pricing tax regulations in selected countries, covered in chapters 9 and 10. Finally, in Part V, a summary and conclusions including the future outlook of transfer pricing issues are explored in chapter 11.

In Part I, I present a general background of the transfer pricing crisis, corporate goals of transfer pricing policies, and methods for pricing the transferred goods and services of MNCs. In chapter 2, I examine the international transfer pricing crisis or challenges facing MNCs and tax authorities around the world. In chapter 3, I focus on the corporate goals or objectives of international transfer pricing and whether MNCs can achieve all or some of them simultaneously using the same transfer pricing system. Chapter 4 is a discussion of transfer pricing methods that are appropriate and acceptable objectives of MNCs and the impact of Section 482 of the United States Internal Revenue Code on activities of MNCs.

In Part II, I cover management accounting and transfer pricing. In chapter 5, I stress effective, practical, and the most convenient tools of management for accountants to successfully defend and win the game of reducing or eliminating the risk of transfer pricing tax audits. Chapter 6 is a discussion and an investigation of transfer pricing and performance evaluation of foreign subsidiary managers of MNCs.

In Part III, I cover e-commerce, intangible assets, and transfer pricing. In chapter 7, I present the e-commerce activities of MNCs and their impact on designing transfer pricing techniques and strategies. In chapter 7, I explore the related issues of international transfer pricing and intangible assets.

In Part IV, I cover transfer pricing tax regulations in the selected countries of Canada, France, Germany, Japan, Mexico, Netherlands, the United Kingdom, and the United States. Chapter 9 covers the arm's-length standard of transfer pricing and advance pricing agreement programs of these eight selected countries. In chapter 10, I cover documentation and penalties of transfer pricing in these selected countries.

Part V is a summary and conclusion, which discusses the future outlook of transfer pricing systems of MNCs in the twenty-first century. In chapter 11, I explore the future of transfer pricing in MNCs, emphasizing the effect of e-commerce and the Internet on the global business environment. I make recommendations for transfer pricing in the twenty-first century.

REFERENCES

Abdallah, Wagdy M. 1986. Change the environment or change the system. *Management Accounting* (October), 33–37.
———. 2001. *Managing multinationals in the Middle East: Accounting and tax issues* (Westport, Conn., Greenwood Press, Inc.).

———. 2002. Global transfer pricing of multinationals and e-commerce in the twenty-first century. *Multinational Business Review* 10, no. 2 (fall): 62–71.

Abdallah, Wagdy M., and Donald Keller. 1985. Measuring the multinational's performance. *Management Accounting* (October): 26–30.

Abdel-Khalik, A. Rashad, and Edward J. Lusk. 1974. Transfer pricing: A synthesis. *Accounting Review* 69: 15–17.

Anctil, Regina M., and Sunil Dutta. 1999. Negotiated transfer pricing and divisional vs. firm-wide performance evaluation. *Accounting Review* 24, no. 1 (January): 87–104.

Borkowski, Susan C. 1999. International managerial performance evaluation: A five country comparison. *Journal of International Business Studies* 30, no. 3 (3rd Quarter): 533–55.

Boyle, M. P., J. M. Peterson, Jr., W. J. Sample, T. L. Schottenstein, and G. D. Sprague. 1999. The emerging international tax environment for electronic commerce. *Tax Management International Journal* (Washington) (June): 357–82.

Burns, P. 2000. United States. *International Tax Review*, no. 1 (Supplement, Transfer Pricing): 131–37.

Eccles, R. G. 1985. *The transfer pricing problem*, Lexington, Mass.: Lexington Books.

Emmanuel, C. R., and M. Mehafdi. 1994. *Transfer pricing*. London: Academic Press.

Felgran, Steven D., and Mito Yamada. 2001. Transfer pricing: A truly global concern. *Financial Executive* (Morristown, N.J.) (November): 21–27.

Grabski, S. V. 1985. Transfer pricing in complex organization: A review and integration of recent empirical and analytical research. *Journal of Accounting Literature* 4: 33–75.

Hamilton, D. 2000. A heavy price to pay. *CA Magazine* (Canada) 133 (May): 14–15.

Hines, J. R., Jr. 1999. Lessons from behavioral responses to international taxation. *National Tax Journal* (Washington) (June): 305–22.

Johnson, Robert E. 2001. The role of cluster analysis in assessing comparability under the U.S. transfer pricing regulations. *Business Economics* 36, no. 2 (Washington) (April): 30–38.

Leitch, R. A., and K. S. Barrett. 1992. Multinational enterprise transfer-pricing: Objectives and constraints. *Journal of Accounting Literature* 11: 47–92.

Levey, Marc M. 2001. Transfer pricing—What is next. *International Tax Review* Supplement, The Best of the Best 2001 (London) (June): 91–92.

Maguire, N. 1999. Taxation of e-commerce: An overview. *International Tax Review* (London) (September): 3–12.

Merrill, P. R. 2001. International tax of e-commerce. *The CPA Journal* (New York) 3, no. 11 (November): 30–45.

Miesel, Victor H., Harlow H. Higinbotham, and Chun W. Yi. 2002. International transfer pricing: Practical solutions for intercompany pricing. *The International Tax Jounral* 28, no. 4 (Fall): 1–22.

Organization for Economic Cooperation and Development Committee (OECD). 1995. *Transfer pricing guidelines for multinational enterprises and tax administrations.* Paris: OECD.

Park, William W. 2002. Income tax treaty arbitration. *Tax Management International Journal* (Washington) 31, no. 5 (May): 219–53.

Tang, Roger Y. W. 1997. *Intrafirm trade and global transfer pricing regulations.* Westport, Conn.: Quorum Books.

Transfer Pricing:
Critical Issues
in General

The Transfer Pricing Crisis

Chapter 2 discusses the international transfer pricing crisis facing multinational companies (MNCs) and tax authorities around the world. The definition of transfer pricing in the new millennium is discussed first. The problems created as a result of using the right price for transferred goods and/or performed services are analyzed next. Third, factors affecting transfer pricing techniques and strategies of MNCs are covered. Finally, the importance of establishing well-designed transfer pricing policies for MNCs investing and operating in foreign countries and the dilemma of implementing the right strategy are discussed.

Over the past two decades, growing international trade has brought into sharp focus the problem of international transfer pricing. At issue are prices paid in cross-border business transactions—whether for tangible property, intellectual property, or provision of services—between companies under related party control. These prices are pressure key points for international taxation by governments, as well as international trade regulation.

MNCs are highly motivated to invest in foreign countries by many factors that are different from one industry to another and even from one firm to another within the same industry. An MNC may find it cheaper to manufacture its products where materials and labor costs are the lowest—such as in Korea, India, Egypt, or Jordan—and then export and sell them in German, Japanese, European, or American markets where selling prices are the highest, thus achieving higher profits.

MNCs may start to look for new markets in Europe, South-Asia, South America, or in other regions of the world for many reasons. These reasons include improving their competitive position in both domestic and international markets, exploring new markets in South-Asian countries, maximizing profits, meeting tariff and quota restrictions in foreign countries, securing otherwise unobtainable raw materials for the home country such as oil products, exploring the scarce economic resources in less developed countries, choosing countries with low tariff and quota restrictions, choosing countries with low income taxes on foreign companies or foreign investments for the purpose of minimizing the sum of its U.S. and foreign taxes, and manufacturing their products in the least cost-producing countries, especially the less developed countries (LDCs), and selling the products in the best selling markets.

The fast increase in business globalization means that both MNCs, IRS-U.S., Inland Revenue-U.K., Japanese, and other foreign tax authorities need to consider transfer pricing carefully. MNCs should ensure that their transfer pricing policies can achieve certain objectives and that at the same time they are fair. IRS and foreign tax authorities need to ensure that they collect a fair amount of corporate income taxes from MNCs operating in their jurisdictions (Elliott 1998a).

Moreover, several governments may impose high tariffs on all imports getting into their countries either to protect their local industries from the competition against the foreign companies or to increase revenues for the government. MNCs must keep abreast of the changes and developments to ensure that they are able to demonstrate compliance with the relevant U.S. and foreign countries' tax regulations. They should avoid any transfer pricing misstatement for tax reporting with the IRS. The U.S. court case of DHL reaffirms that MNCs should plan to properly document and defend the transfer pricing method used to transfer intangible assets to their controlled parties. The courts are willing to uphold the assessment of the 20 to 40 percent penalties in appropriate situations because the IRS will carefully scrutinize situations involving transfers of intangible assets from U.S. to any related foreign parties anywhere on the globe (Shapland and Major 1999).

The growth of MNCs has created new issues for national economies as well as international economies. These include international location of production and distribution territories, their effect on national and international stock and commodity markets, their significant effects on both home and host governments' revenues, and the balance of payments of both foreign and home countries.

However, to maximize profits, an MNC should produce in the least cost-producing countries and sell in the best market countries. To achieve this, top management must have an attitude of globalism that makes it as concerned and involved with each of its foreign operations around the world as with home-country operations, and that makes it attempt to rationalize and manage its operations on a global rather than a domestic basis within the constraints of its social, economic, political, legal, and educational conditions. Consequently, the production and marketing operations in all foreign countries are integrated and coordinated on a global basis within the host and home national governments' restrictions.

One of the major characteristics of a successful MNC in doing business in foreign countries is having a highly efficient organizational tool for utilizing scarce economic resources on a worldwide basis and using a cost-effective alternative for allocating internal resources (Scharge 1999). Moreover, if the headquarters at the home office is to achieve the goals set out in the strategic plan, the international activities of all its foreign and domestic operations need to be planned, organized, coordinated, integrated, and controlled on a global basis.

A transfer price is defined as the price at which a business entity transfers goods, intangible assets, or provide services to a related entity, such as a parent company to a subsidiary. The price is usually set and used by an MNC to quantify the goods transferred or value the service rendered from one subsidiary domiciled in a specific country to a subsidiary located in another country. Transfer prices are set for internal objectives, such as motivating subsidiary managers, monitoring foreign subsidiaries' performance, and achieving goal harmonization between subsidiary managers and the parent. Transfer prices are also set for external objectives; such as taxes and tariffs minimization; foreign exchange risk control; cash movement control; and avoiding foreign government interference. However, the Internal Revenue Service and foreign tax authorities are concerned that MNCs could use these transfer prices to shift profits, between related parties through cost of goods sold, from high tax jurisdictions to low tax jurisdictions.

THE CRISIS OF USING THE RIGHT TRANSFER PRICING

One of the most important and complex considerations in coordinating and integrating production and marketing strategies of MNCs is that of intracompany pricing of their operations in foreign countries. MNCs with large international networks make pricing decisions with a global perspective and in a global context; this affects the sovereignty of both host and home countries. Corporate executive officers (CEO) of MNCs face the following questions:

- Should the product be transferred among a company's own subsidiaries in and outside the foreign country at the world market or arm's-length price?
- Should each manager of foreign subsidiaries be given freedom in making production and marketing decisions and consequently in maximizing profits?
- How much tax will be paid to both Internal Revenue Service (IRS) and foreign tax authorities?
- Is there an acceptable transfer pricing policy for all foreign countries' tax regimes?
- How does one secure compliance with complex rules operated by different accountants in foreign locations?
- Do we assume that the arm's-length price will lead domestic and foreign subsidiaries to make production and marketing decisions in the best interest of the MNC as a whole? Or should full costs, variable costs, cost plus a percentage for markup, profit split method, marginal costs of production, or marginal costs plus opportunity costs when there are neither intermediate price nor competitive markets in foreign countries?
- How often do we have to review and update our international transfer pricing policy to ensure compliance with the most recent tax developments in foreign countries?

CEOs may find answers to these questions through an understanding of this and the following chapters, which can be useful in illustrating the real problems of transfer pricing policies, the factors that affect establishing successful pricing policies, and different techniques to choose the right transfer pricing within the use of e-commerce tools in the global market in the new millennium.

MNCs are usually organized into different subsidiaries, in foreign countries, whose managers are allowed considerable autonomy in day-to-day decision making. Each subsidiary transfers goods or services to others that are located in different countries under different political, legal, taxation, and governmental systems. The prices at which these goods are transferred affect subsidiary managers in making their divisional decisions, and some decisions may achieve divisional profits in the short run at the expense of the global profits in the long run when factors such as transportation costs, taxes paid to either home- or host-country governments, import duties, cash movement restrictions, or governmental rules, among others, are ignored.

Making pricing decisions for MNCs' products or services, in general, is an important, complex, flexible, and complicated task because these decisions affect other major functions of MNCs such as marketing, production location, transportation, and finance that directly affect total sales and profits. Moreover, there is no clear-cut or easy way to establish an effective pricing policy. MNCs cannot just add a standard percentage as a markup to full, variable, or marginal costs to come up with a price that they have to charge for goods sold externally or transferred internally among their own subsidiaries. In reality, the transfer pricing policies of most MNCs have evolved, as the international businesses "have grown either organically or by acquisition in response to a number of competing and often conflicting commercial considerations. The minimization of direct tax is one of such consideration" (Elliott 1998a).

For all domestic activities of MNCs, intracompany transfers of goods or services can be determined by one of the traditional techniques: market or arm's-length price, full actual cost method, full standard cost, actual variable cost, standard variable cost, cost plus, or negotiated price. Under the cost method, the transfer price can be determined on the basis of actual or standard full costs, actual or standard variable costs, or variable or fixed costs plus a fixed amount or a percentage of cost.

Under the market or arm's-length price method, the transfer price is the price at which significant quantities of goods and services are generally sold to third parties who are external to the firm and dealing at arm's length with one another. The market or arm's-length price is the only price that the IRS would accept if it is available. A negotiated transfer price is determined by bargaining between buyer and seller subsidiaries, presuming that both subunits have freedom or equal power or authority to bargain.

The choice of the appropriate technique for transfer pricing should be based on the following four criteria: how well it promotes goal congruence and consequently profit maximization, how well it provides an adequate profit yardstick for performance evaluation of subsidiaries and their managers, how well it guides top management in making decisions, and how well it promotes more autonomy for divisional or subsidiary managers in decision making (Benke and Edwards 1980; Atkinson, Banker, Kaplan, and Young 1997).

MNCs face a major problem as they transfer goods and services between their subsidiaries—that of deciding at what price to transfer goods and services among their subsidiaries or between the parent and its foreign subsidiaries. A survey on transfer pricing practice, sponsored by CIMA and supported by Deloitte & Touche, was conducted to know more about the way in which MNCs approach international transfer pricing (Elliott 1998a and 1998b). In the survey, it has been found that the most important factors impacting on the determination of MNCs transfer pricing policies are maximization of global profit, simplicity and ease of use, aggressiveness of tax authorities, market penetration, and stability of transfer price over time.

Transfer pricing is a critical issue for both MNCs and tax authorities around the world. Transfer pricing is the number one international tax concern of MNCs in the new millennium, according to a 2001 Ernst & Young LLP biennial survey of more than 800 tax and finance officers. Interviews with various revenue authorities around the globe indicate that tax authorities also view transfer pricing as a top audit issue, scrutinizing MNCs' pricing for related party transactions to make sure that the market or arm's-length price is used (Ackerman and Hobster 2002).

MNCs have a global reach, whereas governments are limited by their geographic boundaries to a national border limit. Because the MNC has common overheads and resources, it has additional advantages of economies of scale and scope not available to domestic firms. These resources allow the MNC to cross national jurisdiction. They can also cause problems for tax authorities in deciding where the tax base is located and how to allocate the income and deductions of the MNC group among various national jurisdictions.

The transfer pricing issue is so contentious because MNCs create particular problems for tax authorities that do not occur in taxing domestic firms. These problems arise because the MNC is an integrated global business. The MNC consists of two or more entities, located in different countries but under common control with a common pool of resources and common objectives. The company is an interlocking network of organized global activities, working in tandem depending on the control exercised by the parent company. Its goals are to survive, compete, increase sales, make profits, increase market share, and grow in the global market. Its actions are developed as strategic reactions to competitors in an environment of market imperfections and high risk combined with uncertainty.

On the other hand, the IRS is concerned that transfer pricing strategies could be used by MNCs to shift income from high tax jurisdictions like the United States to low tax jurisdictions. The proper transfer price from tax authorities' perspective is the market value price. In 1992, U.S. tax authorities, followed by other tax authorities, had to give incentives for MNCs to use the right price by offering the Advanced Pricing Agreement (APA) program. The IRS's APA provides MNCs an opportunity to avoid costly audits and litigation by allowing them to negotiate a prospective agreement with the IRS regarding the facts, the transfer pricing methodology, and an acceptable range of results. The program is aimed at MNCs interested in avoiding penalties, managing risk, and determining their tax liability with confidence.

MNCs are responding to these challenges by reconfiguring their business model to implement optimized structures and take advantage of new technologies. However, the new structures and technologies that change the internal business organization often are in conflict with the diverse tax regulations of different countries. At the same time, if tax and transfer pricing are properly managed in conjunction with the business and technology changes, opportunities exist to implement significant tax savings and at the same time dramatically simplify transfer pricing arrangements and compliance (Durst, Stone, Rofle, and Happell 1999).

MNCs' tax directors need to have a fresh look at transfer pricing in the new millennium. As well as deal with the growing trend of formal documentation requirements, the new world of e-business will create fresh challenges. Those that tackle transfer pricing planning in an integrated way with supply chain re-engineering will be the winners in terms of tax savings and simplicity (Ibid.).

Transfer price strategies or manipulation is the charge of high or low transfer prices so as to avoid (from MNCs' perspective) or evade (from tax authorities' perspective) government regulations and policies. That is, transfer pricing strategies or manipulation is the deliberate setting of transfer prices either too high or too low so as to avoid tax or other government regulations. Manipulation must occur, with related parties, relative to some benchmark or standard—for example, your price must be too high or too low relative to the transfer price that would have been set by unrelated parties engaged in similar transactions (the arm's-length price).

MNCs, through their strategies or manipulation of transfer pricing, can take advantage of differences in tax rates and other factors in taxation systems of different countries to reduce their global tax liability. International investors often have at their disposal several alternative methods of structuring and financing their investments, arranging transactions between related parties located in different countries, and returning profits to investors. These alternatives have important tax implications, and there is considerable evidence that tax considerations strongly influence the choices that MNCs make (Hines 1999). A very simple example would be a steel company with a manufacturing unit in country A (subject to a 50 percent tax rate) that sells to an affiliated sales unit in Country B (subject to a 30 percent tax rate). The company can lower its overall tax rate by reducing the transfer price to the sales unit, thereby shifting profits to the tax heaven country.

The taxing authorities in Country A would be expected to object to a pricing structure that results in what they believe to be an artificial shifting of income and consequent erosion of their tax base.

What are the external factors that could motivate an MNC to use certain transfer price strategies or lead the company to engage in transfer pricing manipulation? Table 2.1 illustrates some of the external motivations that MNCs have to manipulate transfer prices. These include differentials in corporate income tax rates between countries, host

TABLE 2.1   External Factors and the Relevant Transfer Pricing Strategies

External Factors	Techniques for Transfer Price Strategies
High tariffs on imported goods	Low transfer price to avoid paying customs duties
Differences in corporate income taxes between countries	Shift tax deductions to the high-tax country and taxable revenues to the low-tax country so as to minimize total tax liability to the two countries.
Cash movement restrictions	If an MNC wants to move cash out of the country, sell to other foreign subsidiaries outside of the country at high transfer prices.
Host government foreign exchange restrictions	If can't directly remit profits to MNC parent because of host country restrictions on foreign exchanges, high transfer price of exports to the foreign affiliate and low transfer price on imports from the foreign subsidiary as an alternative method to shift profits out of the country.
Global or local competition	If competitors' selling prices are low, use low transfer prices on imported goods or provided services to the foreign subsidiary.
Expected government intervention	If host governments use price control policies, charge high prices for purchased materials from other related subsidiaries and sell at low prices.

government interference, competition in local and global markets, restrictions on remitting foreign exchange, customs duties, and so on.

Thus, it is the fear that MNCs will engage in transfer pricing strategies (or manipulations) that will have a significant effect on government tax and customs duty revenues; home- and host-country balance of payments; and the location of international production, marketing, and employment, that leads governments to regulate and control transfer prices used by MNCs. It is not transfer pricing, per se, that is the problem; it is the expected consequences and the significant effect of transfer price manipulation that governments fear and want to prevent through regulations.

THE FACTORS AFFECTING INTERNATIONAL TRANSFER PRICING POLICIES OF MULTINATIONALS

International transfer pricing of an MNC is the process of setting prices for intracompany transactions when the buying subsidiary is in a different country from the selling subsidiary. There are many factors that affect international transfer pricing policies in foreign operations and make them more complicated than those used for domestic operations.

The most important factors can be grouped into two categories: the internal factors that have impact on several functions inside the firm, such as performance evaluation, motivation, stability over time, simplicity, ease of use, and goal harmonization; and global or international environmental variables that are external to the firm. Examples of external factors are foreign and U.S. corporate income taxes, tariffs, aggressiveness of foreign tax authorities, cash movement restrictions, foreign currency exchange risk, foreign market penetration strategies, and the conflict with host governments' policies.

If an MNC uses its transfer pricing policies for performance evaluation of its domestic and foreign subsidiaries and their managers, the MNC pricing method must be at market or competitive prices, which is an essential factor under the concept of decentralization. The resulting net income or loss should be the yardstick for the measurement of a foreign subsidiary manager's ability to manage and control his or her area of responsibility (or his or her profit center). However, when the worldwide market for the transferred product is not competitive or does not exist for the intermediate product transferred, any transfer price other than the negotiated price will neither maintain autonomy or freedom in decision making nor motivate managers to adhere to the objectives of the company as a whole, which in turn will impair goal harmonization.

However, when the performance of each foreign subsidiary is evaluated as a separate profit center, this high transfer price will show lower profits for the buyer subsidiary and a higher profit for the seller subsidiary. This will lead to conflicts between goals of foreign subsidiaries and those of the MNC (Choi, Frost, and Meek 1999). Elliott (1998a, 49) concluded from the results of a CIMA-sponsored survey into the transfer pricing practices of both U.K. and non-U.K. MNCs that transfer pricing policies have evolved, as the businesses have grown either organically or by acquisition in response to a number of competing and often conflicting commercial factors. The minimization of direct tax is only one such factor.

Of foreign environmental or external variables that affect MNCs in deciding on the appropriate transfer pricing policy to be used, one of the most important is the taxes to be paid to both foreign and home governments as a result of transferring the goods or services across the borders of two different countries. The tax authorities of foreign countries and the Internal Revenue Service (IRS) of the United States are very much aware of the effect of the transfer price set by an MNC on taxes paid to each of the two tax authorities as a result of the existence of different tax structures of different countries. For example, an MNC can set a low transfer price for goods transferred from a Japanese subsidiary, which is assumed to have a high corporate income tax rates, to sell at cost to a Singaporean subsidiary, which is assumed to have lower corporate income tax rates. The result is that global tax liabilities of an MNC are less than before and consequently the global profits will be higher.

Significant evidence indicates that taxation significantly influences decisions on locating foreign direct investment, transfer pricing, and dividend and royalty payments. Reactions to worldwide tax rate differences, as well as to changes in international tax rules, provide important information concerning the extent to which MNCs respond to different incentives. The generally high degree of responsiveness in turn carries implications for the design of domestic as well as international tax policy and regulation (Hines 1999). The taxation of cross-border transactions differs from the taxation of domestic activity primarily due to the complications that stem from the taxation of the same income by two or more governments. In the absence of some kind of corrective mechanism, the efficiency costs of double or multiple taxation are potentially quite severe, because domestic tax rates are high enough to eliminate most international business activity if applied two or more times to the same taxable income.

Countries differ not only in their tax rates and systems but also in their commercial and regulatory policies, the characteristics of their labor markets, the nature of competition in product markets, the cost and local availability of intermediate products or services, proximity to final markets, and a host of other attributes that influence the desirability of an investment location (Ibid.).

Another factor considered to be important when an MNC is setting up international transfer pricing policies in a foreign country is cash movement restrictions of host governments on moving cash outside the country. When a foreign country is suffering from a problem of foreign exchange, the government may prohibit such movement or impose strong controls that limit the amount of cash, profit, or dividends that can be repatriated. This problem can be illustrated by assuming that China, which is suffering from a lack of American dollars, imposes controls on all dollar transactions. A seller subsidiary in Paris, where there is dollar or another currency convertible into dollars, sells to a buyer subsidiary in China at a higher price than the cost. The outcome of the transaction is to transfer the profits from China to France and then from France to the United States.

Important duties, tariffs, or customs of foreign countries can be high or low from one country to another and complicate the policies to establish the appropriate international transfer prices. If Singapore, Egypt, Japan, or Canada imposes import duties at the rate of 20 percent on the invoice (transfer) price, a subsidiary selling its goods from the United States to another subsidiary in Singapore could reduce the import duties paid by lowering the transfer price below cost. However, the Singaporean government may intervene, because the government may believe that lowering transfer prices is tax evasion, and at the same time, the customs authorities in Singapore may believe that there are revenues forgone.

As can be seen from this discussion, the appropriate international transfer price used by an MNC in several countries and the one required to achieve certain objectives, such as performance evaluation and motivation, income tax minimization, avoidance of foreign exchange controls, or competitiveness, may or may not be the same. It is important to note that five criteria must be met for establishing an efficient international transfer pricing system for foreign operations.

1. The international transfer pricing policy should provide an adequate profit measurement to evaluate the performance of foreign subsidiaries and their managers in terms of their controllable divisional contributions to global profits.
2. It should provide adequate information to top management to be used as guidelines in managerial decision making.
3. It should increase the overall profit rate of the MNC; in other words, the MNC's overall performance must be improved by the use of the international transfer pricing system.
4. It should motivate foreign subsidiary managers to increase their efficiency and maximize their divisional profits in harmony with the objectives of top management.
5. It should minimize the international transaction costs for an MNC by minimizing border and income tax liabilities, foreign exchange risks, currency manipulation losses, and conflict with foreign government's regulations and policies.

As discussed earlier, globalization and fast technological changes are having a profound effect on the way MNCs manage business and compete in the global marketplace. With respect to the transfer of goods and services, MNCs are being pressured to embrace fundamental changes in their business model. Pressure for change emanates from multiple sources. MNCs need simultaneously to access and compete in an ever-growing number of geographically dispersed markets. At the same time, new and emerging technologies are increasing information flow and accessibility. This in turn is inducing geographic price transparency, raising the sophistication and expectations of consumers, and significantly reducing business start-up costs (Durst et al. 1999).

E-commerce, as another factor, makes it easier for MNCs to engage in global product development, increased market share, high demand on their products, collaboration, and sales. It is expected that there be an increase in global cross-border activities, and an increase in the tax problems inherent in global endeavors. The transfer pricing problem is an important one of these problems. Tax authorities around the world are ever-watchful for manipulation of transfer prices between related parties that result in income manipulations and lost revenues for foreign governments.

In general, when MNCs select the foreign structure of an operation, the key tax goal of the U.S. MNC is to minimize the sum of its total tax liability for U.S. and foreign countries. Relevant factors in making the structure selection for the foreign operation include its anticipated profitability, the use of excess cash generated from the operation, the source of financing, the foreign tax credit position of the U.S. operation, and local business requirements (Lau, Auster, and McCotten 1998).

ESTABLISHING SUCCESSFUL TRANSFER PRICING SYSTEMS FOR MNCs

A transfer price is set and used by MNCs to quantify the goods transferred or services provided from one subsidiary domiciled in a specific foreign country to another foreign subsidiary located in another country. The dynamic growth of most MNCs by going abroad and exploring more and more business opportunities in foreign countries necessitated more delegation of authority and responsibility with more autonomy for foreign subsidiary managers, which opened the door for more decentralization and intracompany pricing problems.

Because the transfer price for the product has an important effect on performance evaluation of individual foreign subsidiary managers, their motivation, divisional profitability, and the global profits as well, top management should devote special attention to designing international transfer pricing policies. A soundly developed policy could lead to better goal harmonization, better performance evaluation measures, fewer taxes and tariffs, more motivated managers, fewer exchange risks, and better competitive positions in foreign countries and international markets.

Another important issue is the transfer pricing policy review. How often should MNCs review their transfer pricing system? What are the main pros and cons of the current transfer pricing system? In a survey by Jamie Elliott (1998b, 49), it was evident that a large proportion of the sample either had a very recent internal review of their transfer pricing system or the review is on a continual basis. Moreover, one of the problems encountered by MNCs in reviewing their transfer pricing systems included lack of comparable systems and concerns about the acceptability of their pricing systems by foreign tax authorities. Also, one main advantage of an internal review of the transfer pricing system is increased confidence in the MNCs' policy and documentation (Elliott 1998b, 50).

In designing international transfer pricing systems of MNCs, four major characteristics should be considered: input, process, corporate goals, and output. The relationship among these four components of the system is illustrated in Figure 2.1.

The input stage includes relevant cost information, differentiation of income tax rates and systems in foreign countries, exchange rate risks, restrictions on cash movements or transfers, import/export tariffs, competition in foreign markets, and inflation rates in countries where MNCs are active. The process of an international transfer pricing system includes three components: requirements for an international transfer pricing system, factors affecting the system, and the methods that can be used for international transfer pricing. Finally, the output of a well-designed international transfer pricing system would be an appropriate and effective international transfer price that will achieve most, if not all, of management objectives and will be the optimum one.

The Inputs of International Transfer Pricing Systems

The inputs of an International Transfer Pricing system (ITP) consists of seven factors considered as inputs for deciding what is the appropri-

Figure 2.1
The Relationship among the Components of the International Transfer Pricing System

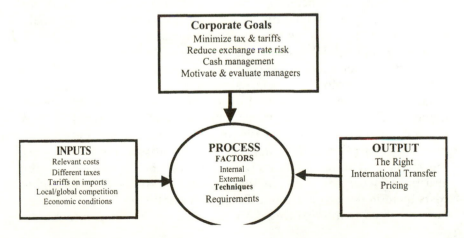

ate price to be charged for goods transferred through the border from a foreign country to another: relevant cost information, differential foreign countries' income tax rates, exchange risks, restrictions on cash transfers, tariffs, competition, and inflation rates of foreign countries.

Relevant Cost Information

Cost information is needed as a major input for ITP systems; it is used as one of the major factors in making decisions on transfer pricing. The question is: What cost information is relevant to the parent or foreign subsidiary manager's decision on pricing of goods transferred out of his subsidiary or services provided to other foreign subsidiaries? Relevant costs are defined as those expected future costs that will make the difference between charging a higher or lower price for goods transferred among subsidiaries of the same MNC in different countries. A foreign subsidiary manager must have the relevant cost information, the ability to use it in the decision-making process, and the understanding of its effect on both his subsidiary's profitability and the global profits of his firm as well.

A cost objective is the product whose cost is to be determined; it includes direct materials, direct labor, and manufacturing overhead. Other costs include selling and administrative expenses that are related to a foreign subsidiary plus other costs allocated by the headquarters of the MNC. Those costs are classified into variable and fixed. Variable costs vary directly and proportionately with the activity level, whereas fixed costs do not change with the activity level. Variable costs include such items as direct raw materials, direct labor, sales commissions, and transportation costs. Fixed costs include such items as factory rent, salaries for supervisors, and depreciation of factory equipment.

Some costs cannot be described by a single cost behavior pattern because they are partially variable and partially fixed. There are many techniques that have been developed for identifying the variable portion and fixed portion including industrial engineering, account analysis, visual fit, high-low, and regression analysis.

In designing an ITP system, managers must decide on which inventory-costing alternative to choose. This decision will have an effect on net income of both the foreign subsidiary unit and the global net income, on the evaluation of foreign subsidiary managers' performance, and on international transfer pricing decisions (Horngren, Foster, and Datar 2000). There are two inventory-costing methods used in practice: absorption and variable costing. The absorption (or full) costing method includes direct materials, direct labor, and both variable and fixed factory overhead as the cost of a product—that is, product costs include both direct and indirect manufacturing costs. Under this method, fixed manufacturing costs are absorbed by the product transferred and are part of the costs of goods sold or transferred and ending inventories.

The variable (or direct) costing method includes only variable manufacturing costs as the cost of a product—that is, product costs include direct materials, direct labor, and variable manufacturing costs. All fixed manufacturing costs are excluded from the inventoriable costs and expensed during the fiscal year in which they are incurred together with all selling and administrative expenses.

As an example, let us assume that a foreign subsidiary of an American MNC in Singapore produced 25,000 units of its product. Fixed manufacturing costs were $25,000, variable manufacturing costs were $3.50 per unit ($2 for direct material, $1 direct labor cost, and $.50 variable factory overhead), and variable selling costs were $.50 per unit sold, fixed selling and administrative expenses are $7,000. Sales for 2003 were 20,000 units at $10 per unit. Generally, the absorption costing method is the accepted method of product costing for external reporting, and the variable costing method is used to prepare internal purpose financial reports to assist in making economic decisions. The net income of the Egyptian subsidiary for the year under the absorption costing methods can be seen in Table 2.2.

TABLE 2.2 The Income Statement Using the Absorption Costing Method for the Singaporean Subsidiary (in U.S. Dollars)

Sales 20,000 at $10		$200,000
Less: Cost of goods sold & transferred		
Beg. inventory	0	
Direct materials used 25,000 x $2	50,000	
Direct labor 25,000 x $1	25,000	
Factory overhead		
Variable 25,000 x $0.50 = 12,500		
Fixed 25,000 x $1.00 = 25,000	37,500	
Cost of goods available for sale	112,500	
-Ending inventories		
(25,000-20,000) 5,000x$4.50	(22,500)	
Cost of goods sold		(90,000)
The foreign subsidiary gross profit		110,000
Less: selling & administrative expenses		
Variable expenses $0.50 x 20,000	10,000	
Fixed expenses given	7,000	(17,000)
The Singaporean subsidiary net income		**$93,000**

Differential Income Tax Rates in Foreign Countries

The income tax policies and regulations of different governments of foreign countries are not the same or even close to each other. International taxation has a significant effect on MNCs in making their management decisions. Taxation affects where an MNC invests, how it markets its products, what form of business organization it selects, when and where to remit cash, how to finance, and—of course—the choice of a transfer price (Mueller, Gernon, and Meek 1997, 181). If tax rates of different countries were the same, there would be no impact of preferring a higher country transfer price over a lower one for the global profits of an MNC.

Both foreign and U.S. governments are interested in profits realized by an MNC, and transfer prices make a big difference between the amounts of income taxes paid to either government. Tax authorities of both countries have become very much aware of the significant impact of the differences in the two tax structures on MNCs in deciding at what price to transfer goods or services from one country to another. From an MNC's point of view, the transfer of goods and services from one subsidiary to another in a different country generates taxable revenues and tax deductible costs in different countries.

Section 482 of the U.S. Internal Revenue Code gives the internal revenue commissioner the authority to reallocate gross income, deductions, credits, or allowances in intracorporate transactions in order to prevent tax evasion or to reflect more clearly a fair allocation of income. The right price from the IRS's perspective is the market or arm's-length standard. Because it is difficult to prove that the transfer price was equal to the market price, MNCs often find themselves in disputes with the IRS regarding the transfer pricing methodology and an acceptable range of results. Therefore, the IRS's Advance Pricing Agreement (APA) program, since its inception, has evolved from a dream approach to resolving transfer pricing disputes into the forum of choice for resolution of the most dramatic and challenging issues (Wrappe and Soba 1998).

Exchange Rate Risks

Foreign exchange risk is defined as "the risk of a change (gain or loss) in the company's future economic value resulting from a change in exchange rates" (Oxelheim 1985, 61). For MNCs, the exchange risk is connected with the firm's cash flows in different currencies, and any change in exchange rates between two different currencies has a direct effect on the value in the base currency of funds to be converted from one currency to another (Ibid., 61). Devaluation of the currency of the home countries pushes the foreign sale of goods up and pushes the home country sales down. This directly affects MNCs because it increases the foreign currencies they are holding.

Because MNCs' activities involve many countries, they must deal with many currencies. The value of currencies frequently change by either devaluation or appreciation. Foreign exchange risk affects both companies with international operations and those with receivables and payables to be collected or paid in foreign currencies (Robock and Simmonds 1983, 536).

Restrictions on Cash Movements in Foreign Countries

Host governments devise different policies such as profit repatriations and/or tax exchange control to exercise control over MNCs' activities for the purpose of protecting their own local industries. MNCs set international transfer pricing policies as a way to overcome these restrictions (Kim and Miller 1979, 72). Sidney Robbins and Robert Stobaugh (1973, 72) in their interview with 39 U.S.-based MNCs concluded that although income tax minimization is a major objective of using transfer pricing, avoiding exchange controls is more important.

Exchange controls with profit repatriation restrictions have been ranked as one of the most important factors in setting international transfer prices by MNCs. Most developing countries have been using exchange control restrictions to avoid outflows of foreign funds outside the country (Kim and Miller 1979, 72). However, MNCs use their international transfer pricing policies to overcome these restrictions imposed by host governments and to decide how much cash flows out of the host countries or to the home country as part of their profits.

Tariffs on Imports in Foreign Countries

The words tariffs, customs, and import duties are used interchangeably. Transfer pricing policies can be used to reduce tariffs of foreign countries imposed on imports into the country or exports on goods to be transferred out of the country. Low transfer prices for imports reduce the payments of high tariffs.

In foreign countries, the effect of using low transfer pricing on imports may significantly affect the balance of payments of those countries especially when they import huge quantities from the same MNCs. On the other hand, MNCs may impose a higher transfer price for goods transferred to subsidiaries of foreign countries with low duty rates.

However, combining both foreign tariffs and income taxes together complicates the decision in setting up the appropriate transfer prices—as is discussed in the next chapter—especially in countries where there are low duties with high income tax rates. In addition, both export duties of the country where the foreign subsidiary (the seller) is located should be considered with the import duties of the country where the buying subsidiary is located, which in turn will never coincide with the transfer pricing strategies of MNCs.

The trade-off between foreign tariffs and income taxes is more diffi-cult than it looks. An MNC cannot charge two different subsidiaries of the same country two different transfer prices for the same goods. Host governments have started to look closer at the transfer pricing policies of MNCs investing in their countries until they make sure that the tax revenues of the country are not affected significantly and consequently the balance of payments as well.

Competition in the Local and Global Markets

When a new foreign subsidiary is starting a new business overseas, competition is another factor that should be considered in establishing international transfer pricing policies. An MNC can set a low transfer price for goods shipped to the new foreign subsidiary to strengthen its financial and competitive position in the first years of business. How-ever, this may open the door for the intervention of host foreign gov-ernments to protect their local industries if the selling prices of the new subsidiary are much lower than those of other domestic industries of the host country. An MNC can charge high international transfer prices for imported goods to report lower profits on its foreign subsidiaries to avoid host governments' interference when they show higher profit-ability, or charge low transfer prices to discourage any new firms from entering the market to compete with them.

International transfer pricing policies have become the most contro-versial issues in MNCs in reporting the results of their foreign business transactions. The top management of an MNC tries to accomplish the following:

1. To minimize their foreign exchange losses.
2. To avoid exchange control restrictions on cash outflows.
3. To pay less tariffs on both imports and exports.
4. To minimize total income tax liability to be paid for both home and foreign governments by charging low international transfer prices for goods and services transferred into low income tax rate countries for the buying subsidiaries and charging high prices for goods and services transferred into big income tax rate countries.
5. To help foreign subsidiaries to compete with other firms in foreign countries. MNCs, at the same time, try to achieve goal congruence between foreign subsidiary objectives and overall MNC objectives; to provide subsidiary managers with relevant information for decision making; to evaluate the performance of foreign subsidiaries and their managers on an objective basis; and to allocate their financial, economic, and human resources efficiently.

An MNC, when trying to establish its international transfer pricing policies for foreign activities, may find a great degree of conflict among all these factors. Countries with low income tax rates may impose higher tariffs on goods transferred into the country. Countries with serious problems with foreign exchange may use restrictive monetary policies to completely prohibit or place restraints on cash movements that can be repatriated. Moreover, there is conflict between charging low international transfer prices to help foreign subsidiaries, newly established, to compete or survive in that country by showing more artificial profits and then using them for performance evaluation of foreign subsidiary managers.

Inflation Rates of Foreign Countries

The possibility of major currency devaluation, which can happen after periods of rapid and sustained inflation, often require MNCs to adopt precautionary strategies. The future inflation rates are not known. It is a possible contributing factor to the makeup of the term structure of interest rates. MNCs may have difficulties setting transfer prices and adjustments to exchange rate fluctuations resulting from inflation. In fact, inflation in foreign countries is the most influential factor on prices.

For political or economic reasons, when inflation rates in foreign countries go out of control, MNCs must counteract by holding a net monetary position on foreign investments. In this respect, international transfer pricing is the only management tool for withdrawing excess funds from countries at risk. For example, it may be desirable for an MNC to establish artificially high transfer prices in certain countries so as to minimize risk by removing funds from foreign countries that are experiencing highly inflationary and volatile exchange rate conditions.

The Process of International Transfer Pricing Systems

A process can be a series of actions, changes, or functions that bring about a particular result. The process of an International Transfer Pricing system includes a series of factors affecting the decision to choose the appropriate international transfer pricing technique that should meet specific requirements to achieve the MNC's objectives.

In discussing the process of the ITP systems, four elements are to be included: the factors affecting the decision, different techniques to choose from, specific requirements needed to be met, and corporate goals of ITP systems. (The first and third elements are discussed in detail in this chapter; the second and fourth elements are discussed later in two separate chapters.)

Factors Affecting Transfer Pricing Systems of MNCs in Foreign Countries
There are many factors that have a significant effect on designing an appropriate international transfer pricing system for foreign business activities. These factors can be classified into internal factors and external factors. In designing International Transfer Pricing policies, all internal as well as external factors should be considered; otherwise, many problems such as suboptimal decisions, disruption in the operating process, and negative behavioral actions may result.

Internal factors are behavioral, organizational, managerial, and motivational issues. Degree of decentralization, interdependence, management control system, goal congruence, motivation, and performance evaluation are just examples. These and other related issues that have an effect on establishing a well-designed international transfer pricing system that fits the foreign business units are discussed here.

First, the degree of decentralization or centralization of managerial decision making for transfer pricing is an important issue. Complete decentralization that includes the delegation of authority for decision making of production and sales is used only when foreign subsidiaries buy and sell on the market. Foreign or domestic subsidiary managers are assumed to have their freedom in making decisions for productions and sales—making their decisions faster, relieving top management of making operating decisions, and being evaluated on the basis of operational measurement performance.

However, decentralization has its own drawbacks or side effects for an MNC. The biggest problem is dysfunctional decision making, which may occur as the result of conflict between foreign subsidiary and corporate objectives. Another problem is that relevant information for making decisions is gathered at the subsidiary level for transfer pricing rather than in the home country; however, because of the independence of each foreign or U.S. subsidiary from one another, the relevant information is not fully communicated among subsidiary managers (Knowles and Mathur 1985, 18).

Second, the degree of interdependence among foreign and U.S. subsidiaries is another issue that affects establishing a well-designed ITP system. If the decisions or actions of one subsidiary affect the foreign business of one or more of the others in other countries, a high degree of interdependence of international operations exists. With highly interrelated international operations, subsidiary managers may make their decisions without considering the effects on other subsidiaries of the same MNCs. As a result, these managerial decisions may optimize the individual manager's profits at the expense of others, which in turn does not lead to optimal global profits.

Third, many MNCs as the main basis of domestic performance evaluation have used the profit center concept. A foreign subsidiary manager under this concept makes the major decisions relating to profit center costs and revenues. Because the manager is able to influence the results of operations, he or she is accountable for and evaluated on the basis of those results, which are the profits of the profit centers.

Independence, autonomy, and freedom in decision making usually characterize a profit center. A foreign subsidiary manager should try to achieve the highest possible profits for the subsidiary by buying from other subsidiaries of the same MNC or from the market at the lowest price and selling to others at the highest price. They are actually using the international transfer prices that maximize their profits, and consequently show better performance for their foreign subsidiaries. However, the profit center concept in an MNC may not work well for the following reasons.

1. Transfer pricing policies are usually set in MNCs to facilitate cash movements in foreign countries where currency restrictions exist and to minimize taxes. Therefore, transfer pricing policies are not complementary to the profit center concept. Consequently, performance evaluation cannot be achieved properly using the traditional management techniques.
2. With the existence of different inflation rates and other sociological, economic, legal, political, social, and educational conditions among foreign countries, top management may have trouble understanding each foreign country's situation and so be less able to evaluate what is good or bad profit performance abroad. Profit centers are likely, therefore, to have more utility for domestic rather than foreign subsidiaries.
3. Domestic company activities are often organized by independent profit or investment centers. Under these decentralized systems, subsidiary managers are given the authority to make decisions directly affecting their activities. Under these conditions, the rate of return on investment (ROI) as a measure of performance may be acceptable. However, such performance evaluation systems may not function well for MNCs because foreign operations are often established for strategic marketing and economic reasons rather than for profit maximization; thus many of those foreign operations cannot be measured precisely or quantitatively by ROI.
4. Many times the units of an MNC are integrated and managed as a coordinated whole, which means that the major decisions affecting foreign profits are made centrally for all international units. Therefore, the profit center concept may not be relevant for foreign activities.

If there is no high degree of independence and the foreign subsidairy has no control on the transfer price, then the pseudo-profit center concept is used. A pseudo-profit center is "a responsibility center in which profit is based on internal sales or purchases at artificial prices" (Benke and Edwards 1981, 385). Foreign managers of the pseudo-profit center use artificial profits and have control only over costs, and it is more likely to be considered as a cost center. In this case, international transfer prices are used only for performance evaluation purposes.

Fourth, the management control process (MCP) is another factor affecting ITP systems. There are two major objectives of the process: to guide foreign subsidiary managers to achieve the MNC's objectives, and to measure the results of the foreign subsidiary's performance against the MNC's objectives. It is essential for an MNC to operate and manage its foreign operations within the objectives of its management control process and make sure that the objectives of both management control process and ITP are consistent (Knowles and Mathur 1985).

The main purpose in designing the MCP is to achieve goal congruence, which is the equality between the sum of individual goals with those of the MNC. The international transfer price should help both the buying and selling foreign subsidiaries to make the right decision to maximize their own profits and at the same time the global profits of the MNC as a whole. However, it is more likely that transfer prices may create conflicts between the buying and the selling foreign subsidiaries because the buying subsidiary tries to use the lowest possible transfer price to maximize that subsidiary's profits while the selling subsidiary tries to sell at the highest possible price.

Fifth, the use of ITP systems may motivate foreign subsidiary managers to work in their own divisional self-interest because they are motivated by the presumed behavioral advantage of operating with a high degree of autonomy. At the same time, organizational objectives should be achieved by being motivated to work for the best interest of the MNC as a whole. However, subsidiary managers may choose transfer pricing methods that are not compatible with the MNC's long-term objectives (Knowles and Mathur 1985).

Finally, performance evaluation of a foreign subsidiary's performance and its managers is among the important factors affecting international transfer pricing policies. Subsidiary managers should not use transfer pricing techniques to manipulate their costs or profits for the purpose of creating "the illusion of better or worse performance" than has actually happened (Benke and Edwards 1980).

Performance evaluation reports, based on a transfer price set by top management, do not reflect how much the foreign or domestic subsidiary or its manager contributes to the global profits unless the international transfer price among subsidiaries is identical to the market or arm's-length price of the intermediate product. Under these circumstances, the contribution of the subsidiary, measured by the market price, will be important for managers and central management who use it for the evaluation of the subsidiary's profitability and make decisions either to continue or discontinue their investments in these subsidiaries.

However, when there is no market for the intermediate products transferred internally among the subsidiaries, conflict is likely to arise in MNCs between subsidiary managers because of the conflict of interest between the buyer subsidiary who wants to be charged with the lowest possible transfer price and the selling subsidiary who wants to achieve the highest possible divisional profits by charging the highest possible transfer price.

The problem is more complicated when we look at all factors affecting transfer pricing policies combined together. Different income tax rates and rules of different foreign countries, different tariffs, different market penetration strategies, and different cash flow restrictions are on the one hand, and motivation, performance evaluation, goal congruence, and profit center or pseudo-profit centers are on the other. Both require different transfer prices for the same goods or services transferred across the border.

It is obvious that international transfer prices as used now in practice, at which goods or services are transferred internally among different subsidiaries of MNCs in different countries, can significantly distort the profitability of foreign subsidiaries and their managers.

In addition to internal factors, as discussed earlier, there are external factors that can have an effect on the decision of what transfer price should be charged. These are market conditions in foreign countries, economic conditions, and currency appreciation or devaluation.

Foreign countries' government interventions put many restrictions on MNCs as they do business there. There are many ways for foreign governments to intervene in the business of MNCs. They may increase or decrease prices of imports and exports through tariffs, quotas, and taxes. They may intervene in foreign exchange rates. They also may restrict the amount of profits an MNC can transfer to reduce pressure on the balance of payments of the host country. All these factors have a significant effect on MNCs in setting appropriate transfer prices.

Transfer prices are also affected by the competitive position of subsidiaries in foreign countries either to be strengthened by charging low transfer prices for the input or high prices for the output, or to be weakened to avoid any potential government intervention.

Requirements for International Transfer Pricing Policies in Foreign Countries
An international transfer pricing policy in the foreign country should meet specific requirements if an MNC wants to achieve its objectives. These requirements are discussed next. Any transfer pricing method

should provide an adequate measurement of the performance of both foreign subsidiaries and their managers. It should measure the manager's controllable contribution toward the global profit in an objective and operational way that must be consistent with the global objectives of the MNC and, at the same time, must motivate managers toward instituting better performance.

The policy should provide top management with relevant information to decide to expand, continue, or discontinue its operation in specific locations of foreign countries. International intracompany pricing information plays a major role as input for the decision making process and in presenting a realistic profit picture of foreign subsidiary performance.

The policy should minimize income tax liability that MNCs pay for both foreign and U.S governments and/or tariffs (import/export duties). In this case, the appropriate international transfer price should come up with the lowest possible total tax liability of MNCs to be paid including income taxes and tariffs combined, not separately.

Finally, the policy should reduce or alleviate the conflict between the MNC's objectives and foreign governments' objectives. MNCs should understand the needs of foreign governments and try to utilize the total economic and human resources in both their own best interest and that of foreign governments to avoid any possibility of profit repatriation, restrictions on cash movements or exchange control, expropriations, or any possible limitations that may be imposed on an MNC's foreign activities—all of which has a significant negative impact on global profits over the long run.

SUMMARY AND CONCLUSIONS

MNCs face the dilemma of choosing the right price as they transfer goods and/or services among their own subsidiaries between two different countries with different tax rates, regulations, tariff systems, and many other factors. In general, making pricing decisions for MNCs is an important, complex, flexible, and complicated task because these decisions have significant effects on other major functions of MNCs. Moreover, MNCs have a global reach, whereas governments, especially tax authorities, are limited by their geographic boundaries to a national border limit.

MNCs may use their own strategies, or manipulation, of transfer pricing to take advantage of differences in tax rates and other factors in different countries to reduce their global tax liability and achieve their other corporate goals. International investors often have at their disposal several alternative methods of structuring and financing their investments, arranging transactions between related parties located in different countries, and returning profits to investors. These alternatives have important tax implications, and there is considerable evidence that tax considerations strongly influence the choices that MNCs make (Hines 1999).

When MNCs choose the right transfer pricing, the following four criteria should be considered: how well the transfer pricing system promotes goal congruence and consequently profit maximization, how well it provides an adequate profit yardstick for performance evaluation of foreign subsidiaries and their managers, how well it guides top management in making decisions, and how well it promotes more autonomy for divisional or subsidiary managers in decision making.

Four major characteristics of ITP systems of MNCs investing in foreign countries are identified in this chapter: input, process, corporate goals, and output. The inputs of an ITP system consist of seven factors that are considered as inputs for deciding what is the appropriate price to be charged for goods transferred through the border from one country to another. These inputs are relevant cost information, differential foreign income tax rates, foreign exchange risks, restrictions on cash transfers, tariffs, competition, and inflation rates of foreign countries.

The process of an ITP system of MNCs includes a series of factors affecting the decision to choose an appropriate ITP technique, which should meet specific requirements to achieve the MNC's objectives. In discussing the process of an ITP system, four elements should be considered: the factors affecting the decision, different techniques from which to choose, specific requirements needed to be met, and the corporate goals of ITP systems. The first and third elements were analyzed and discussed in details in this chapter; the second and fourth elements are discussed later in the following chapters.

Finally, the most important factors in establishing successful and effective transfer pricing policies for MNCs' businesses are maximization of global profits, avoidance of foreign exchange risks, simplicity, ease of use, reduction of restrictions on cash transfers, and performance evaluation of foreign subsidiaries. These factors include the trade-offs that MNCs must consider when establishing or revising their transfer pricing policies. To be successful in their overseas business activities, MNCs should put more emphasis on designing their transfer pricing policy to fit into foreign countries' cultural, legal, and economic environment. Moreover, it is very important for MNCs to prepare social responsibility reports to show how much they contribute into the welfare and the social and economic conditions of foreign countries.

REFERENCES

Ackerman, Robert E., and John Hobster. 2002. Managing transfer pricing audit risks. *The CPA Journal* 72 (New York), no. 2 (February): 57–59.

Atkinson, Anthony A., Rajiv D. Banker, Robert S. Kaplan, and S. Mark Young. 1997. *Management accounting*, 2nd Edition. Upper Saddle River, N.J.: Prentice-Hall.

Benke, Ralph L., Jr., and James Don Edwards. 1980. *Transfer pricing techniques and uses*. New York: National Association of Accountants.

Benke, Ralph L., Jr., and James Don Edwards. 1981. Should you use transfer pricing? *Management Accounting* (February): 385.

Choi, Frederick D.S., Carol Ann Frost, and Gary K. Meek. 1999. *International accounting*, 3rd Edition. Upper Saddle River, N.J.: Prentice-Hall.

Durst, Michael, Garry Stone, Chris Rofle, and Michael Happell. 1999. The new world of transfer pricing. *International Tax Review*, Supplement, Guide to the World's Leading Transfer Pricing Advisers (London) (December): 4–6.

Elliott, Jamie. 1998a International transfer pricing: A survey of UK and non-UK group. *Management Accounting* (CIMA-London) (November): 48–50

———. 1998b. International transfer pricing: A survey of UK and non-UK group: Part 2. *Management Accounting* (CIMA-London) (December): 48–50.

Hines, James R., Jr. 1999. Lessons from behavioral responses to international taxation. *National Tax Journal* (Washington) (June): 305–22.

Horngren, Charles T., George Foster, and Srikant M. Datar. 2000. *Cost accounting: A managerial emphasis*, 10th Edition. Upper Saddle River, N.J.: Prentice-Hall.

Kim, Seung, and Stephen W. Miller 1979. Constituents of the international transfer pricing decisions. *Columbia Journal of World Business* (spring): 71–72.

Knowles, Lynette L., and Ike Mathur. 1985. Factors influencing the designing of international transfer pricing systems. *Managerial Finance* 11: 17–20.

Lau, Paul C., Rolf Auster, and Tom McCotten. 1998. Entity decisions for overseas operations after TRA '97. *Journal of Corporate Taxation* 25, no. 2 (summer): 149–79.

Mueller, Gerhard G., Helen Gernon, and Gary Meek. 1997. *Accounting: An international perspective*, 4th Edition. Chicago: Richard D. Irwin, Inc.

Oxelheim, Lars. 1985. *International financial market fluctuations*. New York: John Wiley & Sons.

Robbins, Sidney M., and Robert B. Stobaugh. 1973. *Money in the multinational enterprise*. New York: Basic Books.

Robock, Stephan H., and Kenneth Simmonds. 1983. *International business and multinational enterprises*, 3rd Edition. Chicago: Richard D. Irwin.

Scharge, Michael. 1999. Smart, works hard, in mint conditions. *Fortune* (July 19): 134–35.

Shapland, Rick, and Bill Major. 1999. 40% transfer pricing penalty upheld. *The Tax Adviser* (April): 224–25.

Wrappe, Steven C., and George H. Soba. 1998. A practical guide to the U.S. Advance Pricing Agreement process. *Tax Executive* 50, no. 6 (November/December): 454–64.

3

Corporate Goals of Transfer Pricing Policies

This chapter examines the corporate goals or objectives of international transfer pricing policies and whether MNCs can achieve all or some of them simultaneously using the same transfer pricing system. It divides the corporate goals into internal and external sets. The external set of goals is analyzed first, and they include reducing income tax liability, tariffs, exchange rate risk, avoiding conflicts with host governments, cash flow management, and competition. Then the internal set of goals is discussed, and they include performance evaluation of foreign subsidiaries and their managers, motivation, and goal harmonization.

Over the years, transfer pricing of tangible and intangible goods has undeniably become a major international business issue of MNCs and a nightmare problem for CEOs. MNCs, in theory, have the ability to use their international transfer pricing policies to maximize their global profits. Practically, developing these policies is a most difficult and sophisticated pricing decision, one more complicated than developing domestic transfer pricing policies. An MNC has to manage its overseas production and marketing policies in a world characterized by different international tax rates, foreign exchange rates, governmental regulations, currency manipulation, and other economic and social problems. Such market characteristics create high transaction costs for an MNC when it uses its regular marketing policies. It is important for MNCs to create an internal market if they want to avoid these problems and any costs associated with them. Allocation of resources among domestic and foreign subsidiaries requires the central management of an MNC to set up the appropriate transfer price for global activities to achieve certain corporate goals.

Top management of MNCs and both domestic and foreign subsidiary managers must understand the corporate goals for using transfer pricing policies within their organizations. They need to know how these usually interrelated corporate goals can affect each other (Knowles and Mathur 1985).

An international transfer pricing (ITP) system of an MNC should achieve two different sets of goals. The first set includes consistency with the system of performance evaluation of foreign subsidiaries, motivation of foreign subsidiary managers, and achievement of goal harmonization. The second set of goals consists of certain corporate goals that are more relevant to the foreign operations. These goals include reduction of income taxes, reduction of tariffs on imports and exports, minimization of foreign exchange risks, avoidance of a conflict with foreign countries' governments, management of cash flow, and competitiveness in the international markets.

However, any manipulation of transfer pricing systems by MNCs may have a significant impact on many areas of the worldwide economy, including both the home and host countries. The impact of transfer pricing systems includes effects on balance of payments and foreign and domestic formation of capital investment. By charging higher transfer prices on goods transferred into or services performed for a foreign subsidiary, the MNC can limit a subsidiary's export abilities or avoid controls on foreign remittance by "tapping-off excess profits" (Greenhill and Herbalzheimer 1980). Imposing low transfer pricing on sales of foreign subsidiaries will reduce customs duty payments and help subsidiaries to compete in foreign markets against other local competitors (Ibid.). Also, Jamie Elliott (1998) conducted a survey and found out that local management may be remunerated in part by results, and artificial transfer prices would undermine the MNC objective and may damage the business by demoralizing management.

The purpose of this chapter is to identify, at the international level, different corporate goals of establishing transfer pricing systems for foreign business activities; to investigate how MNCs can achieve all, most, or a few of these goals; and to point out significant problems MNCs might face when they try to achieve these goals. The second group of objectives is discussed first because of their significant impact on foreign operations.

REDUCTION OF INCOME TAXES

One of the most important corporate goals of an international transfer pricing policy is believed to be reducing the global income tax liability of an MNC. Tax reduction can be achieved by transferring goods to countries with low income tax rates at the lowest possible transfer prices and by transferring goods out of these countries at the highest possible transfer prices. In countries with high income tax rates, goods transferred into the country should be at the highest possible prices, so that the cost to the buying subsidiary will be high, to minimize its eventual tax liability.

International transfer pricing policies are generally set to maximize the after-tax profitability of worldwide business transactions. The minimization of income tax liabilities for an MNC has been considered as the most significant factor or objective in designing ITP policies in the foreign country, and consequently, if a transfer price shifts profits from a country with high tax rates to a country with low tax rates, the global profits will be maximized. However, the IRS and tax authorities of other countries are concerned that MNCs could use these transfer prices to shift profits between related parties through cost of goods sold.

MNCs often have at their disposal several alternative methods of structuring and financing their foreign investments, arranging transactions between related parties located in different countries, and returning profits to investors in the home country. These alternatives have important tax implications, and there is considerable evidence that tax considerations strongly influence the choices that firms make. International tax avoidance typically entails reallocating taxable income from countries with high tax rates to countries with low tax rates, and may also include changing the timing of income recognition for tax purposes. Many of these methods are quite legal (Hines 1999).

To illustrate the income tax effects on setting international transfer prices for cross-border activities, let us assume that the Singaporean subsidiary of an American MNC produces 25,000 units and sells 20,000 units to the Japanese subsidiary, another subsidiary owned by the same American MNC, at US$20.00 a unit. The Japanese subsidiary, in turn, sells these units for US$50.00 a unit to an unrelated customer.

As can be seen from Table 3.1a, the income tax rate of Singapore is 30 percent and that of Japan is 50 percent. In this case, Singapore, with the lower income tax rate, is considered as a tax haven country. As a result of using higher transfer prices between the Singaporean and the Japanese subsidiaries, there is a significant change in the net income of both foreign subsidiaries and the consolidated net income of the American MNC as a whole. With the low, original, transfer price, the Singaporean subsidiary sells at $20.00 per unit and pays income taxes of $49,500, the Japanese subsidiary pays income tax liability of $160,000, and the MNC pays a total income tax liability of $209,500. Under the next high transfer price of $25.00 per unit, as can be seen from Table 3.1b, the Singaporean's income taxes go up by $30,000 to $79,500, the Japanese's

TABLE 3.1a   The Tax Effect of Transfer Pricing Strategies

Transfer Price @ $20	Singaporean Subsidiary	Japanese Subsidiary	The MNC
Sales (20,000 units @$20)	$400,000	$1,000,000	$1,000,000
Less CGS	$150,000	$ 400,000	$ 150,000
Gross profit	$250,000	$ 600,000	$ 850,000
Less operating expenses	$ 85,000	$ 280,000	$ 365,000
Net income before tax	$165,000	$ 320,000	$ 485,000
Income taxes (30% & 50%)	$ 49,500	$ 160,000	$ 209,500
Net income after tax	$115,500	$ 160,000	$ 275,500

taxes go down by $50,000 to $110,000, the combined tax liabilities of the MNC go down by $20,000 from $209,500 to $189,500, and the consolidated net income goes up by the same amount of $20,000 from $275,500 to $295,500. The consequences of charging a higher transfer price are a decrease in total tax liabilities by $20,000 ($209,500 – $189,500) and an increase in the consolidated net income by the same amount of $20,000, from $275,500 to $295,500.

An important question may be asked: What is the best or optimum transfer price that can be used in our example of cross-border intracompany transactions between the Singaporean and the Japanese subsidiaries? As can be seen from Table 3.1c through Table 3.1f, any increase of transfer price up to $35.00 may be acceptable for foreign tax authorities and very profitable for MNCs. At the transfer price of $35.00, as can be seen from Table 3.1e in our example, the MNC achieves a net income after tax of $335,000 (allocating $325,000 for the Singaporean subsidiary, the tax haven country, and $10,000 for the Japanese subsidiary. However, any transfer price higher than $35.00 per unit will likely not be acceptable to the Japanese tax authorities because it reduces the net

TABLE 3.1b   The Tax Effect of Transfer Pricing Strategies

Transfer Price @ $25	Singaporean Subsidiary	Japanese Subsidiary	The MNC
Sales (20,000 units @$25)	$500,000	$1,000,000	$1,000,000
Less CGS	$150,000	$ 500,000	$ 150,000
Gross profit	$350,000	$ 500,000	$ 850,000
Less operating expenses	$ 85,000	$ 280,000	$ 365,000
Net income before tax	$265,000	$ 220,000	$ 485,000
Income taxes (30% & 50%)	$ 79,500	$ 110,000	$ 189,500
Net income after tax	$185,500	$ 110,000	$ 295,500

TABLE 3.1c   The Tax Effect of Transfer Pricing Strategies

Transfer Price @ $30	Singaporean Subsidiary	Japanese Subsidiary	The MNC
Sales (20,000 units @$30)	$600,000	$1,000,000	$1,000,000
Less CGS	$150,000	$ 600,000	$ 150,000
Gross profit	$450,000	$ 400,000	$ 850,000
Less operating expenses	$ 85,000	$ 280,000	$ 365,000
Net income before tax	$365,000	$ 120,000	$ 485,000
Income taxes (30% & 50%)	$109,500	$ 60,000	$ 169,500
Net income after tax	$255,500	$ 60,000	$ 315,500

TABLE 3.1d   The Tax Effect of Transfer Pricing Strategies

Transfer Price @ $35	Singaporean Subsidiary	Japanese Subsidiary	The MNC
Sales (20,000 units @$35)	$700,000	$1,000,000	$1,000,000
Less CGS	$150,000	$ 700,000	$ 150,000
Gross profit	$550,000	$ 300,000	$ 850,000
Less operating expenses	$ 85,000	$ 280,000	$ 365,000
Net income before tax	$465,000	$ 20,000	$ 485,000
Income taxes (30% & 50%)	$139,500	$ 10,000	$ 149,500
Net income after tax	$325,500	$ 10,000	$ 335,500

TABLE 3.1e   The Tax Effect of Transfer Pricing Strategies

Transfer Price @ $36	Singaporean Subsidiary	Japanese Subsidiary	The MNC
Sales (20,000 units @$36)	$720,000	$1,000,000	$1,000,000
Less CGS	$150,000	$ 720,000	$ 150,000
Gross profit	$570,000	$ 280,000	$ 850,000
Less operating expenses	$ 85,000	$ 280,000	$ 365,000
Net income before tax	$485,000	$ 0	$ 485,000
Income taxes (30% & 50%)	$145,500	$ 0	$ 145,500
Net income after tax	$339,500	$ 0	$ 339,500

TABLE 3.1f   The Tax Effect of Transfer Pricing Strategies

Transfer Price @ $37	Singaporean Subsidiary	Japanese Subsidiary	The MNC
Sales (20,000 units @ $37)	$740,000	$1,000,000	$1,000,000
Less CGS	$150,000	$ 740,000	$ 150,000
Gross profit	$590,000	$ 260,000	$ 850,000
Less operating expenses	$ 85,000	$ 280,000	$ 365,000
Net income before tax	$505,000	$ (20,000)	$ 485,000
Income taxes (30% & 50%)	$151,500	$ (10,000)	$ 141,500
Net income after tax	$353,500	$ (10,000)	$ 343,500

income to zero or net loss instead of net income as can be seen from Table 3.1e and Table 3.1f.

The general rule for the pricing strategy of MNCs is that if the sole corporate objective is to minimize total tax liability, transfer most of the profits to the foreign subsidiaries in the tax-haven countries, as can be seen in Figure 3.1. However, the manipulation of international transfer pricing policies only for reducing income taxes has caused the governmental tax authorities—including the U.S. Internal Revenue Service (IRS), the Japanese tax authority, the Singaporean tax authority, and other industrial countries' tax authorities—to intervene to ensure that there is no tax evasion and that the country does not lose its tax revenue under the transfer pricing shield.

Moreover, there are many factors besides foreign income tax minimization that should be considered by MNCs in designing their ITP systems, such as motivation and performance evaluation of foreign subsidiary managers, competitiveness in foreign markets, and foreign exchange risks.

A survey by H. Seung Kim and Stephen W. Miller indicated that in the past, MNCs considered reducing income taxes as the most important corporate goal in designing their ITP systems. Now, tax reduction is only a minor factor among many others, and the company's overall goal rather than income tax liability should be a major concern (Kim and Miller 1979). Another survey, by Jamie Elliott (1998), found that an important factor that places constraints on a group's freedom to minimize direct taxes by fixing artificial transfer prices is the possible knock-on effect that this could have on indirect taxes.

The evidence of tax-motivated transfer pricing comes in several forms. Though it is possible that high tax rates are correlated with other location attributes that depress the profitability of foreign investment, competitive conditions typically imply that after-tax rates of return should be equal in the absence of tax-motivated income shifting. The

Figure 3.1
Transfer Pricing Strategies under Different Tax Rates of Different Countries

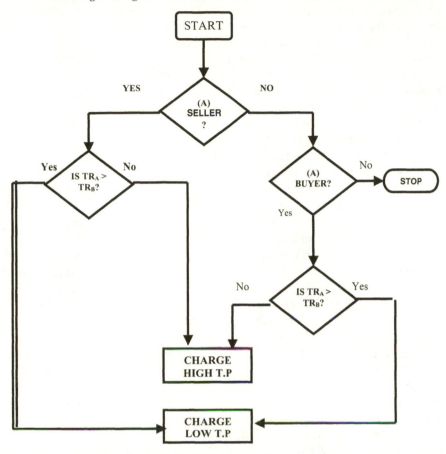

fact that before-tax profitability is negatively correlated with local tax rates is strongly suggestive of active tax avoidance (Hines 1999, 311).

Along with the reduction of global income tax liability, a major problem is how to coordinate the tax effect of transferred goods among different foreign countries to come up with the optimal transfer price. To set the appropriate transfer price for tax reduction, it is very important to determine the tax effects of different ways of taxing imports and exports by imposing duties and customs on them, and different tax rate structures and the methods of taxing MNCs' profits used by foreign countries.

It is not an easy task to determine the results of these effects on MNCs' global profits because there are frequent and rapid changes by host- and home-country governments to achieve some economic, political, or social objectives for their own countries. In the United States the IRS is concerned that MNCs may rescue their tax liabilities by using transfer prices to shift profits from multinational local businesses to businesses in countries with low tax rates. Section 482 of the Internal Revenue Code gives the IRS the power to reallocate income and deductions among subsidiaries of an MNC if it finds that this is necessary to prevent any illegal reduction of taxes (that is, tax evasion). Under this section, all transfer prices should generally be established according to arm's-length market values on any transactions between affiliates.

MNCs, under Section 482, are not allowed to use any transfer price that will maximize their global profits other than an arm's-length: the comparable uncontrolled price method, the resale price method, and the cost-plus method. However, if the ITP policies of an MNC were designed only to comply with Section 482 of the Internal Revenue Code, there would not be effective systems to measure foreign managers' performance, motivate them to control the costs of their foreign subsidiaries, or maximize the global profits of the MNC as a whole.

In general, contractual arrangements between related parties located in foreign countries with different tax rates offer several possibilities for successful tax strategies or tax avoidance. MNCs typically can benefit by reducing prices charged by affiliates in high-tax countries for goods and services provided to affiliates in low-tax countries. Almost all countries require firms to use transfer prices that would be paid by unrelated parties or the so-called arm's-length price or standard, but enforcement is difficult by tax authorities—particularly when pricing issues concern unique items such as in pharmaceutical companies where products and ingredients are unique, and many of which are patented. Given the looseness of the resulting legal restrictions, it is entirely possible for firms to adjust transfer prices in a tax-sensitive fashion without violating any laws (Hines 1999).

REDUCTION OF TARIFFS

Tariffs are the most widely used trade restrictions by foreign countries and can be imposed on either imports or exports. Tariffs on imports are used as a way of reducing the volume of imports coming into the country and to protect local industries. MNCs use transfer pricing strategies as a way to reduce import or export tariffs and to avoid paying high tariffs to foreign governments, and consequently to reduce their global production costs and maximize their global profits. However, the use of transfer pricing for both reduction of income taxes and tariffs at the same time complicates the transfer pricing system.

As an example, let us assume that the American subsidiary in Japan must pay tariffs at the rate of 15 percent, and that the income tax rates of Singapore and Japan are still at 30 percent and 50 percent, respectively. Then increasing the transfer price will increase the tariffs that the Japanese subsidiary must pay, assuming that the tariffs are imposed on the invoice transfer price. The combined effect of tax and tariff with the increased transfer price is shown in Table 3.2a through Table 3.2e.

Under the low transfer price strategy of $20.00 per unit, import tariffs of $60,000 (15 percent of $400,000) are paid to the Japanese government, while the income tax paid declines by a $30,000 tax shield (50 percent of $60,000), because import tariffs are assumed to be tax-deductible in Japan. Global income taxes and import tariffs to be paid are $239,500 ($179,500 + $60,000, respectively), and the global net income is $245,500 ($115,500 + $130,000), as can be seen from Tables 3.2a and 3.2b.

Under a higher transfer price strategy of $25.00, three items have been affected: the net income, income tax liability, and tariffs. First, the net income of the Singaporean subsidiary increased by $70,000 (from $115,500 up to $185,500), and it was offset by a decrease in the Japanese subsidiary's net income of $57,500 (from $130,000 to $72,500), and the outcome is an increase of the global profit by the difference of $12,500 (from $245,500 to $258,000). Second, the corporate income tax liability of the Singaporean subsidiary increased by $30,000 (from $49,500 to $79,500); the income tax liability of the Japanese subsidiary decreased by $57,500 (from $130,000 to $72,500), and the outcome is the decrease in the global income tax liability of the MNC by $27,500 (from 179,500 to $152,000). Third, import tariffs of the Japanese subsidiary increased from $60,000 to $75,000 (a difference of $15,000), and the import tariff of the MNC increased by the same difference of $15,000, as can seen from Table 3.2b. However, global tax liability and tariffs decreased by

TABLE 3.2a   The Effect of Low Transfer Pricing, Income Taxes, and Tariffs on Net Income

Transfer Price @ $20	Singaporean Subsidiary	Japanese Subsidiary	The MNC
Sales (20,000 @$20 & $50)	$400,000	$1,000,000	$1,000,000
Less CGS	$150,000	$ 400,000	$ 150,000
Less tariffs of 15%-Japan	0	$ 60,000	$ 60,000
Gross profit	$250,000	$ 540,000	$ 790,000
Less operating expenses	$ 85,000	$ 280,000	$ 365,000
Net income before tax	$165,000	$ 260,000	$ 425,000
Income taxes (30% & 50%)	$ 49,500	$ 130,000	$ 179,500
Net income after tax	$115,500	$ 130,000	$ 245,500

TABLE 3.2b The Effect of Low Transfer Pricing, Income Taxes, and Tariffs on Net Income

Transfer Price @ $25	Singaporean Subsidiary	Japanese Subsidiary	The MNC
Sales (20,000 @$25 & $50)	$500,000	$1,000,000	$1,000,000
Less CGS	$150,000	$ 500,000	$ 150,000
Less tariffs of 15%-Japan	0	$ 75,000	$ 75,000
Gross profit	$350,000	$ 425,000	$ 775,000
Less operating expenses	$ 85,000	$ 280,000	$ 365,000
Net income before tax	$265,000	$ 145,000	$ 410,000
Income taxes (30% & 50%)	$ 79,500	$ 72,500	$ 152,000
Net income after tax	$185,500	$ 72,500	$ 258,00

TABLE 3-2c The Effect of Low Transfer Pricing, Income Taxes, and Tariffs on Net Income

Transfer Price @ $30	Singaporean Subsidiary	Japanese Subsidiary	The MNC
Sales (20,000 @$30 & $50)	$600,000	$1,000,000	$1,000,000
Less CGS	$150,000	$ 600,000	$ 150,000
Less tariffs of 15%-Japan	0	$ 90,000	$ 90,000
Gross profit	$450,000	$ 310,000	$ 760,000
Less operating expenses	$ 85,000	$ 280,000	$ 365,000
Net income before tax	$365,000	$ 30,000	$ 395,000
Income taxes (30% & 50%)	$109,500	$ 15,000	$ 124,500
Net income after tax	$255,500	$ 15,000	$ 270,500

TABLE 3.2d The Effect of Low Transfer Pricing, Income Taxes, and Tariffs on Net Income

Transfer Price @ $31	Singaporean Subsidiary	Japanese Subsidiary	The MNC
Sales (20,000 @$31 & $50)	$620,000	$1,000,000	$1,000,000
Less CGS	$150,000	$ 620,000	$ 150,000
Less tariffs of 15%-Japan	0	$ 93,000	$ 93,000
Gross profit	$470,000	$ 287,000	$ 757,000
Less operating expenses	$ 85,000	$ 280,000	$ 365,000
Net income before tax	$385,000	$ 7,000	$ 392,000
Income taxes (30% & 50%)	$115,500	$ 3,500	$ 119,000
Net income after tax	$269,500	$ 3,500	$ 273,000

TABLE 3.2e   The Effect of Low Transfer Pricing, Income Taxes, and Tariffs on Net Income

Transfer Price @ $32	Singaporean Subsidiary	Japanese Subsidiary	The MNC
Sales (20,000 @$32 & $50)	$640,000	$1,000,000	$1,000,000
Less CGS	$150,000	$ 640,000	$ 150,000
Less tariffs of 15%-Japan	0	$ 96,000	$ 96,000
Gross profit	$490,000	$ 264,000	$ 754,000
Less operating expenses	$ 85,000	$ 280,000	$ 365,000
Net income before tax	$405,000	$ (16,000)	$ 389,000
Income taxes (30% & 50%)	$121,500	$ -	$ 121,500
Net income after tax	$283,500	$ (16,000)	$ 267,500

the net difference of $27,500, from $179,500 to $152,000, and the global net income increased by $12,500 from $245,500 to $258,000. Therefore, the high transfer price strategy is still preferable because of the $12,500 increase in global profits.

As a result of another $5.00 increase in the transfer price to $30.00 per unit, the result is the same as just discussed. However, as the transfer price moves up from $31.00 to $32.00, the outcome will not be favorable for the MNC, as can be seen from Table 3.2d and Table 3.2e. The increase in the net income of the Singaporean subsidiary is $14,000 (from $269,500 to $283,500), the Japanese subsidiary's net income of $3,500 decreases to a net loss of $16,000 (net effect of a reduction of $19,500), and this results in the reduction of the global profit of $5,500 (from $273,000 to $267,500), Then the final effect will cost the company a payment of additional tariffs to be paid to the Japanese government of $3,000 (from $93,000 to $96,000) and a payment of higher corporate income tax for the Singaporean government by $6,000 (from $115,500 to $121,500).

Because the tax rate in Japan is higher than in Singapore, the tax shield will be $1,500 of the tariffs (50 percent of the $3,000), to be subtracted from the difference of avoiding paying 20 percent more of $20,000, which is $4,000. Therefore the global profits will be increased by $2,500 ($4,000 – $1,500). We can conclude from this analysis that as long as the tax rate differential (which is 20 percent in our case as the difference between the tax rates of the two countries) is higher than the net effect of tariff rates (which is 15 percent of the costs of goods transferred reduced by the tax shield of 50 percent of the 15 percent = [15 percent – (50 percent of 15 percent) = 7.5 percent] imposed by the country with the higher tax rate, the higher transfer price will always generate net savings for the MNC (12.5 percent for each $1.00 increase in the transfer price per unit).

However, if the management (either the Singaporean subsidiary manager or the headquarter of the MNC) increases the price for goods transferred from the Singaporean subsidiary to the Japanese subsidiary by $1.00 more (from $31.00 to $32.00), it will have a negative effect on both the global profits of the MNC and on the net income of the Japanese subsidiary, as can be seen from Table 3.2e.

In concluding this section, it is important to notice that there is a limit for any increase in the transfer price. When the higher transfer price results in showing a net loss for the buying subsidiary, the global profits of the MNC will decrease by the difference between the maximum tax savings the MNC could get, which is the tax shield of 50 percent of the increase in the cost of the goods transferred (50% of $20,000 = $10,000) plus the 50 percent tax shield of the increase in the tariffs (50% of $3,000 = $1,500), and the maximum tax reduction allowed (which is $1,500) because of achieving net loss and paying zero tax. Assuming that no losses are allowed to be carried forward to the next year according to the tax regulations of Japan, the net effect, as indicated in the example, will be a $7,500 decrease in the global profits, resulting from paying more tariffs ($96,000 – $93,000 = $3,000) and more income taxes of $5,500 ($273,000 – $267,500).

MINIMIZATION OF EXCHANGE RATE RISK

The risk of the foreign exchange rate arises from doing international business denominated in currencies other than the domestic currency. High fluctuations in foreign exchange rates cause high risk of loss or gain. International transfer prices may be used to reduce an MNC's foreign exchange risk, which is the risk of a gain or loss in the MNC's future economic value resulting from a change in the foreign exchange rates (Oxelheim 1985, 61).

Transfer pricing is one of the best means to be used to minimize foreign exchange losses from currency fluctuations or to shift the losses to another subsidiary by moving assets from one country to another under the floating exchange rates system. This can be done by determining what currency is to be used for payment and whether the buying or selling subsidiary has the foreign exchange risk. If this is done, the appropriate transfer price for foreign activities will have a significant effect on the net exposure of the foreign subsidiary. In this case, funds in weak-currency countries are moved through the use of transfer pricing, especially when the foreign currency is not allowed to move out of the country.

As an example, let us assume that an American subsidiary sold merchandise worth US$20,000 in merchandise in January 2003 to a French subsidiary and that the payment was in American dollars within 60 days, at a time when the exchange rate was US$1 = One euro. Let us also assume that the MNC headquarters imposed the transfer price of US$22,000. The American subsidiary would receive $2,000 (or e2,000) more, but the assets of the Canadian subsidiary would have been reduced by e2,000 or $2,000. The difference in the price does not affect the global profit of the MNC.

Funds in weak-currency countries can be siphoned off by using international transfer price adjustments. To use international transfer pricing effectively in gaining through the exchange rates, it must be coordinated with the currency-hedging techniques of leading or lagging, which allow MNCs to avoid exchange risks and extract more funds out of a weak currency for conversion into a strong currency (Plasschaert 1994).

At the time of payment, March 2003, if the exchange rate was $1.00 = e1.50, the French subsidiary had to pay the American subsidiary $22,000, which is equivalent to e33,000 at the time of payment. In this case, the MNC moved the profits from France (which is assumed to have a soft currency) to the U.S. currency. Subsidiary A, the American, received e11,000 more than the original transfer price and e2,000 more than the original market price. The result was e11,000 foreign exchange loss for the French subsidiary on a relatively small transaction.

Generally, assets in weak-currency countries are moved through the use of international transfer price adjustments. An MNC can change the transfer price to take advantage of expected movements in the exchange rate. This allows the MNC to charge high transfer prices when the currency is expected to decline. By doing so, it maintains the gross profit margins in terms of U.S. dollars, even though in local currencies the gross profit margin has increased. However, price controls or government intervention may limit the use of this technique.

AVOIDING A CONFLICT WITH FOREIGN COUNTRIES' GOVERNMENTS

Transfer pricing policies of MNCs have a direct effect on foreign countries' economies where they are foreign subsidiaries. MNCs need to set their transfer pricing policies to charge for goods and services transferred into and out of foreign countries on a basis that host governments will consider justified. To avoid a conflict with the host country's government, an MNC should not charge high transfer prices for any goods and services transferred, because high prices mean more cash or fund outflows from the country than cash inflows, which will have a direct impact on the country's balance of payments and consequently on its economy. Therefore, MNCs need to determine what price to charge for their own products manufactured in one country and transferred to another country to achieve reasonable global profits.

Foreign governments, on the other hand, may concentrate on devising different tools, techniques, or regulations to minimize the effect of transfer pricing policies of MNCs on their countries. Host-country governments want to make sure that the long-term cash or fund outflows, such as dividends, royalties, and especially intracompany pricing manipulations, do not significantly exceed the value of goods, services, funds, or cash inflows. Therefore, MNCs need to make a balance between maximizing their global profits by charging very high transfer prices and avoiding conflict with the host-country government by charging low transfer prices.

CASH FLOW MANAGEMENT IN FOREIGN COUNTRIES

MNCs may need to withdraw funds from their foreign subsidiaries either because it is expected that a new political group is moving into the foreign government and an expropriation of most investments is anticipated, or because there are restrictions on moving cash out of the country due to balance of payments or exchange rate problems. International transfer pricing, dividends, royalties, interest on loans, and management service fees are the most important techniques for withdrawing cash from foreign countries. An MNC may raise transfer prices on goods or services transferred to a foreign subsidiary by another within the same organization by withdrawing funds from countries. Charging high transfer prices may be the only way to shift funds out of the country, as stated by an officer of a large MNC: "If I cannot get dividends out and my royalty rate is fixed, and I want to remit more money, then I do this on an uplift of my transfer prices" (Robbins and Stobaugh 1973, 91). Another officer indicated that his firms, even though they did not use transfer pricing for tax purposes, would push transfer prices up or down if exchange restrictions blocked the transfer of funds (Ibid.).

MNCs can control their cash flow in foreign countries through the use of transfer pricing techniques. In cash flow management, the transfer pricing strategy of MNCs comes into play. For example, if a U.S. corporation has a subsidiary in China and through an IRS examination is required to shift $400 million of income from the Chinese subsidiary to the U.S. parent corporation, there obviously would be major tax and cash flow effects. "Tax liabilities and foreign tax credits would change, and the company might need to pay a dividend. When this enormous shift in income happens, cash flow planning goes out the window. The idea that all this could be controlled through an APA so a company could plan makes sense not only from a tax perspective but from a corporate management perspective as well" (Wrappe, Milani, and Joy 1999, 40).

COMPETITIVENESS IN FOREIGN MARKETS

An MNC must help its subsidiaries in their first stages of business in foreign countries. ITP systems can be used to help them in competition against other businesses by charging a low transfer price for goods shipped into those countries to keep these foreign subsidiaries competitive with other local businesses.

Competition can be in the final selling markets, the raw materials market, the intermediate market, or in the parent company's market. However, a conflict may arise between host governments and MNCs that charge very low transfer prices for goods transferred into the foreign country, especially when there are import customs or duties imposed on the invoice price of goods and/or the low transfer price helps foreign subsidiaries to compete against local firms and may drive them out of the market. In this case, foreign governments may intervene to protect their domestic industries and their tax or tariff revenues as well.

MOTIVATION

Motivation is considered as one of the objectives of setting an international transfer pricing policy for domestic and foreign subsidiaries. Foreign subsidiary managers need to be motivated to maximize (or increase) their subsidiary's profits and transfer their products or services in and out of their areas of responsibility within the MNC at appropriate transfer prices. Transfer prices, in this case, can be used to motivate foreign subsidiary managers to achieve their subsidiaries' goals (by maximizing their own local profits) and at the same time achieving their MNC's goals (by maximizing the global profits).

For an international transfer pricing system to be a motivator, it must be tied to performance of foreign subsidiary managers. In order to be used as a measure of performance, an international transfer pricing system must meet the following four criteria:

1. It must be a result of the foreign manager's behavior.
2. It must include all the actions or activities that need to be performed.

3. It must be accepted by foreign subsidiary managers as a valid measurement of their performance.
4. It must include practical attainable goals for foreign subsidiary managers.

Does the transfer price completely measure the foreign subsidiary manager's performance? That is, does the transfer pricing system reflect all the actions that should be performed by the foreign subsidiary manager in selling his products to another subsidiary? Certainly the answer is no, because a foreign subsidiary manager does not have control over the fluctuations of the exchange rate of the local currency of the country in which he or she is doing business. The manager can easily achieve translation gains or losses to be included in his or her performance report because of political, legal, economic, or social factors over which he or she does not have any degree of control. The manager's profits can go up or down because of sudden increases in inflation rates and/or commodity or stock prices, and the outcome will be an increase or decrease in the market price when it is used as a transfer price.

MNCs must analyze the potential impact of using a transfer pricing system as a motivator for the foreign subsidiary manager's performance. Actions or decisions that are made by managers to improve their performance can have a negative effect on the global goals or profits of the MNC as a whole. Whenever international transfer pricing corporate goals lead to conflicting consequences, MNCs are forced into trade-offs between achieving different goals and must accept lower global profits when one objective has a priority over others, especially for achieving long-term goals.

GOAL HARMONIZATION

Goal harmonization exists when the goals of the MNC's foreign subsidiary managers, so far as feasible, are consistent with the global goals of the MNC. In establishing the right transfer pricing policy, top management would like to motivate foreign subsidiary managers to achieve the subsidiary's goals by contributing toward the achievement of the MNC's goals. It is almost impossible to achieve perfect congruence between foreign subsidiary managers' goals and the MNC's goals. However, at least the ITP policies should not motivate foreign subsidiary managers to make decisions that may be in conflict with the MNC's goals.

Motivation and goal harmonization are important factors in designing ITP systems. If an MNC desires to have its foreign subsidiary manager strongly motivated toward achieving congruent goals, it is necessary to consider the effect of the transfer pricing on divisional profitability or performance. However, if there is a conflict between foreign subsidiary managers' goals and the global goals, it may be preferable to have as little motivation and autonomy of foreign subsidiary managers as possible.

Generally, an ITP system should be designed in such a way that a foreign or domestic subsidiary manager is motivated to make decisions that are in the best interest of the MNC as a whole. When foreign subsidiary managers increase their subsidiaries' profits and at the same time increase global profits, then foreign subsidiary managers are in the MNC's best interest if the ITP system does not mislead managers about what the MNC's interests really are. However, both subsidiary manager and central management must be aware that the measurement of the subsidiary's net income (or contribution) under this ITP system is inherently imperfect, and the limited usefulness of that performance measure is further complicated by the existence of common resources used within the MNC.

SUMMARY AND CONCLUSION

This chapter has identified and discussed nine different objectives of establishing an international transfer pricing policy for MNCs: reduction of income taxes, reduction of tariffs, minimization of foreign exchange risks, avoidance of a conflict with host countries' governments, management of cash flows, competitiveness, performance evaluation, motivation, and goal harmonization. For the first two objectives combined, as long as the tax rate differential is higher than the net effect of the tariff rate imposed by the country with the higher tax rate, the higher transfer price will always generate net savings for the MNC. However, if the higher transfer price results in showing artificial losses for the buying subsidiary, the net effect will be detrimental for the MNC as a whole.

With the fluctuations in foreign exchange rates, assets in weak currencies can be moved through the use of higher transfer prices. However, host-government intervention with or without price controls will certainly limit the MNC's use of this technique. When performance evaluation systems combine with fluctuations in foreign exchange rates, transfer pricing policies will lead to misleading and imperfect financial measures of performance. A new transfer pricing system (dollar-indexing technique) was suggested and is believed to help in evaluating foreign subsidiary managers' performance and avoid any distorted financial results for performance evaluation.

Motivation, goal harmonization, and autonomy of foreign subsidiaries and their managers always lead to conflicting results with performance evaluation, reduction of income taxes, reduction of tariffs, and avoidance of foreign exchange risks. However, when different objectives lead to conflicting consequences, MNCs have to make trade-offs between achieving different objectives and must be satisfied with lower global profits when one objective has a priority over others, especially for achieving long-term objectives.

In designing an international transfer pricing policy to fit the foreign country, business literature, especially accounting, does not provide MNCs with any unique technique or model to help them arrive at the appropriate transfer price. Therefore, MNCs are in urgent need of a practical and objective technique or model that can avoid conflicts between different objectives of the system and, at the same time, achieve the global goals of MNCs to continue their overseas business activities under different political, economic, and social environmental conditions.

REFERENCES

Elliott, Jamie. 1998. International transfer pricing: A survey of UK and non-UK group. *Management Accounting* (CIMA-London) (November): 48–50

Greenhill, C. R., and E. O. Herbalzheimer. 1980. International transfer pricing: The restrictive business practice approach. *Journal of World Trade Law* (May-June): 232.

Hines, James R., Jr. 1999. Lessons from behavioral responses to international taxation. *National Tax Journal* (Washington) (June): 305–22.

Kim, H. Seung, and Stephen W. Miller. 1979. Constituents of the international transfer pricing decisions. *Columbia Journal of World Business* (spring): 71.

Knowles, Lynette L., and Ike Mathur. 1985. International transfer pricing objectives. *Managerial Finance* 11: 12.

Oxelheim, Lars. 1985. *International financial market fluctuations.* New York: John Wiley & Sons.

Plasschaert, Sylvain R. F. 1994. The multiple motivations for transfer pricing modulations in multinational enterprises and governmental counter measures: An attempt at clarification. *Management International Review,* 34, no. 1: 36–50.

Robbins, Sidney M., and Robert B. Stobaugh. 1973. *Money in the multinational enterprise.* New York: Basic Books.

Wrappe, Steven C., Ken Milani, and Julie Joy. 1999. The transfer price is right . . . or is it? *Strategic Finance* (July): 38–43.

4

Methods for Pricing Transferred Goods or Services of Multinational Companies

This chapter discusses transfer pricing methods that are appropriate and acceptable to achieve certain internal objectives of MNCs in managing their foreign activities. It also analyzes Section 482 of the U. S. Internal Revenue Code and its impact on the foreign activities of MNCs. It examines the IRS's Advanced Pricing Agree (APA) program and its effect on transfer pricing policies of foreign activities. Finally, the OECD guidelines for transfer pricing policies are discussed.

MNCs use transfer pricing policies as a way to achieve certain objectives of managing their foreign business operations. There are two sets of objectives in business literature: internal and external. Internally, MNCs use transfer prices in the accounting sense as accounting prices, to account for transactions transferred between different subsidiaries within the same organization. They are also used for making decisions regarding the allocation of resources between different subsidiaries in different countries, and to help top management in managing a decentralized organization by integrating and coordinating autonomous (or pseudo-autonomous) subsidiaries all over the world. Motivation, control, and performance evaluation of foreign subsidiaries within MNCs are also other objectives for using transfer prices. At the top of the objectives stands goal harmonization, which requires that all actions and decisions made by a foreign subsidiary manager be in the best interest of the MNC as a whole.

The second set of objectives relates to factors outside the home country. From the viewpoint of an MNC, transfer prices are used to allocate net income among different subsidiaries in different countries under different legal, social, and economic regulations. Externally, MNCs face other problems, such as different income tax rates of different countries, tax structures and regulations, quotas and import duties, cash movement restrictions, currency exchange control, and conflicts with host governments. From the viewpoint of the United States or any other foreign government, transfer pricing policies create problems with the belief that they do not reflect open market prices. Host governments, like others, believe that MNCs set their own transfer pricing policies to avoid paying taxes. Therefore, MNCs are in conflict with both home and host governments.

The two sets of objectives are not directly related to each other, and there is no evidence that any single transfer price designed for only one objective will satisfy all other objectives. No practical evidence has been found regarding what is the best or most appropriate transfer price for an MNC to use in managing its businesses in foreign countries. There are three reasons for this problem.

First, changing global environmental factors—such as market conditions, government attitudes, political issues, legal considerations, economic conditions, and different global strategies—force MNCs to use different transfer prices at different times under different circumstances. Second, balance of payments, tax revenues, and market structures of different host countries, among other factors, are affected by the use of transfer prices.

There is no easy way to "ascertain ex post whether a given transfer price level was practiced ex ante with a view to minimize taxes or regulations or primarily on business grounds" (Plasschaert 1979, 12). Third, if the transfer price does not reflect the foreign market conditions or if it deviates from arm's-length price between unaffiliated companies, then it is unacceptable. "The extent of the deviation depends on the yardstick used; . . . the implementation of the yardstick is difficult and frequently gets enmeshed in the issue of the fair price, whatever that concept may mean" (Ibid.).

The basic acceptable international standard for transfer pricing is the arm's-length principle. The notion is that pricing in transactions between related parties should be closely comparable to the pricing that would prevail between related parties. This principle might appear readily susceptible to empirical proof. In practice, it is inherently subjective and difficult to apply confidently. The most difficult issue is obtaining reliable data from comparable transactions between related parties. In the case of new or unique intangible property, such data ordinarily will not exist (unless the company licenses to third parties.) Even in the case of commodities, it may be hard to replicate the circumstances of the controlled transactions. MNCs ordinarily do not share sensitive pricing information with competitors, as that is considered confidential. Moreover, when MNCs publish financial information in their annual reports, they are of limited use because they are presented on a gross and brief basis.

To choose the appropriate transfer pricing policy for foreign activities, it is essential to look at both the appropriate transfer pricing methods used in practice for the internal use of management and the appropriate transfer pricing method for tax purposes. Therefore, this chapter is divided into the following sections: economics and accounting oriented analysis, mathematically oriented analysis (including linear and nonlinear), Section 482 of IRC, the IRS's Advanced Pricing Agreement (APA) program, and the Organization for Economic Co-operation and Development (OECD) guidelines on transfer pricing policies.

ECONOMICS AND ACCOUNTING ORIENTED ANALYSIS

The economic and accounting oriented techniques fall into one of the following subgroups:

- market price
- cost-based and cost-plus methods including: full production cost, full production cost plus profit margin, variable production cost, and variable production cost-plus profit margin
- marginal cost-based
- negotiated price

Market/Arm's-Length Price

The market price is the price that would prevail when a manufacturing subsidiary sells its products to an external customer; or, the manufacturing subsidiary charges the same price to the buying subsidiary as it would charge the external customer in arm's-length transactions. However, four criteria should be satisfied to use the market price as a transfer price.

1. There is a competitive intermediate market.
2. Subsidiary managers have freedom in decision making—that is, they can decide to buy or sell internally or in the open market without any interference of top management.
3. Subsidiary managers have their own autonomy or at least a minimal degree of interdependence among profit centers.
4. There is a known market price that can be quoted at anytime.

There are several advantages to using the market price. First, if a market price can be determined, it is the best price to be used for performance evaluation of the profit centers, because it motivates managers to act as if they were managing their own business, and it consequently reduces costs of production and increases divisional profits. Second, market prices correspond to the arm's-length price, and it is the most acceptable price from IRS's perspective. Using the market price may help MNCs to avoid any conflict with either home- or host-country governments. Third, subsidiary managers, especially in foreign countries, may be well qualified to make quick decisions under certain circumstances to avoid any negative consequences as interference of the government.

However, there are some problems that may result from using market prices. First, the appropriate market price may be difficult to determine. It may be different from one country to another even if it is in the same currency, or it may be different from time to time. Therefore, market price may be difficult to establish. Second, in the international market, transportation costs are significant and are different from one location to another. That makes it impossible to have a uniform market price for the same product of the same MNC that is sold in different countries. Third, the supply and demand in foreign markets require establishing a price that will prevail in that market and will help foreign subsidiaries to compete with other subsidiaries. Therefore, there is no unique market price to be quoted.

Cost-Based and Cost-Plus Methods

Cost-based transfer pricing may be used when market prices do not exist or are not available for MNCs to use for international transfer pricing. Under cost-based methods, cost may mean different things and have different effects on performance evaluation, motivation, decision making, divisional profits, income tax liability, and global profits.

Cost-based methods include the full cost (actual or standard) and variable cost (actual or standard). Full cost includes direct material, direct labor, and factory overhead. This method offers three major advantages.

1. Availability of cost information is provided by the accounting system currently in use by the MNC.
2. It is also in conformity with U.S. generally accepted accounting principles concerning inventory valuation and income determination.
3. It may motivate foreign subsidiary managers to increase their divisional contribution as long as the full absorption cost exceeds

the variable cost and there is additional capacity to accommodate the incoming orders.

However, the use of the full absorption costing method can create many problems, which can be summarized as follows:

1. If the selling subsidiary is assured of covering all full production cost on all goods transferred internally, there is little incentive for foreign subsidiary managers either to have control over their divisional costs, produce efficiently, or make rational decisions related to their area of responsibilities as long as the cost of their inefficient use of resources is passed on to the buying subsidiaries. This can be avoided by using standard costs rather than actual costs for transfer pricing.
2. If the full cost exceeds the market price, the buying subsidiary manager would be motivated to buy from the market outside the MNC and, consequently, create idle capacity for the MNC as a whole.
3. It leads to suboptimal short-run decisions for the MNC as a whole when the buying subsidiary treats the fixed costs of the selling subsidiary as variable costs.

A variable cost-based transfer price leads the buying subsidiary to make optimal decisions in the best interest from the MNC viewpoint. The MNC's variable costs (either actual or standard) are considered as the buying subsidiary variable costs as it acts in the international market. However, using the variable cost-based transfer price forces the selling subsidiary to report zero profit or loss equal to its fixed costs.

For making long-run pricing decisions, variable cost-based transfer pricing will mislead the buying subsidiary managers in making the appropriate pricing decisions to compete in the international market from the MNC viewpoint. In other words, the subsidiary manager's decision may not be in the best interest of the MNC as a whole.

Cost-plus transfer pricing may use actual or standard cost, which should be marked up to allow the selling subsidiary to realize a profit. A markup can be a flat percentage of the cost (actual, standard, full, or variable). A markup should allow the foreign subsidiary to recover its normal operating costs plus an appropriate amount to earn a return on investment equal to that earned in the domestic market (Nagy 1987).

A major reason for the common use of cost-plus transfer pricing is its simplicity, clarity, and its approximation of the market price, especially when the intermediate product has an international market, and it is a justifiable and reasonable transfer price when there is no market for the product. However, it may lead to suboptimal decisions for the MNC as a whole when it is not related to some economic reality.

Marginal Cost-Based Method

Marginal cost is the change in total cost that results from an increase in the production by one more unit.

Under the marginal cost-based method, the transfer price is to be set at the marginal cost of the selling subsidiary. The selling subsidiary should produce when its marginal cost (the transfer price) is equal to its marginal revenue—this will lead to maximization of the profits of the MNC. Marginal cost-based transfer pricing is presumed to result in optimal production for the MNC.

The marginal cost-based method is appropriate when there is neither an external market for the intermediate nor an agreeable negotiated transfer price between the two subsidiaries. However information on marginal cost cannot be practically collected from the MNC accounting system. Several empirical studies showed that marginal transfer pricing, which is a theoretical technique, is of very little use in practice and it is not a realistic technique to be used.

Negotiated Transfer Pricing Method

A negotiated transfer price is used when the buying and the selling subsidiaries are free to negotiate the acceptable transfer price for both of them. This method retains the independence of both managers to make the right decision for their subsidiary and makes both managers accountable for the outcome of their decision. Therefore, it motivates subsidiary managers to have control over their costs and increase their divisional contribution to the MNC.

However, this method may lead to suboptimal decisions, especially when the final product is sold in a different country and other factors—such as different tax rates, different government regulations, different tariffs, and competition—are ignored. Another problem is that negotiations may require too much time, therefore making this a time-consuming process and possibly requiring top management intervention for settlement.

MATHEMATICALLY ORIENTED ANALYSIS

Mathematical programming techniques were introduced after the failure of the traditional economic models to solve transfer pricing problems. The mathematical programming models allocate the resources efficiently and, at the same time, evaluate the efficient use of the resources under a decentralized organization (Abdel-Khalik and Lusk 1974; Baumal and Fabian 1964). These techniques are linear programming models, which deal with allocation problem in which the objective (or goal) and all the requirements imposed are expressed by linear functions; nonlinear programming models which, are used when the goal and/or one or more of the requirements imposed are expressed by nonlinear functions; and a goal programming model, which is used when there are multiple goals for an MNC. Under all these techniques, a mathematical model sets the transfer prices at the opportunity costs (or the shadow prices) of the intermediate product.

However, the suggested mathematical programming techniques have the following drawbacks:

- The MNC must obtain suboptimal divisional information in order to maintain "efficient decentralized operations" (Bailey and Boe 1976, 561). When transfer prices are set centrally, the autonomy of foreign subsidiary managers is ignored completely and the profit center concepts are not applicable under these conditions.
- The problem is enlarged with MNCs because of the existence of different economic, political, and social variables that may require setting a different transfer price in each country where a foreign subsidiary is located. In other words, different tax rates, foreign exchange risks, expropriation risks, government interventions, and avoiding any conflicts with host country governments are just examples of many problems that MNCs face in doing business abroad, and they may make the development of any mathematical programming model for MNCs much more difficult than for domestic firms, if not impossible. Therefore, experimental or empirical studies are badly needed to validate the use of these models within MNCs.
- These models do not give any consideration to the behavioral implications of using transfer pricing; therefore, they do not achieve the objectives of establishing international transfer pricing, described previously.
- In evaluating foreign subsidiary managers' performance as one of the objectives of international transfer pricing policies within these models, performance evaluation is assumed to be a function of profits. However, performance evaluation may be affected by divisional costs, variances between budgeted and actual cost, or any other factors that should be incorporated into the system (Abdel-Khalik, Rashad, and Lusk 1974, 20).

THE U.S. TAXATION OF INTERNATIONAL TRANSFER PRICING TRANSACTIONS AND SECTION 482 OF IRC

For the past three decades, MNCs have experienced no business function that goes so deeply into nearly all international operations— including manufacturing, marketing, management, and financing—as international transfer pricing. International transfer pricing decisions have great impact on foreign operations of MNCs, directly affecting their global revenues and profits, and can help or limit an MNC's ability to operate, manage, and utilize its economic resources on a global basis for the purpose of achieving its ultimate goals.

Recent U.S. tax changes reflect the importance of global competition and devote considerable effort to revising provisions that affect the taxation of foreign income (Hines 1999, 306). Tax regulations of the United States are different from those of foreign countries in many aspects, such as tax rates, tax treaties, tax bases, foreign tax credits, and taxes imposed on any profits resulting from using intercompany transfer pricing policies for goods and services crossing the border of the country. There are great differencees among foreign countries in many aspects in their tax regulations and laws. Developed countries, such as the United Kingdom, Canada, Germany, France, Japan, and Switzerland, have different objectives in their tax structure, policies, and regulations than those of developing countries, such as Egypt, India, Kuwait, Mexico, and Jordan, among many others.

The significant growth of the global market means that both MNCs and tax authorities should consider transfer pricing policies very carefully. MNCs should ensure that their transfer pricing policies and strategies can be supported and that they are deemed to be fair and acceptable. Foreign tax authorities should also ensure that they collect a fair and reasonable amount of corporate tax revenue from MNCs investing and operating in their countries (Elliott 1998, 49).

Developed countries impose taxes on their multinational and foreign corporations for four main purposes:

1. To raise revenues
2. To provide tax incentives
3. To avoid or minimize double taxation
4. To curb tax abuses

Developing countries (DC) use their tax system to achieve, to some extent, different objectives:

- To achieve certain rates of economic growth

- To establish industrial priorities
- To encourage new investments in new industries
- To maintain political and social stability by sustained development of their economy
- To monitor all foreign exchange transactions and enforce stringent control

However, some foreign countries relax their governmental restrictions on the repatriation or remittance of profits, capital, or income of foreign investments to encourage more inward investment in their countries.

It is estimated that almost 60 percent of all international business transactions take place between related partners, so tax authorities worldwide developed four main ways to catch and reduce tax evasion by transfer pricing (Lermer 1998, 30):

1. Including provisions in their legislation with formal, detailed, and binding regulations, similar to the ones in the U.S. Tax Code
2. Including provisions in their legislation with detailed guidelines on reasonable and acceptable techniques of transfer pricing, such as in Germany
3. Providing in their legislation arm's-length standards that help to establish acceptable transfer pricing practices based on the guidelines of the Organization for Economic Cooperation and Development's (OECD) guidelines, such as in the United Kingdom
4. Having no specific transfer pricing legislation, where the ordinary tax laws and evasion prohibitions are relied on to prevent transfer pricing understatement, such as in Netherlands.

Transfer pricing is becoming increasingly important as foreign countries become more accessible to the rest of the world and vice versa. Tax authorities of foreign countries are not well prepared to deal with the complicated issues involved in transfer pricing policies of large MNCs. Different countries do things differently. There are no specific regulations to control transfer pricing issues in most foreign countries. Some host countries' tax authorities may make easy inspections of MNCs investing in the area; however, others may be too tough. This depends on the political party at the time of inspection, the tax officer, and the economic conditions of the country.

Over the long run, different tax structures, different tax rates over foreign investments and subsidiaries, and different foreign exchange control policies may constitute the most basic reason for using the right strategy for international transfer pricing policies in foreign countries.

This can be combined with long-range global tax planning to achieve the global objectives of MNCs within different environmental conditions in the global market.

In general, most governments regulate transfer pricing methods by requiring MNCs to use the arm's-length standard. The most common solution that tax authorities have adopted to reduce the probability of the transfer price manipulation is to develop specific transfer pricing regulations as part of the corporate income tax code. These regulations are generally based on the concept of the arm's-length standard, which specifies that all MNC intracompany transactions should be priced as if they took place between unrelated parties acting at arm's length in competitive markets. The arm's-length price is the price two unrelated parties would use through bargaining in a competitive market.

To ensure the use of the appropriate arm's-length standard, two important questions should be asked: What would the two related parties have done had they been unrelated? What sale price would they have negotiated? Because the companies are related in the transaction under scrutiny by the tax authorities, any answer to these two questions must be hypothetical. The best way to answer is to use a substitute price, done in one of two methods (Eden 1998).

1. A price negotiated by two other unrelated parties that were engaged in the same or comparable transaction under the same or comparable circumstances is a substitute for the arm's-length price in the transaction between the two related firms. The tax authority looks for two other companies that are unrelated and engaged in similar activities as the related parties in question, and then uses the price negotiated by the unrelated companies, adjusted if necessary for differences in product and functional characteristics, as the arm's-length price. The arm's-length price negotiated between unrelated companies is used to substitute the transfer price between the two related companies.

2. A price set by one of the related parties in a comparable transaction under comparable circumstances with an unrelated party could be used as an approximation. Where the MNC either buys outside or sells outside, in comparable circumstances, the price negotiated with unrelated parties can be used as the arm's-length price.

For tax authorities, which method is used will depend on the available information and the prevailing circumstances. Important questions should be asked to determine whether the arm's-length price is appropriate in a given case.

1. Are there unrelated parties that do the same, or almost the same, kind of business and/or transactions under the same circumstances?

2. Does one of the two related parties also do the same business and/or transactions with an unrelated party under the same circumstances?
3. Where there are differences between the related and unrelated transactions, are they quantifiable and justifiable?
4. Do the results seem reasonable and acceptable in the circumstances?

If the answers to these questions are yes, then the arm's-length standard will yield a reasonable and/or acceptable result. If the answers are no, then alternative methods must be used (Ibid.).

SECTION 482 OF IRC

International transfer pricing decisions have a significant impact on global sales, tax liabilities, and profits of MNCs. Tax authorities of most countries throughout the world require that the transfer pricing policies between related entities must be at arm's length. Their objectives are to prevent MNCs from reducing their tax liabilities by shifting profits from one entity to another, to allow tax authorities to adjust income and deductions to reflect clearly the correct taxable income within their territories, and to counter abusive transfer pricing policies. Most legislation of different countries has focused on the concept of comparing intercompany prices with arm's-length third-party prices.

In the United States, Section 482 of the U.S. Internal Revenue Code provides that the Internal Revenue Service (IRS) may allocate gross income, deductions, credits, or allowances among related entities to prevent the evasion of taxes and to reflect clearly the income of each entity of a corporate group. Related entities under Section 482 are defined as two or more trades, organizations, or businesses owned or controlled, either directly or indirectly, by the same group or interests. The purpose of Section 482 is to prevent shifting of income or profits from one commonly controlled entity to another by an MNC.

Section 482 deals with five types of transactions:

1. Interest charged on intercompany loans
2. Services performed for a related party
3. Use of tangible property by a related party
4. Intercompany transfers of intangible property
5. Intercompany sales of tangible property

Intercompany pricing on sales of tangible property is the most widely known problem; therefore, it is the one that is discussed most in this book.

The application of Section 482 of the U.S. Internal Revenue Code of 1986 has tended to focus on the concept of comparing intragroup transfer prices with arm's length third-party prices. The arm's-length standard is defined by the Code as "the amount which would have been charged in independent transactions with unrelated parties under the same or similar circumstances." In other words, Section 482 insists that intercompany transactions be priced at arm's-length, or as if they involved unrelated parties in the open market.

Currently there is evidence of tax-motivated transfer pricing, which comes in several forms. Though it is possible that high tax rates are correlated with other location attributes that depress the profitability of foreign investment, competitive conditions typically imply that after-tax rates of return should be equal in the absence of tax-motivated income shifting. It is true that before-tax profitability is negatively correlated with local tax rates, which is strongly suggestive of active tax avoidance (Hines 1999, 313).

Many problems may arise in translating Section 482 into practice by MNCs, because the regulations are ambiguous and vague. Consequently, facts and circumstances of what constitute the appropriate arm's-length price to be used among related entities can give plenty of scope for debate and negotiations. Therefore, most cases between the IRS and MNCs require courts to settle disputes, and there is not one general rule arrived at among courts. A research study by Jane D. Burns (1980) concluded that 53 percent of the sample group of MNCs had Section 482 reallocations in at least one year and the average annual deficiency proposed by the IRS was about $1 million, of which 70 percent was agreed to and paid, 16 percent was reduced, and 14 percent was being disputed.

Section 482 prescribes three specific methods for determining arm's-length prices, to be used in order, and a fourth method that may be used for all other situations in which none of the first three is considered appropriate and reasonable. The three methods set forth in the regulations, to be used in order, are comparable uncontrolled price method, resale price method, and cost-plus method.

The IRS, in allocating profits or income, should look, first, for an uncontrolled transaction, second for a resale price, and third at cost of a tangible property plus a reasonable profit. Only if none of these three methods applies, a fourth method is used. This method was included in the regulations after great objections by businesses when the original regulations were issued with only the three methods mentioned here. This fourth method allows MNCs an alternative if they can fully justify the appropriateness and reasonableness of the method selected for their circumstances. In allocating the income or profits of foreign subsidiaries, MNCs have the responsibility to justify their international transfer pricing methods and to prove that they are reasonable. Otherwise, income reallocations made by the IRS must be accepted by the courts unless the MNC proves them to be unreasonable or arbitrary allocations (Burns 1984, 140).

Generally, it is not necessary for an MNC to use only one pricing method for all of its products under all circumstances. It may be acceptable for an MNC to sell different products at different stages of completion in different markets using different pricing methods. The methods prescribed in Section 482 of the IRC are discussed next.

THE COMPARABLE UNCONTROLLED PRICE (CUP) METHOD

An uncontrolled sale is defined in the IRS regulations as a sale in which the seller and buyer are not members of the same controlled group. In other words, it uses prices charged in comparable sales to third unrelated parties as the appropriate prices for intercompany transactions.

Uncontrolled sales can be comparable to the conditions surrounding the sale that are either identical to the controlled sales or so nearly identical that differences can be reflected by adjustments to the price. Adjustments are to be made when they reflect differences that have a definitive and reasonable effect on price. The uncontrolled sale, as adjusted, makes up the comparable uncontrolled sale price.

A comparison with sales to third parties is deemed the most appropriate method. However, a major problem, which opens the door for disputes, is how can an MNC validly prove a comparable uncontrolled price? Factors in doing so would include the terms of sale, the timing of sale, the conditions prevailing in the market place, transportation costs, and different qualities of products (Liebman 1987). Generally, the most important issue, under this method, is whether the sale is truly comparable.

The transfer pricing system requires that MNCs certify that their tax returns are in accordance with the arm's-length price. However, there are two problems: MNCs are not confident that foreign tax authorities would necessarily be in accord with MNCs' view of arm's-length pricing; and it is difficult to obtain support from senior management assigned to overseas locations for short periods of time (Elliott 1998, 49).

In brief, the CUP method can be determined in one of three ways.

1. If the MNC sells or buys the same product under the same circumstances to or from an unrelated third party, that price can be used to approximate or as a substitute for a CUP.

2. If two unrelated parties trade the same product under the same circumstances, the price they set is a CUP.
3. If there are some differences in the products traded or in the circumstances in either of the two first cases and adjustments can be made to the price to take account of these differences, then that adjusted price can be used as a CUP.

However, all the facts, documents, and circumstances that could materially affect the price must be considered—for example, the characteristics of the product, the market location, the economic conditions, the trade level of the companies, and the risks involved. Adjustments are made to the external price to more closely reflect or estimate the arm's-length price.

Assume that JAPCO sells DVD players directly to its U.S. subsidiary AMCO located in New York City. JAPCO and other Japanese firms also sell VCRs in the United States to unrelated parties through a U.S. department store chain FARCO located in Fargo, North Dakota. JAPCO's product is sold FOB (free on board—i.e., without freight or insurance added) to both AMCO and FARCO. The average U.S. retail price, based on sales by FARCO, is $300 per DVD player. FARCO charges, on average, 10 percent of the retail price as its commission for selling the DVD player.

Under the CUP method, the arm's-length price should be the price that JAPCO sells to unrelated customers, assuming the same or comparable transactions under the same or comparable circumstances. JAPCO sells the same product to its U.S. subsidiary and to the unrelated department store FARCO, so these unrelated U.S. sales can be used to generate an arm's-length price that can be used to provide a CUP. We know that the retail price of DVD players in the U.S. market is $300. We also know the markup charged by FARCO. Because we want the FOB transfer price from JAPCO to AMCO, we must also subtract the freight costs of moving the DVD players from Japan to FARCO in the United States. Table 4.1 provides a numerical illustration of the CUP method.

In an example of an MNC that sells the same product under the same circumstances both inside and outside the enterprise, the outside price can be a substitute for the transfer price. In this case, the products are the same but the circumstances are slightly different (i.e., there is a sales agent, and freight costs are incurred in the outside sales), so some adjustment is required to find the right transfer price. Most tax authorities prefer the CUP method over all other pricing methods because it incorporates more information about the specific transaction than does any other method. CUP is transaction and product specific. Because the arm's-length standard is a transactional approach to valuing the MNC,

TABLE 4.1   The Comparable Uncontrolled Price (CUP) Method

The Transfer Pricing per DVD player:	
Average retail price of a DVD player in the United States	$300.00
Less FARCO commission agent	–$ 30.00
Less freight adjustment (from CIF to FOB)	–$ 20.00
Transfer pricing using the CUP method	$250.00

the best method is the method that focuses most closely on the product and the transaction under consideration.

However, several problems are encountered in applying the CUP method in practice (Schindler 1989). One of the most serious is the absence of unrelated transactions in some industries such as the petroleum industry, where there is vertical integration of global operations handling exploration, production, refining, and shipping. It is seldom practical to find unrelated parties to handle some of the major transactions. Another is that intercompany transfers of intangible property does not fit into the arm's-length standard as required by the regulations. It is difficult, if not impossible, for a firm to sell its valuable advanced technology, marketing know-how, or any intangible assets such as patents to both its own foreign subsidiaries and to unrelated parties who may be its own competitors.

An excellent example of some of the problems associated with the use of comparable prices is cited in the survey conducted by Jamie Elliott (1998, 50). It was stated in the survey that to use the transfer pricing guidelines prescribed by the tax authorities, pharmaceutical companies must conduct comparability studies; however, it is almost impossible for pharmaceutical companies to find comparable transactions between independent parties. The products and ingredients of the pharmaceutical MNCs are unique and patented.

THE RESALE PRICE METHOD (RPM)

If an arm's-length price cannot be determined through the use of a comparable uncontrolled price, the regulations specify that the resale price method must be used. Arm's-length price is computed by looking at a sale by a related buyer to its customers, reduced by an appropriate markup percentage. The RPM, as an alternative method, focuses on one side of the transaction, either the manufacturer or the distributor, and to estimate the transfer price using a functional approach. Under the resale price method, the tax officer looks for firms at similar trade levels that perform similar distribution transactions.

The RPM is best used when the distributor adds relatively little value to the product, so the value of its functions is easier to estimate. The assumption behind the RPM is that competition among distributors means that similar margins on sales are earned for similar transactions. A distributor is likely to charge the same or a similar sales margin for carrying DVD players as for carrying televisions or other similar goods. Given a large number of distributors, averaging over these unrelated firms can be used to substitute the margin that the distribution affiliate would have earned in an arm's-length transaction. Subtracting this margin from the retail price, one can estimate the transfer price under the RPM.

Recall AMCO, the American distributor for its Japanese parent company's established line of DVD players. Comparable independent distributors in the United States earn gross profit margins of 10 percent. What should the transfer price be for exports from the Japanese parent to AMCO? Under the resale price method, the transfer price to AMCO for a particular DVD player should be calculated as the final retail price in the United States minus the gross margin earned by comparable American distributors. This assumes that the arm's-length price for AMCO is the same gross profit margin as is earned by other distributors in the United States of similar products under similar circumstances. If other comparable distributors earn 10 percent margins, on average, the arm's-length margin for AMCO should also be 10 percent. Table 4.2 illustrates the resale price method for the case of an American distributor of Japanese-made DVD players.

The RPM is appropriate where a sale transaction is made to a controlled party that then resells to an unrelated party and there is no comparable uncontrolled price. A portion of the resale price may be attributable to value added by the related party. In that case, adjustments are to be made to the resale price.

Unlike the CUP method, the RPM evaluates the transaction only from the buyer's perspective. The method ensures that the buyer receives an arm's-length margin consistent with margins earned by similar companies engaged in similar transactions. But nothing is done to ensure that the manufacturer's profit margin is consistent with margins earned by other manufacturers. Under the RPM, having determined the buyer's arm's-length margin, all excess profit on the transaction is assigned to the seller. Therefore, the RPM tends to overestimate the transfer price

TABLE 4.2   The Resale Price Method (RPM)

The transfer pricing per DVD player:	$300.00
Final retail price of a DVD	
Less margin earned by comparable American distributors	
(10% of retail price)	–$ 30.00
= Transfer pricing using the RPM	$270.00

because it gives all unallocated profits on the transaction to the current manufacturer.

Different guidelines as to the appropriateness of any markup may be used. However, the appropriate markup percentage can be determined from uncontrolled sales made by other resellers under similar circumstances. Generally, there are two methods to compute the markup percentage: the gross profit percentage and the net profit percentage. The regulations prescribe the gross profit percentage method to be used in allocating the income of subsidiaries. However, the net profit percentage can be used as the fourth method.

COST-PLUS METHOD (CPM)

The seller's price is computed by multiplying the cost of production by an appropriate gross profit percentage to cover the functions it carries out. The appropriate gross profit percentage can be determined from comparable uncontrolled sales of the seller, another party of the uncontrolled sale, or unrelated parties. This method is usually used by MNCs with major activities in exports of manufacturing components or unfinished goods that have substantial values added to them by the purchasing foreign subsidiaries.

In the CPM, the tax officer looks at the other side of the transaction: the manufacturer. The method starts with the costs of production, measured using known accounting standards, and then adds an appropriate markup to the costs. The assumption is that in a competitive market the percentage markups over cost that could be earned by other arm's-length manufacturers would be roughly the same. The CPM works best when the producer is a simple manufacturer without complicated activities so that its costs and returns can be more easily estimated. For example, KALVCO, a wholly owned subsidiary of an American Calvin Kline for women perfume multinational, produces an expensive perfume for sale in Paris using active ingredients purchased at arm's length. The active Calvin Kline ingredients cost $5.00 per ounce of perfume; KALVCO's standard manufacturing cost is $12.00. The industry average markup for bulk formulations performed by other perfume manufacturers in France is 25 percent above standard cost.

Under the cost-plus method, the tax authority looks to see what comparable companies in France would have been willing to manufacture the product for; that is, what gross markup over standard costs would they have demanded to be paid? If the MNC had simply contracted out the manufacturing function, what would the company have had to pay on the competitive market to get the product made? In this case, comparable perfume manufacturers demand a gross markup of 25 percent over standard manufacturing cost (excluding material input costs). Therefore, to KALVCO's standard manufacturing cost we need to add the same markup that other perfume manufacturers demand, plus the cost of the active ingredients. The transfer price per ounce of perfume for a particular shipment by KALVCO to one of the foreign affiliates is calculated as shown in Table 4.3.

In order to use the cost-plus method, the tax authority or MNC must know the accounting approach adopted by unrelated parties. For example, what costs are included in the cost base before the markup over costs is computed? Is it actual cost or standard cost? Are only manufacturing costs included or is the cost base the sum of manufacturing costs plus some portion of operating expenses? The larger the cost base, the smaller should be the profit markup, or gross margin, over costs. As a one-sided method, the CPM focuses only on the profit markup of the seller and insists that the seller should earn only what arm's-length sellers engaging in similar transactions would earn in a competitive market. Therefore the CPM tends to underestimate the transfer price because it gives all unallocated profits from the transaction to the buyer.

However, the term "cost of production" as prescribed in the regulations should be consistent with sound accounting practices for allocating costs. According to the regulations, if the seller used its full costs to compute its gross profit percentage, then the cost of production would be the full production costs. If the seller used direct costs to compute its gross profit percentage, the cost of production would be equal to the direct costs.

The manner in which direct costs are computed may be inconsistent with the regulations' definition of cost of production. In management (or cost) accounting practices, direct costs are defined as those costs that can be traceable into and are identified specifically with a particular product or process for a particular purpose. However, direct costing, sometimes called variable costing, is a method of product costing that charges only the variable costs of manufacturing to the product. Variable manufacturing costs include direct materials, direct labor, and variable manufacturing overhead.

Section 482 is not specific as to what is meant by direct costs. Is it the term "direct costs," which includes direct materials and direct labor

TABLE 4.3   The Cost-Plus Method (CPM)

The transfer pricing per ounce of women's perfume:	
KALVCO standard per ounce (excluding active ingredients costs)	$12.00
Plus gross markup received by fuctionally comparable manufacturers in France (25 percent of standard cost)	+$ 3.00
Plus cost of active ingredients	+$ 5.00
Equals transfer pricing using the cost-plus method	$20.00

costs only, or is it the product costing method called "direct costing"? The difference between the two is variable manufacturing overhead, which may be between 10 and 30 percent of production costs.

In general, the CUP is the preferred transactional method for determining the transfer price. Where it cannot be used, functional comparables methods (RPM, CPM) are the second alternative. The disadvantage both the RPM and the CPM have is that they only focus on one side of the transaction, either that of the seller or the buyer The CUP has the advantage of focusing on both sides of the business transaction. However, finding a CUP is almost impossible. Moreover, high-tech goods and services (intangibles), where there are not good substitutes, are by their nature the most difficult to evaluate.

THE ALTERNATE METHOD

The regulations provide that when none of the three methods can reasonably be applied under the usual circumstances of a particular case, an alternate method should be used. The alternate method can be a variation of one of the three, or an entirely different method that may be appropriate under certain circumstances.

For many years Section 482 has been used as the standard tax treatment of intercompany transfers. It was first adopted in the Revenue Act of 1921 and has remained essentially unchanged since then. A few clarifications and some additional authorities have been given to the IRS over more than 65 years of statutory history.

Today U.S.-based and non-U.S corporations and their international activities have expanded from only imports and exports to more and more direct involvement in different international markets using many different tactics. The growth of U.S.-based and foreign MNCs has brought significant changes in the structure of international markets and has created significant economic interdependence between most nations (Schindler 1989, 9). A survey by Jamie Elliott (1998, 50) indicated that the most applicable transfer pricing methods for U.K., U.S., and European-owned companies were cost-plus, the comparable uncontrolled price (CUP), and resale price.

The U.S. Tax Reform of 1986 reduced U.S. corporate tax rates. The Act significantly affects international operations of U.S.-based MNCs and U.S. taxation of foreign MNCs that have subsidiaries in the United States. Although the Act changed the corporate tax rates, it also made the international transfer pricing policies more complicated than before. The majority of accounting practitioners and MNCs' key top executives believed that lowering the U.S. corporate tax rates below those of other industrial developed and developing countries would encourage the U.S.-based MNCs to minimize their global tax liability and consequently maximize their global profits. This could be done by bringing more and more of their taxable income to the United States. However, Section 482 still insists on the use of arm's-length pricing for intercompany transactions.

Since MNCs do not deal with their foreign subsidiaries as if they were unrelated, proving the reasonableness of their international transfer pricing in dealing with IRS may be nearly impossible, especially if their production and marketing techniques are not comparable with any other techniques throughout the world.

Another problem with the new U.S. Tax Reform Act of 1986, which creates a potential problem on the transfer price for goods imported into the United States, is that a U.S. importer may not claim a transfer price for income tax purposes on goods purchased from a related party that is higher than was claimed for U.S. custom purposes. This restriction prevents companies from reporting a lower transfer price for customs purposes, and consequently, paying lower custom duty, than was reported for income tax purposes. On the other hand, the higher the cost of goods sold used for transfer pricing, the lower U.S. taxable income that would be used as a basis for income tax liability.

It may be concluded from this analysis that as long as the tax rate differentials are higher than the net effect of tariff rates imposed by the higher tax rate country, the higher transfer price will always generate net savings for the MNC.

However, if the top management increases the price for goods transferred from a subsidiary to another by a specified amount of money, the higher transfer price may have a negative effect on both the global profits of the MNC and on the net income of the buying subsidiary. Generally, the higher the import tariffs relative to the difference in net income tax rates between different countries, the more likely that a low transfer price is preferrable.

THE IRS'S ADVANCED PRICING AGREEMENT (APA) PROGRAM

The expansion of global business activity in recent years made inevitable a significant increase in transfer pricing enforcement by tax authorities around the world. The United States was the first country to adopt substantial penalties relating to transfer pricing and to require that companies maintain detailed documentation of their transfer pricing systems. Many MNCs, fearful of penalties, responded by seeking to reduce risk exposures in the United States (Durst 1999).

From the IRS's perspective, the acceptable price is the market value price. Because it is difficult to prove that the transfer price was equal to the market price, companies often find themselves in disputes with the

IRS. But now there is a way out. The IRS's Advanced Pricing Agreement (APA) program provides companies an opportunity to avoid costly audits and litigation by allowing them to negotiate a prospective agreement with the IRS regarding the facts, the transfer pricing methodology, and an acceptable range of results. The program is aimed at multinational corporations interested in avoiding penalties, managing risk, and determining their tax liability with certainty.

In the APA program, you as a financial professional and representative of your company would work proactively with the IRS in a cooperative negotiating environment rather than in an adversarial examination or litigation environment. The APA's goal is to agree on the best method to use arm's-length prices, which allows you to determine your transfer price and, ultimately, your tax liability with certainty. An APA results in no surprises for the taxpayer. Because the IRS has agreed prospectively, you do not find yourself involved in transfer pricing disputes later as long as you comply with the agreement, which can cover as many as five years and can also be applied to prior years. Since the start of the program, the IRS had completed 164 APAs, and 181 were in process as of 1999 (Wrappe, Milani, and Joy 1999).

The story of the APA program started on March 1, 1991, when the IRS released the official procedures for obtaining an APA in Revenue Procedure 91-22.

On May 24, 1995, the IRS explained the general objectives of the APA program, in its proposed revenue procedure, as follows:

1. To enable taxpayers to arrive at an understanding with the IRS on three basic issues:
   - The factual nature of the intercompany transactions to which the APA applies;
   - An appropriate transfer pricing methodology (TPM) applicable to those transactions; and
   - The expected range of results from applying the TPM to the transactions. However, in appropriate cases, the IRS will consider APAs that set forth a TPM without the specification of any range;
2. to do so in an environment that encourages common understanding and cooperation between the taxpayer and the IRS and that harmonizes and incorporates the opinions and views of all the IRS functions involved with the taxpayer;
3. to come to an agreement in an expedited fashion, as compared with the traditional method, which entails separate and distinct dealings with the Examination, Appeals, and Competent Authority functions and/or possible subsequent litigation; and
4. to come to an agreement in a cost-effective fashion for both the taxpayer and the IRS.

Therefore, the APA program's goal is to agree upon the best method to calculate market-driven prices, which allows MNCs to determine the acceptable transfer price and, ultimately, their tax liability with certainty.

Some MNCs have experienced the suffering of not getting the right transfer prices from the point of view of the IRS. In December 1998, DHL, the package delivery service, lost a transfer pricing battle with the IRS over the valuation of its trademark. DHL valued the trademark at $20 million, whereas the Tax Court concluded that $100 million was the right price. Unfortunately, DHL was fined with a 40 percent penalty for this error in judgment. The APA program not only lets MNCs avoid the payment of such penalties, but it also lets them gain certainty regarding their expected tax liability (Robak 1999).

The APA process may be long and tedious; however, it has many benefits to both taxpayers and IRS, as explained in the program description released by the IRS.

1. For MNCs, they can avoid penalties and gain substantial certainty with respect to how the desired transfer pricing activities will be treated for U.S. tax purposes and, in the case of a bilateral APA, how U.S. transfer pricing activities will be treated by foreign tax authorities as well.

2. The APA process provides an environment in which the taxpayer, the IRS, and, where appropriate, the competent authorities cooperate to determine which transfer pricing method should apply to transfer pricing activities. The APA process stimulates a free flow of information between all parties involved in the process so as to come to a legally correct and practically and workable result.

3. The APA can reduce the taxpayer's record-keeping burden. Taxpayers will have to keep records to substantiate only one reasonable methodology (the TPM agreed upon), and generally do not have the burden of keeping all documents potentially relevant to other methodologies that the IRS could consider in an examination.

4. The APA process may help taxpayers avoid extended litigation, subjects the TPM to extensive review, and retains legal merit.

5. The APA process provides the opportunity to resolve open years by rolling back the APA pricing methodology to resolve transfer pricing issues in prior years, with consent of the appropriate district, appeals, or competent authority.

In summary, the advantages of APAs include friendly collaboration between the MNC and IRS, possible avoidance of costly and time-consuming audits and litigation, and the reduction of uncertainty about the tax treatment of international transfer pricing activities.

However, MNCs expose themselves to the following risks by applying for an APA (Tang 1997, 102):

1. The IRS may scrutinize the industry and taxpayer-specific information submitted and the annual reports for each taxable year of an MNC covered by the APA.
2. An APA does not shelter the taxpayer from the IRS's subsequent scrutiny regarding transfer pricing activities of the business entity.
3. The significant assumptions may change. What was acceptable TPM at the time the APA was signed may be quite disadvantageous in later years.
4. The cost of obtaining an APA may be significant.

MNCs are the target of tax authorities of all governments all over the world. Most MNCs are based in the highly industrialized and developed countries such as the United States, the United Kingdom, Japan, Germany, and Canada.

The United States was the first country to respond to domestic political pressures for tax enforcement of MNCs in the 1980s and early 1990s and adopted new regulations designed to make enforcement easier, to adopt substantial penalties relating to transfer pricing, and to require that companies maintain detailed documentation of their transfer pricing policies. Many MNCs, fearful of penalties, responded by seeking to reduce risk exposures in the United States (Durst 1999, 57).

Initially, the other tax authorities generally perceived the increased U.S. enforcement as a potential assault on their own tax bases, which the non-U.S. countries feared they could not realistically counter with increased enforcement regimes of their own. Other countries, therefore, did not agree on the U.S. initiatives. However, the major developed countries, including trading partners of the United States, held the view that global political and economic realities called for an appropriate uniform international approach to transfer pricing enforcement. Today, an international environment exists in which many countries are implementing enforcement, documentation, and penalty regimes similar to the regime that now is implemented in the United States (Durst 1999, 57).

The APA programs in Canada, Germany, Japan, the United States, and the United Kingdom vary by degree of complexity and formality. A survey examined the status of APAs in the five countries. APA programs are more popular with tax authorities than with MNCs. The principal reasons cited by TNCs for nonparticipation involve documentation, the costs involved, and confidentiality concerns with the information contained in the documentation

Tax authorities all over the industrialized countries tend to consider transfer pricing as a soft target because of the difficulties involved and the fact that most MNCs are ready to pay. The simultaneous increase in scrutiny of transfer pricing by governments around the world places new pressure on the tax executive of the multinational company. More than ever before, effective management of a company's transfer pricing policies requires a global approach in which, perhaps, the greatest danger consists of focusing too closely on the enforcement risks in a single country, or small group of countries, while ignoring equally significant risks in others (Durst 1999, 57).

In the United Kingdom, all U.K.-based MNCs are liable for a tax rate of 35 percent on their worldwide profits. A foreign tax credit is allowed for foreign income taxes paid on foreign income taxable in the United Kingdom with the U.K. tax actually charged on that foreign income as a maximum. Branches of non-U.K. MNCs are liable for income tax at a rate of 35 percent, the same as the domestic, on the British-source income. A few years ago, the Revenue decided that an advance ruling system would be too time-consuming and too costly to operate. But, almost unnoticed, a reasonably comprehensive ruling system is now springing up in the United Kingdom (Symons 1998, 62). At this time, the U.K. government has no statutory arrangements in effect to help taxpayers to participate in Advance Pricing Agreements (APAs). The government intends that the Inland Revenue of the United Kingdom should consult on APAs. In recent years, the Inland Revenue has used powers granted under the terms of Double Taxation Conventions to participate in APAs with tax authorities of other countries that have introduced legislation helping them to join APAs (Elliott 1998, 49).

In the United Kingdom, the objective of a ruling system is to give MNCs certainty about their tax obligations. The system will only work if the tax authorities are able to deal with the rulings in a helpful, efficient, and business nonhostile way. That will cost money. This comparison is particularly stark if you look at the opportunity cost of diverting highly trained inspectors away from compliance work. However, anything less could lead to a serious culture clash that would be contentious and confusing (Symons 1998, 62).

Japan requires its MNCs to aggregate the loss or income of foreign branches with income or loss of the corporation and pay the Japanese corporate income tax of 33.3 percent on distributed income or 43.3 percent on undistributed income on their worldwide income. Branches of foreign MNCs are only taxed on the Japanese source-income in the same manner as the Japanese corporations. The allowed methods for determining an arm's-length price are the classic transaction-based methods of comparable uncontrolled price method, resale price method, and cost-plus method. None of these methodologies is preferable over another. Japanese transfer pricing rules prescribe a fourth method in the event that none of the three methods can be used. Specifically, this is a method that corresponds to one of the three methods or a method prescribed by the official tax authority. The Tax Administration does not recognize the comparable profits method, transactional net margin method, or similar profits methods as permissible transfer pricing methods (Acceptable 1998). The Tax Administration recently prepared a series of questions and answers regarding the profit split method. The first of these questions and answers clearly states that the Tax Administration does not accept, in current form, the comparable profits method or modified resale price being used in APAs (Ibid.).

For MNCs, goods and services transferred between two different countries may be priced at two different prices using two different approaches by two different tax authorities for the same item. In addition, different objectives and policies of the tax regulations of the two countries could lead to completely conflicting results.

Despite the tax treaties among countries, MNCs are still required to pay high income tax liabilities over their global profits as a cost of doing business across the border. Every revenue authority tries to come up with the arm's-length price, which may not be in existence in reality when the product is unique in the international market.

However, tax treaties are applied only to dividends, interest, rent, or royalties. Business profits, which does not include these four items, are taxable at corporate tax rates applicable by the host country to business profits in general. Tax treaties do not eliminate double taxation completely; in most cases, they only reduce the tax rate on income. Dividends, for example, are taxed by both host and home countries, who are parties to tax treaties, but at different lower rates.

THE ORGANIZATION FOR ECONOMIC COOPERATION AND DEVELOPMENT (OECD) GUIDELINES

In 1995, the OECD released revised guidelines on transfer pricing (OECD 1995). The revised guidelines, which replace those contained in the OECD's 1979 report (OECD 1979), continue to support the arm's-length standard as the best approach of transfer pricing methods, and confirm the role and superiority of traditional transfer pricing methods (Ibid.). In 1998, the OECD recommended the use of traditional transaction methods, such as the comparable uncotnrolled price (CUP), the cost plus (CPM), and the resale price (RPM) methods—which therefore should be used in cross-border transactions whenever these methods can be reliably applied (OECD, 1998).

If traditional methods are not applicable for e-commerce transactions or for such a high level of integration between related parties, the OECD guidelines permit the transactional profit method. Using this method, the overall profit of the group is divided among entities engaged as third parties would have been. The profit-split method has already been established in some counries in the area of innovative financial trans-actions. The OECD has examined profit-split mehtods and concluded that both the profit split (PSM) and the transactional net margin (TNMM) methods are becoming more widespread.

SUMMARY AND CONCLUSIONS

The chapter discussed transfer-pricing methods that are appropriate to achieve certain internal objectives of MNCs in managing their overseas activities. It also analyzed Section 482 of the U. S. Internal Revenue Code and its impact on foreign activities of MNCs. Finally, it examined the IRS's Advanced Pricing Agreement (APA) program and its effect on transfer pricing policies of foreign activities. Finally, the OECD revised guidelines on transfer pricing mehtods were discussed.

The objective of an appropriate ITP technique for either internal reporting, external reporting, or both is determined largely by the objectives of establishing an ITP policy. Transfer pricing methods are divided into two groups: economic and accounting oriented analysis includes the market price, cost-based, cost-plus, marginal cost-based, and negotiated price; and mathematically oriented analysis includes linear, nonlinear, and goal programming models.

The transfer of goods and services between two different countries may be priced at two different prices using two different approaches by the two different tax authorities for the same item. Also, different objectives and policies of tax regulations of different countries could lead to conflicting results. When different tax authorities of two coun-tries adjust the appropriate transfer price according to their belief on what is called the appropriate arm's-length price, an MNC may be liable for more than a double tax liability on the same item.

A technique or method useful for one group of objectives or for one purpose may not be the best choice for another. The two sets of objectives, as discussed in the chapter, are not directly related to each other, and there is no evidence any single transfer price designed for only one of the ITP objectives will satisfy all others. No practical evidence has been found concerning the appropriate (or optimal) transfer price for MNCs to use. There are many reasons for this conclusion:

1. The significance of and fast change in global environmental conditions—such as market conditions, government attitudes and differential global strategies, force MNCs to use different transfer prices at different times under different conditions.
2. Host countries' balance of payments, tax revenues, and foreign market structures, among other factors, are affected by the use of transfer pricing policies.
3. The use of any transfer price other than the arm's-length price is more likely unacceptable to tax authorities.
4. Foreign exchange risks, expropriation risks, government interventions, and avoiding any conflict with host countries' governments are just examples of many problems that face MNCs in developing an appropriate ITP policy and make it much more difficult than for domestic firms, if not impossible.
5. The most important key factors in deciding what transfer pricing method to use are the global strategy of MNCs, exchange controls, income tax liability, and performance evaluation of foreign subsidiaries and their managers.
6. The MNCs, the IRS, and the host countries' tax authorities will get great benefits of Advanced Pricing Agreement (APA) programs including friendly collaboration between the MNC and IRS, possible avoidance of costly and time-consuming audits and litigation, and the reduction of uncertainty about the tax treatment of international transfer pricing activities.

REFERENCES

Abdel-Khalik, A. Rashad, and Edward J. Lusk. 1974. Transfer pricing: A synthesis. *Accounting Review* 69: 3–23.

Acceptable transfer pricing methodologies. 1998. *International Tax Review* (February): 25.

Bailey, Andrew D., Jr. and Warren J. Boe. 1976. Goal and resource transfers in the multigoal organization. *The Accounting Review* 1(3) (July): 559–573.

Baumal, W. J., and T. Fabian. Decomposition, pricing for decentralization, and external economies. *Management Science*, 1–32.

Burns, Jane O. 1980. How IRS applies the intercompany pricing rules of Section 482: A corporate study. *Journal of Taxation* 52 (May): 308–14.

Burns, Jane O. 1984. The multinational enterprise: U.S. taxation of foreign source income. In *International Accounting*, edited by H. Peter Holzer and others (New York: Harper and Row Publishers).

Durst, Michael C. 1999. United States. *International Tax Review* (February): 56–62.

Eden, Lorraine. 1998. *Taxing multinationals: Transfer pricing and corporate income taxation in North America*. Canada: University of Toronto Press.

Elliott, Jamie. 1998. "International transfer pricing: A survey of UK and non-UK group. *Management Accounting* (CIMA-London) (November): 48–50

Hines, James R., Jr. 1999. Lessons from behavioral responses to international taxation. *National Tax Journal* (June): 305–22.

Lermer, David. 1998. Pitfalls of transfer pricing. *Finance Week* (December 4): 30–31.

Liebman, Howard. 1987. International transfer pricing and recent development: Part I. *Tax Planning International Review* (August): 4.

Nagy, Richard J. 1987. Transfer price accounting for MNEs. *Management Accounting* (January): 35.

Organization for Economic Cooperation and Development Committee on Fiscal Affairs. 1979. *Transfer Pricing and Multinational Enterprises*. Paris: OECD.

——. 1995. *Transfer Pricing Guideline for Multinational Enterprises and Tax Administrations*. Paris: OECD.

——. 1998. *Taxation of Global Trading of Financial Instrucments*. Paris: OECD.

Plasschaert, Sylvain R. F. 1979. *Transfer pricing and multinational corporations: An overview of concepts, mechanisms and regulations*. New York: Praeger Publishers.

Robak, Epsen. 1999. Son of Solomon: Tax court splits the baby in DHL Corp. *Taxes* (September): 20–31.

Schindler, Guenter. 1989. Intercompany transfer pricing after Tax Reform of 1986. *Tax Planning International Review* (November): 9–10.

Symons, Susan 1998. US corporate tax: The dawn of a new era. *International Tax Review* (September): 61–63.

Tang, Roger Y. W. 1997. *Intrafirm trade and global transfer pricing regulations*. Westport, Conn.: Quorum Books.

Wrappe, Steven C., Ken Milani, and Julie Joy. 1999. The transfer price is right . . . or is it? *Strategic Finance* (July): 38–43.

II

Management Accounting and Transfer Pricing

5

Management Accountants and Transfer Pricing Tax Audits

It does not take very long for management accountants of multinational companies (MNCs) to be hit with transfer pricing audits of either the IRS (the United States) or some host country's tax authority. Unlike other tax planning issues, transfer pricing is very much linked to day-to-day operational and financial decisions. Traditionally, transfer pricing stimulates the complicated and conflicting objectives of avoidance of foreign exchange risks, tax minimization, cash flow management, and performance evaluation of foreign subsidiary managers.

This chapter discusses and analyzes the problems that management accountants face in designing their companies' transfer pricing systems. It also provides them with effective, practical, and the most convenient tools to be ready for any transfer pricing audits by tax authorities. First, the new challenges for management accountants in designing and using transfer pricing systems for global operations are discussed. Second, seven strategic issues of transfer pricing systems that should be considered by management accountants in designing, preparing, and reducing the risk for transfer pricing tax audits of their companies are analyzed. Finally, tax authorities' requirements and especially advance pricing agreement programs, as one of the key solutions for transfer pricing conflicts between MNCs and U.S.-IRS, are covered.

NEW CHALLENGES FOR MANAGEMENT
ACCOUNTANTS OF MNCs

Every minute, at least one intracompany transaction of goods or services of a multinational company, somewhere around the globe, moves across the border from one country to another. One of the most important and complex considerations in coordinating and integrating production, marketing, and tax strategies for MNCs is that of intracompany pricing of their worldwide operations. Should the product be transferred among the company's own subsidiaries in and outside of China, Mexico, Egypt, France, or the United Kingdom at the world market or at arm's-length price? Should each manager of foreign subsidiaries be given freedom in making production and marketing decisions and consequently in maximizing divisional profits? How much tax will be paid to both the IRS and foreign tax authorities? Is there an acceptable transfer pricing method for all countries' tax regimes? How does a multinational company secure compliance with complex rules operated by different accountants of various countries? Do we expect to have a transfer pricing audit from IRS or foreign tax authorities soon? How often do we have to review our transfer pricing systems to ensure a compliance with all countries' tax authorities' requirements? Answers to these questions can be found through an understanding of what management accountants of MNCs need to do to get ready for expected transfer pricing audits of the U.S. and host countries' tax authorities in the near future.

The growth of MNCs has created new issues for foreign countries' national economies as well as international economies. These include the international location of production and distribution territories, their effect on national and international stock and commodity markets, their significant effects on both home and host governments' revenues, and the balance of payments of both foreign and home countries.

MNCs are highly motivated to go across the border by many factors that vary from one industry to another and even from one firm to another within the same industry. In this case, an MNC may manufacture its products at home and then export them to European markets to achieve higher profits. On the other hand, an MNC may find it less costly to manufacture its products where labor costs are the lowest, such as in in China, Egypt, Mexico, or Jordan, and sell them where selling prices are the highest, such as European countries or Japan.

A transfer price is set and used by MNCs to quantify the goods and services transferred from one subsidiary domiciled in a specific country to another subsidiary in another country. The dynamic growth of most MNCs by going abroad and exploring more and more business opportunities in foreign countries necessitated increased delegation of authority and responsibility with more autonomy for foreign subsidiary managers, which opened the door for further decentralization and intracompany pricing problems.

Traditionally, for management accountants of MNCs, transfer pricing stimulates the complicated and conflicting issues of avoidance of foreign exchange risks, cash flow management, the funding of investments overseas, the evaluation of foreign subsidiaries' performance, and effective tax management. Making pricing decisions for MNCs' products or services, in general, is an important, flexible, and complicated task, because these decisions affect other major functions of MNCs, such as marketing, production location, transportation, and finance, which directly affect its total sales and profits. Moreover, there is no clear-cut or easy way to establish an effective pricing policy. MNCs cannot merely add a standard percentage as a markup to a full or variable cost to come up with a price they have to charge for goods transferred internally among their own subsidiaries. In reality, the transfer pricing policies of most MNCs have evolved as international businesses "have grown either organically or by acquisition in response to a number of competing and often conflicting commercial considerations. The minimization of direct tax is one of such consideration" (Elliott 1998).

MNCs face a major problem as they transfer goods and services between their subsidiaries—deciding at what price to transfer goods and services between them or the parent company. A survey on transfer pricing practice, sponsored by Chartered Institute of Management Accountants (CIMA) and supported by Deloitte & Touche, was conducted to discover more about the way in which MNCs approach international transfer pricing (Elliott 1998). In the survey, it was found that the most important factors impacting the determination of MNCs' transfer pricing policies were the maximization of global profit, simplicity and ease of use, aggressiveness of tax authorities, market penetration, and stability of transfer price over time.

As we see a tremendous growth in global trade, more and more business takes place across the border between related parties. Consequently, in efforts to protect their tax bases, tax authorities have become more on the alert in enforcing the rules of transfer pricing. As global trade grows and more countries increase scrutiny, it is more likely that MNCs could face inconsistent and unfair treatment of cross-border transactions and double taxation, plus penalties for noncompliance (Hamilton 2000).

The rapid increase in business globalization means that MNCs, the Internal Revenue Service (IRS)-U.S., Inland Revenue-U.K., South-Asian, Foreign, and other foreign tax authorities must consider transfer pricing carefully. MNCs should ensure that their transfer pricing policies achieve certain objectives and at the same time are fair. IRS and foreign tax authorities must ensure that they collect a fair amount of corporate income tax from MNCs operating in their jurisdiction (Elliot 1998). Consider this example in the pharmaceutical industry: Smith-Kline Beecham pays close attention to transfer pricing issues these days, because their Canadian subsidiary appeared before the Tax Court of Canada in 1995 to dispute a $66-million tab. The Canadian tax authority believed the subsidiary paid too much for an ingredient from related offshore suppliers in low-tax countries, allowing it to reduce its tax burden (Hamilton 2000).

Moreover, foreign governments may impose high tariffs on all imports coming into their countries, either to protect their local industries from competition against foreign companies or to increase revenues for the government. MNCs must keep abreast of the changes and developments to ensure that they are able to demonstrate compliance with relevant American, Canadian, German, and British tax regulations. They should avoid any transfer pricing misstatement for tax reporting with the tax authorities. The U.S. court case of DHL reaffirms that MNCs should plan to properly document and defend the transfer pricing method used to transfer intangible assets to their controlled parties. The court was willing to uphold the assessment of the 20 to 40 percent penalties in appropriate situations, because the IRS will carefully scrutinize situations involving transfers of intangible assets from the United States to any related foreign parties, including South Asia and other foreign countries (Shapland and Major 1999).

Recent changes in transfer pricing legislation are presenting new challenges for MNCs' management accountants. The principal legislative change of developed countries now calls on taxpayers to demonstrate the use of arm's-length prices. In addition, the introduction of advance pricing agreements (APA), increased power to penalize noncompliance, and increased documentation requirements will all have significant implications for MNCs' management accountants.

MNCs have to be concerned about transfer pricing audits. Transfer pricing remains the number one tax issue for MNCs. They must pay close attention to transfer pricing issues. A survey by Ernst & Young showed that 75 percent of MNCs believed that they would be hit with a transfer pricing audit (Hamilton 2000). MNCs were most likely to be audited in their home country, and nearly three quarters of MNCs conducting business in Europe report being hit with transfer pricing audits in the past two years. This compares with 64 percent in Canada and 62 percent in the United States. But, despite this activity, 37 percent still consider transfer pricing to be a compliance issue, and only 30 percent of MNCs include it in their strategic planning (Hamilton 2000).

Another important issue is the transfer pricing policy review. How often do MNCs need to review their transfer pricing systems to be ready for any transfer pricing audit by tax authorities? What are the main pros and cons of the current transfer pricing system? In a survey by Jamie Elliott (1998), it was evident that a large proportion of the sample either had a very recent internal review of their transfer pricing system, or that the review was done on a continuous basis. Moreover, one of the problems encountered by MNCs in reviewing their transfer pricing systems included lack of comparable systems and concerns about the acceptability of their pricing systems by British, French, Chinese, Is-raeli, or other foreign tax authorities. A main advantage of an internal review of the transfer pricing system is increased confidence in the MNC's policy and documentation (Elliott 1998).

REDUCING THE RISK OF TRANSFER PRICING AUDITS FOR MNCs

It is the responsibility of management accountants to design and implement an effective transfer pricing system (TPS) to help their companies achieve the specific objectives of their TPS. In the twenty-first century, tax management of transfer pricing, as the number one tax issue for MNCs, has become the most difficult area of international taxation. A survey by Ernst & Young showed that 8 in 10 multinationals expected to be hit with transfer pricing audits of either home or foreign tax authorities (Hamilton 2000). On top, U.S. and foreign tax authorities justify their heightened transfer pricing audit activity by citing the magnitude of taxable income related to transfer pricing (Borkowski 2000). Management accountants need to prepare an effective TPS sup-ported by facts and be ready to meet the IRS or go to the court, if needed, to successfully present and defend the used price or value of all aspects of across-the-border transactions.

Based on our consulting experience and transfer pricing practices of MNCs, we include the strategic issues of transfer pricing and the criteria that should be considered by management accountants in preparing and getting ready for transfer pricing audits from either IRS or foreign tax authorities. Strategic transfer pricing issues, discussed in detail later and in chapter 7 as they relate to e-commerce cross-border business transactions, should include TPS, transfer pricing methods (TPM), eq-uitable allocation, documentation, presentation, confidentiality, and review, as summarized in Table 5.1.

Transfer Pricing System

If the accountant expects a high probability that the IRS will scruti-nize the company, it is crucial for management accountants to ensure that their TPS is based on facts and supported by appropriate docu-

TABLE 5.1 Strategic Issues and Criteria to Prepare for Transfer Pricing Audit

Strategic Transfer Pricing Issues	Criteria to Be Considered
Transfer Pricing System (TPS)	• Do you have an effective TPS supported by facts and documents? • Do you intend to seek an APA with the tax authorities? • Do you have sufficient data of profitability of joint ventures as a whole?
Transfer Pricing Method (TPM)	• Does your TPM satisfy the arm's-length standard? • Is your TPM the most convincing for IRS? • Is your TPM the same as the CUP or CPM? • If you used the CPM, did you use the same markup percentage as unrelated comparable transactions? • Have you ever confirmed the CUP analysis of your products or services to convert from CPM to CUP to come up with a comparable set of transactions to which it could apply a CUP analysis? • Did you consider the degree of comparability between controlled and uncontrolled transactions? • Have you ever tested the arm's-length standard under different TPM?
Equitable Allocation	• Are management fees, services, or royalties allocated properly between the parent and foreign subsidiaries? • Is income allocated between related parties on an equitable basis?
Documentation	• Do you have sufficient documentation to support your compliance with the arm's-length standard? • Are all intracompany transactions to which the APA applies based on facts?
Presentation	• Can you present a persuasive, strong, and readily understood story or a fully coherent economic analysis to explain and prove your compliance with Section 482? • Have you prepared reports based on comparable profits analysis? • Can you present some organizing principles to provide analysis based on a comparable unit of payment? • Can you effectively explain why the results of using TPM are reasonable?
Confidentiality	• Is all information provided to tax authorities confidential? If not, what information should be revealed to tax authorities?
Review	• How often do you review and update your TPS to comply with all recent changes in tax regulations of all countries involved? • What assumptions did you use for acceptable TPM? Are the assumptions still the same? Have you considered any changes in the assumptions and their effect on tax liability?

ments. In addition, facts and clear documents on the industry practices and market conditions should be available to support TPS (Lubkin 2000). Success in reducing or eliminating the risk of transfer pricing audit for many years is had by going for an APA with the tax authorities of the countries in which your company has income tax liability. By looking at the APA programs of different countries, you may find them not similar to the U.S. tax regulations. Whereas many foreign tax authorities have established either formal or informal APA programs, MNCs face the reality that the procedures, cost, difficulty, and length of time associated with negotiating an APA are not consistent across borders (Borkowski 2000).

Many countries follow OECD transfer pricing guidelines, either explicitly or as the basis for developing their own more specific legislation. However, those guidelines include only a general discussion about APAs as an alternative administrative approach to avoiding and resolving transfer pricing issues (Ibid.). Consider the United Kingdom's regulations on the APA. They differ from those of the United States in three important issues. First, the IRS allows only transactions between related taxpayers, whereas Inland Revenue also includes branch transactions, attribution on income to a permanent establishment, and purely domestic APAs. Second, the Inland Revenue limits APAs to the complex cases of large MNCs, whereas the IRS encourages MNCs of any size and complexity to go for the APA program. Finally, the IRS encourages rollbacks, if it is feasible, whereas the Inland Revenue allows the rollback as a way to resolve a transfer pricing issue in earlier years (Borkowski 2000).

It is true that transfer pricing practice is based on facts rather than restricted tax regulations. So long as your TPS is based on facts and the facts are acceptable by IRS or tax courts—if necessary—the law is satisfied (Lubkin 2000). As management accountants start to investigate and redesign their TPS to be appropriate and ready for any expected transfer pricing tax audit, the following questions (or a checklist) may be used as guidelines.

1. Has the MNC determined its goals of TPS (such as tax minimization with certainty of fair tax treatment, MNC involvement in competent authority negotiations, reduction of tariffs on imports and exports, minimization of foreign exchange risks, avoidance of conflicts with foreign countries' governments, simplicity of the selected TPM, speed of an APA over a tax audit, avoidance of double taxation, and resolution of transfer pricing examinations)?
2. Do MNCs need to adopt different tax strategies for their TPS in different countries to emphasize the need for better documentation and better justifiable systems to reduce the risk of being first targets for tax authorities' investigations?

3. Have management accountants considered the variations among different tax years involved in the analysis because of different assumptions, market conditions, political and legal conditions in certain or some foreign countries?
4. Is there a lack of information of profitability of every one of an MNC's joint ventures and on all foreign operations as a whole?

Transfer Pricing Method

From the viewpoint of an MNC, transfer prices are used to allocate net income among different subsidiaries in different countries under different legal, social, tax, and economic regulations. MNCs face several problems, such as different income tax rates for various countries, tax structures and regulations, quota and import duties, cash movement restrictions, and currency exchange control. From the viewpoint of the U.S. government or any other foreign government, transfer pricing policies create problems with the belief that they do not reflect open market prices. Foreign governments believe that MNCs set their own transfer pricing policies to avoid paying taxes.

No practical evidence has been found regarding the best or most appropriate transfer price for MNCs to use in managing their business around the world. However, Section 482 allows MNCs to use the CUP, RPM, CPM, or an alternative method. The IRS of the United States may use Section 482 to make sure that your TPM satisfies the arm's-length standard; therefore, it could dispute your TPM agreed by the parties as distortions of income allocation to the party that is taxable under U.S. tax regulations.

Now, which TPMs are the most acceptable and convincing for IRS and foreign tax authorities? Based on transfer pricing practices, the most traditional method of arriving at the right transfer pricing is the CUP; however, it had been consistently rejected in the tax courts until 1999 (Lubkin 2000). In 1999, there was a clear methodological preference for the CUP in the Compaq case (Ibid.).

Management accountants, especially of MNCs in the service industry consulting businesses, should consider the CPM. It is the most widely used now as an arm's-length transfer price under Section 482. It deals better than the CUP with the allocations related to the value of service or intangible asset as in H Group and GAC Produce court cases (Ibid.). However, you have to make sure that you use the same markup percentage for your foreign subsidiaries as the one used in unrelated comparable transactions.

Equitable Allocation

Section 482 of IRC allows tax authorities to adjust deductions, income, management services, fees, or royalties, and all other expenses to reflect clearly the correct taxable income of MNCs and their domestic and foreign subsidiaries within their territories. Most court cases, regulations, and administrative rulings often focus less on close legal analysis and more on reaching equitable results of allocations among related parties. It is advisable for MNCs to use equitable allocation or charge rates for their foreign subsidiaries as they do for domestic subsidiaries.

Documentation

MNCs should have sufficient documentation based on facts to support and to prove that they are in compliance with tax requirements of all tax authorities, especially for the arm's-length standard. Moreover, they have to maintain updated and convincing documents about their business or industry practice and current market conditions of all countries in which they do business.

Presentation

The successful and conceptually coherent presentation of your TPS before the IRS or foreign tax authorities is the key for winning the game of transfer pricing. The MNC's team must present a strong and clearly understood story to explain the facts that support and prove the company's compliance with the arm's-length standard. The presentation should include the following:

1. A fully coherent transfer pricing analytical report of your TPM, including risk analysis, based on comparable profits of both related and unrelated entities.
2. Consideration of the variations among different tax years involved.
3. Application of some organizing principle and an analysis based on a comparable unit of payments or charges for services provided for related and unrelated parties to be considered as a standard service or franchise payment.
4. In the case of changing the method of transfer pricing, demonstration of strategic changes of methodology to develop and support the analyses.
5. Explanation why the result or outcome of using the selected transfer pricing method is reasonable and acceptable for tax authorities.

Confidentiality

MNCs should ensure that tax authorities will not be disclosing confidential information acquired in the course of tax examination to outsiders except when authorized by MNCs' headquarters or legally obligated to do so. The IRS maintains confidentiality of MNC APA data, whereas other foreign tax authorities, including Inland Revenue, state that information provided in the APA process can and will be used in other circumstances when appropriate (Borkowski 2000). Therefore, American MNCs will not be reluctant to provide foreign tax authorities with confidential financial and production information that might deteriorate the competitive position of the company. Management accountants of MNCs should decide on what information should be disclosed to U.S.-IRS but not to foreign tax authorities.

System Review

Management accountants of MNCs should review transfer pricing policies and supporting documentation on a continuous basis and determine whether both home and most recent foreign tax authorities' requirements are being met. Transfer pricing audits by tax authorities tend to be fact-driven; they are very time-consuming compared with other tax audits (Hamilton 2000). TPS should be reviewed and updated more frequently to make sure that any changes in tax regulations of different countries are included and that your system is modified accordingly.

TAX AUTHORITIES' REQUIREMENTS

Recent U.S. tax changes reflect the importance of global competition and devote considerable effort to revising provisions that affect the taxation of foreign income (Hines 1999, 306). Tax regulations in the United States are different from those in European, South Asian, or foreign countries in many respects, such as tax rates, tax treaties, tax bases, foreign tax credits, and taxes imposed on any profits resulting from using intercompany transfer pricing policies for goods and services that cross a country's border. Among European countries, for example, great differences exist in many aspects of their tax regulations and laws. Developed countries, such as the United Kingdom, Canada, Germany, France, Japan, and Switzerland, have different objectives in their tax structure, policies, and regulations than those of developing countries such as Egypt, Mexico, Bahrain, and Jordan, among many others.

The significant growth of the global market means that both MNCs and tax authorities should consider transfer pricing policies carefully. MNCs should ensure that their transfer pricing policies and strategies can be supported and that they are deemed fair and acceptable. European or South Asia tax authorities should also ensure that they collect a fair and reasonable amount of corporate tax revenue from MNCs investing and operating in their countries (Elliott 1998, 49).

It is estimated that almost 60 percent of all international business transactions takes place between related partners, so tax authorities worldwide developed four main ways to catch and reduce tax evasion by transfer pricing (Lermer 1998, 30):

1. Including provisions in the legislation with formal, detailed, and binding regulations, similar to the ones in the U.S. tax code
2. Including provisions in the legislation with detailed guidelines on reasonable and acceptable techniques of transfer pricing, such as in Germany
3. Providing in the legislation arm's-length standards that will help establish acceptable transfer pricing practices based on the guidelines of the OECD guidelines, such as in the United Kingdom
4. Having no specific transfer pricing legislation, where the ordinary tax laws and evasion prohibitions are relied on to prevent transfer pricing understatement, such as in the Netherlands

Over the long run, different tax structures, different tax rates on foreign investments and subsidiaries, and different foreign exchange control policies may constitute the most basic reason for using the correct strategy for international transfer pricing policies in nations of Europe, China, South America, South Asia, and in other foreign countries. This can be combined with long-range global tax planning to achieve the global objectives of MNCs within their foreign subsidiaries operating in different environmental conditions in the European, Asian, or any other foreign markets.

OECD Guidelines

The OECD, on July 27, 1995, released its final guidelines in *Transfer Pricing Guidelines for Multinational Enterprises and Tax Administration,* which included the 1979 report *Transfer Pricing and Multinational Enterprises* and the 1984 report *Transfer Pricing and Multinational Enterprises: Three Taxation Issues.* The 1995 guidelines are not laws, but member countries are encouraged to follow them. Most member countries do not have their own detailed transfer pricing regulations and have been following prior OECD guidelines on transfer pricing.

Despite some differences, the guidelines are generally consistent with Section 482 of the IRC on transfer pricing regulations. American MNCs that comply with Section 482 regulations should not be exposed to a significant risk of double taxation in OECD member countries. The guidelines emphasize the arm's-length standard and the use of transaction-based methods that rely on comparable uncontrolled transactions.

Section 482 regulations require taxpayers to follow the best method rule: Which facts and circumstances will provide the most reliable measure of an arm's-length result relative to the other potentially applicable methods? Under the guidelines, MNCs must select the method that provides the best estimate of an arm's-length standard (Greenhill and Bee 1996).

The OECD 1995 guidelines also provide extensive discussion on the documentation to be obtained from MNCs in connection with a transfer pricing inquiry. The guidelines suggest that MNCs should make reasonable efforts when establishing their transfer pricing policies to determine whether their transfer pricing results meet the arm's-length standard. The OECD also recognizes that tax authorities should have the right to obtain the documentation to verify compliance with the arm's-length standard. The guidelines encourage member countries to administer penalty systems in a manner that is fair and not unduly onerous for MNCs. Thus U.S. MNCs are not relieved of the need for contemporaneous documentation required under Section 6662(e) to avoid the risk of U.S. transfer pricing penalties.

SUMMARY AND CONCLUSIONS

It does not take long for management accountants of MNCs to be hit with transfer pricing audits of either the IRS (the United States), Inland Revenue (the United Kingdom), Customs and Revenue Agency (Canada), National Tax Administration (Japan), or any other foreign tax authority. Unlike other tax planning issues, transfer pricing is very much linked to day-to-day operational and financial decisions. Traditionally, transfer pricing stimulates the complicated and conflicting objectives of avoidance of foreign exchange risks, tax minimization, cash flow management, and performance evaluation of foreign subsidiary managers. However, transfer pricing is still considered the number one tax issue for financial executive directors of MNCs.

Management accountants are responsible for designing and implementing effective transfer pricing systems based on facts supported by documents to help their companies reduce or eliminate the risk of transfer pricing tax audits. This chapter provided accountants, and management accountants in particular, with effective, practical, and the most convenient tools of transfer pricing systems.

In brief, to determine the best transfer pricing method, two important steps should be taken:

1. Consider the degree of comparability between controlled and uncontrolled transactions.

2. Test the arm's-length standard under different transfer pricing methods to see whether there are significant differences among them and then decide which one is the most convincing and most acceptable for most tax authorities that are involved.

There are two keys for MNCs to win the game of transfer pricing audit; the first one is to go for an advanced pricing agreement program with the tax authorities of the countries in which they have income tax liability; and the second one is to make a successful and conceptually coherent presentation of your transfer pricing method to prove compliance with the arm's-length standard. However, MNCs should be aware of the confidentiality issue. In most countries, all information disclosed to tax authorities under the advance pricing agreement programs might be available to the public.

REFERENCES

Borkowski, Susan C. 2000. Transfer pricing advance pricing agreements: Current status by country. *The International Tax Journal* (Greenvale) 26 (Spring): 1–16

Elliott, Jamie. 1998. International transfer pricing: A survey of UK and non-UK group. *Management Accounting* (CIMA-London) (November): 48–50.

Greenhill, Mitchell, and Charles W. Bee, Jr. 1996. Transfer pricing guidelines issued by the OECD. *The Tax Adviser* (New York) (May): 265–66.

Hamilton, Dwight. 2000. A heavy price to pay. *CA Magazine* (Toronto) 133 (May) 14–15.

Hines, James, R., Jr. 1999. Lessons from behavioral responses to international taxation. *National Tax Journal* (June): 305–22.

Lermer, David. 1998. Pitfalls of transfer pricing. *Finance Week* (December 4): 30–31.

Lubkin, Gregory P. 2000. Section 482: Major developments in 1999. *Tax Management Memorandum* (Washington) 41 (March 27): 103–12.

Organization for Economic Cooperation and Development Committee on Fiscal Affairs. 1979. *Transfer pricing and multinational enterprises.* Paris: OECD.

———. 1984. *Transfer pricing and multinational enterprises: Three taxation issues.* Paris: OECD.

———. 1995. *Transfer pricing guidelines for multinational enterprises and tax administrations.* Paris: OECD.

Shapland, Rick, and Bill Major. 1999. 40% Transfer pricing penalty upheld. *The Tax Adviser* (April): 224–25.

6

Transfer Pricing and Performance Evaluation of Foreign Subsidiary Managers

To date, the literature on the use of transfer pricing as a tool for performance evaluation of foreign subsidiary managers has not been discussed to the same extent as other tools of managerment, international accounting, and tax issues. Most research efforts of management accounting scholars have addressed either the issue of international transfer pricing or performance evaluation measurements in the United States and different countries around the world. Moreover, the management accounting literature is full with universal remedies but often impractical solutions (Abdel-Khalik, Rashad, and Lusk, 1974; Abdallah and Keller, 1985; Eccles, 1985; Grabski, 1985; Abdallah, 1986; Leitch and Barrett, 1992; Emmanuel and Mehafdi, 1994; Anctil and Dutta, 1999; Borkowski, 1999; Abdallah 2001; and Abdallah 2002). Current theory does not address the more global view of the MNC where foreign subsidiaries act all together according to a global decision by top management to maximize profits and therefore can be evaluated in a similar fashion. Borkowski (1999) has found out that there is some evidence, however, that specific performance evaluation criteria do vary in importance by country.

In recent years, extended research has not been undertaken on the use of international transfer pricing techniques that are founded on performance evaluation of foreign subsidiary managers. In multinational companies, however, international taxation complicates transfer pricing and performance evaluation problems. These problems have been addressed using traditional performance evaluation measures. Although this has attracted a tremendous theoretical and empirical research effort to solve its technical issues, its equally pertinent combination of performance evaluation of foreign subsidiary managers and transfer pricing issues has been overlooked.

Transfer pricing systems of MNCs are expected to achieve certain internal and external objectives. The internal objectives include consistency with the system of performance evaluation of foreign subsidiaries and their managers; motivation; and goal harmonization. External objectives include reduction of global income taxes; reduction of tariffs; minimization of foreign exchange risk; avoidance of any conflict with host countries' governments; management of cash flows; and competitiveness in the global market. However, to set up the same transfer price for an intermediate product or service may create a conflict of objectives leading to managerial dissension rather than harmonization, because the transfer price, which leads to minimizing global income tax liabilities, may result in showing artificial profits for one foreign subsidiary in a tax haven country while understating profits of another subsidiary in a country with high income tax rates. Therefore, top management of MNCs and foreign subsidiary managers must understand the objectives of using transfer pricing systems within their organizations. This chapter focuses on the use of transfer pricing as a tool for performance evaluation of MNC foreign subsidiaries and their managers.

INTRODUCTION

MNCs usually invest in foreign countries to improve their global competitive position in the international market in accordance with the company's long-run strategic mission, to meet tariff and quota restrictions in selling their products, and to secure otherwise unobtainable raw materials. Another important reason is to take advantage of differences in taxation, capital markets, product costs, and product selling markets. To achieve these objectives, management must have an attitude of globalization that makes it as concerned and involved with each of its foreign operations around the world as with its U.S. operations, and that makes it attempt to rationalize and manage its operations on a global rather than domestic basis within the constraints of the international social, economic, political, legal, and educational conditions.

However, MNCs may have relatively little influence and no direct control over environmental factors. Therefore, an MNC needs a separate set of measurements for planning, control, and evaluation of its managers' performance, a set that is substantially different from the one utilized by domestic business units. Traditionally, performance evaluation systems have been used to compare actual performance of foreign subsidiaries with expected performance, to facilitate measurement of subsidiaries in meeting some predetermined set of criteria, to help top management in making resource allocation decisions so that corporate resources are directed to subsidiaries where expected returns are the highest, and to motivate decision makers to achieve their goals and overall corporate objectives.

In this chapter, the traditional performance evaluation measures used by American MNCs in managing their foreign subsidiaries and their managers are examined first. A suggested performance evaluation system for foreign countries is presented second. The proposed system estimates foreign subsidiary managers' relative performance after considering the effects of noncontrollable foreign environmental factors on the measured performance of foreign subsidiaries. Third, this suggested environmental model is applied to one of the foreign subsidiaries of an American MNC [name is omitted] to illustrate how MNCs can implement the model in practice. Finally, performance evaluation of foreign subsidiaries with frequent fluctuations of both home and foreign currency values is discussed and analyzed.

TRADITIONAL PERFORMANCE EVALUATION MEASURES OF FOREIGN SUBSIDIARY MANAGERS

Historically, many management accounting techniques were oriented toward measuring earnings. Recently, these traditional techniques have been criticized as being too narrow in focus and not reflecting the realities of the international markets of the MNCs. The feeling is that an array of objectives should be considered in the management accounting evaluation process. In addition, many other factors affect the usefulness of currently used techniques of performance evaluation.

1. The organizational structure and environmental factors that interact in a complicated foreign market may make profit measures misleading as the prime criteria for the evaluation of subsidiary performance.
2. The use of a companywide ROI criterion not only may neglect important aspects of foreignt subsidiary operations but also could fail to consider the real objectives for which the subsidiary was established.
3. The selection of an investment base for use of ROI can yield results, which either encourages desirable or undesirable action by subsidiary managers.

4. Because MNCs conduct business in many countries, each using a different currency, management must decide the extent to which foreign subsidiary managers are to be held responsible for foreign exchange losses.

Recently, however, it has been felt that a broader range of objectives should be considered. International accountability measures now in use include rate of return on investment (ROI), operating budget comparisons, and residual income.

Abdallah and Keller (1985) surveyed American MNCs and discovered that internal accountability measures have not been developed to the extent required for proper evaluation and control of MNC managers and subsidiaries. Most American MNCs still use the same basic techniques to evaluate foreign subsidiary manager performance as they use to evaluate foreign subsidiary performance. Moreover, the same performance evaluation techniques are used domestically as well as internationally without regard for the social, political, and economic complexities facing MNCs in foreign countries.

The measure of performance called "rate of return on investment" is increasingly commonly used. Most MNCs require their foreign subsidiaries to use the same budgeting and financial planning techniques as domestic subsidiaries. These MNCs use the profit center concept or the investment center concept to measure ROI as the main performance measure (Mauriel 1969, 37). In some cases, profit compared to budgeted profit is the principal measure of profitability, with ROI the secondary measure (Bursk et al. 1971, 43).

Other measures used to evaluate the managerial performance in MNCs are profit, budgeted sales compared to actual sales, cash flow potential from foreign subsidiary to the United States, return on investment, budgeted ROI compared to actual ROI, and residual income (Morsicato and Radebaugh 1979, 85).

A more appropriate performance evaluation system is needed to estimate foreign subsidiary managers' relative performance after considering the effects of noncontrollable foreign environmental factors.

HOW DO MNCs EVALUATE THEIR FOREIGN SUBSIDIARY MANAGERS' PERFORMANCE?

Almost without exception, American MNCs use more than one criterion to measure the results of their international activities. However, they tend to place more emphasis on one over the other, using the remainder for supplementary purposes (Persen and Lessig 1978, 64). The traditional performance measures used in American MNCs to evaluate the performance of foreign subsidiaries and their managers are discussed next.

Rate of Return on Investment

ROI is a fraction. Its numerator is the profit earned by a foreign subsidiary; its denominator is the investment in the subsidiary. ROI is the generally accepted measure of the long-run profitability of a business entity. ROI is supposed to have the following advantages (Bursk et al. 1971, 17–18):

1. It is a single comprehensive figure influenced by everything that has affected the financial conditions of a foreign subsidiary.
2. It measures how well the foreign subsidiary manager uses the assets of the MNC to generate profits.
3. It is a common denominator that can be compared directly among subsidiaries, among subsidiaries and outside companies, or among subsidiaries and alternative investments.

However, there are many problems facing MNCs in using ROI as the companywide criterion for measuring performance. First, it oversimplifies a very complicated decision process and tries to combine three major elements in one single ratio—planning, control, and decision making (Bierman 1978, 410) Using a single rate of return for each foreign subsidiary is too simple to be used as a base for all trade-offs between investments and profits in an MNC.

Second, with respect to the numerator, the measurement of foreign subsidiary income for the rate-of-return calculation is complicated by intercompany transactions. The effect of one subsidiary on the return streams of other subsidiaries needs to be accounted for; however, such assessments are difficult to do (Choi, Frost and Meek 2002, 364).

Third, with respect to the denominator, it is difficult to obtain a satisfactory monetary basis for the value of the investment. For example, using the gross book value of the investment base may lead to suboptimal decisions, because a manager may increase the ROI by scrapping perfectly useful assets that do not contribute profits equal to the foreign subsidiary's goal.

Fourth, foreign operations are often established for strategic economic motivations for going abroad rather than for profit maximization. However, top-management forgets this fact when evaluating the performance of foreign subsidiary managers. Therefore, using a companywide performance (ROI) criterion to evaluate the profitability of foreign subsidiaries and performance of their managers is inadequate and misleading as well.

Fifth, the reported results of any foreign subsidiary are directly affected by many environmental constraints.

- Social, economic, political, legal, and educational policies and actions of host governments can drastically affect the reported results of a foreign subsidiary.
- Foreign exchange controls have a significant effect on both a subsidiary's and a manager's performance (Persen and Lessig 1978, 45).
- Because MNCs conduct business in many countries, top management must decide the extent to which managers of foreign subsidiaries are to be held responsible for foreign exchange losses (Robbins and Stobaugh 1973, 35).

Operating Budget Comparisons

Comparisons of actual results with operating budgets have been used widely for performance evaluation of foreign activities (Persen and Lessig 1978, 45). Variances between budgeted and actual results can be analyzed for the purpose of evaluating the performance of foreign subsidiaries and their managers, and, finally, corrective actions may be taken.

In an MNC, the same budgetary procedures are often used for both domestic and foreign operations. The budget has been used for supplementary information on foreign subsidiary performance; however, the MNC still selects ROI as a key item in the budget (Robbins and Stobaugh 1973, 83).

The Committee on International Accounting of the American Accounting Association (AAA 1973, p. 253) has indicated that when operating results of foreign subsidiaries are evaluated on the basis of their conformity with budgeted results, the performance evaluation is often less than satisfactory, because the budget is prepared for only key factors such as profit and control that are not considered for exclusion. In addition, this approach does not distinguish between foreign subsidiary performance and foreign subsidiary manager performance. Moreover, Bursk and others have indicated that if the profit budget of a foreign subsidiary does not provide an accurate rate measure of short-term profitability, we need to use other nonfinancial techniques to evaluate the performance (Bursk et al. 1971, 126).

Other Performance Evaluation Measures

Other measures are used by MNCs for performance evaluation, such as cash flow potential from the foreign subsidiary to the United States, residual income, contribution to earnings per share, return on sales, return on investment (adjusted for inflation), and other ratios (Persen and Lessig 1978, 25–33). These other performance evaluation measures have been well covered in the literature, and need not be considered here.

Performance evaluation measures used in MNCs have often failed to consider adequately the environmental variables surrounding foreign operations, because of the difficulty of measuring and incorporating those variables into traditional management accounting approaches. As a result, measuring the performance of foreign subsidiaries and their managers on the basis of ROI or any other currently used measure of performance tends to encourage suboptimal decisions because of a lack of goal harmonization between the foreign subsidiary and top management.

Abdallah and Keller (1985) surveyed 64 MNCs to determine the financial measures currently used to evaluate the performance of foreign subsidiaries and their managers, the use of different performance evaluation systems for domestic operations and for foreign operations, and the relationship between the firm's environmental variables and the firm's performance evaluation systems.

The international division officers were asked to indicate the measure their firms use in performance evaluation of foreign subsidiaries and their managers, and to rate each measure in terms of its importance. Almost 86 percent of the sample group use budgeted profit compared to actual profit to evaluate the performance of foreign subsidiaries. Figure 6.1 compares the four measures in terms of their importance in the evaluation of the foreign subsidiaries' performance.

Figure 6.1
Comparing Financial Measures Used to Evaluate Performance of Foreign Subsidiaries (Based on Abdallah and Keller 1985)

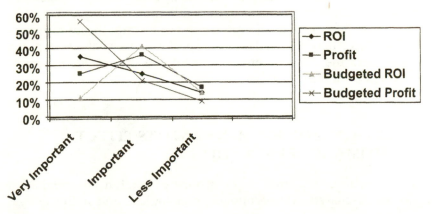

Figure 6.2

Comparing Financial Measures Used to Evaluate Performance of Foreign Subsidiary Managers (Based on Abdallah and Keller, 1985)

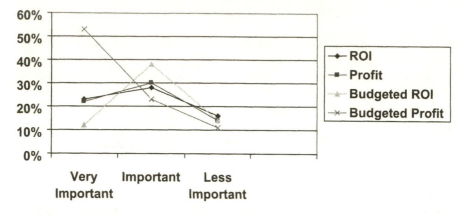

As for foreign subsidiary managers, 87 percent of the sample uses the same criterion, budgeted profits compared to actual profits, as the primary measure of performance, with ROI (67 percent) as a secondary measure. Figure 6.2 provides comparisons between the ROI, profits, budgeted ROI compared to actual ROI, and budgeted profits compared to actual profits as a measure of foreign subsidiary managers' performance. Moreover, it was found that 82 percent of the sample group use the same basic techniques to evaluate foreign subsidiary managers that they use to evaluate foreign subsidiary performance.

Evaluating performance of MNC foreign managers and subsidiaries requires special concern analysis. The distinction that should be made in performance evaluation relates to who has control over revenues, assets, personnel, and expenses. When measuring foreign subsidiary manager performance, the focus of the evaluation technique should be on the factors that the manager can control or has significant influence over. Therefore, there is a need for a new performance evaluation model that considers the effect of environmental constraints on managers' internal accountability.

THE FOREIGN ENVIRONMENT AND ITS EFFECT ON PERFOMANCE EVALAUTION

In this section, the three major groups of foreign environmental factors are discussed first—economic, sociological, and political-legal factors. Then, the proposed performance evaluation model that fits the foreign environment is discussed, analyzed, and applied to one of the foreign subsidiaries of an American MNC.

Economic Environmental Factors

MNCs invest in foreign countries to take advantage of economic differences, such as taxation differences, financial market differences, differences in product costs, and differences in product selling prices in different international markets. The main strategy of MNCs is to produce in the countries where production costs are the least and to sell in the countries where selling prices are the highest.

MNCs may sometimes utilize resources more effectively than domestic enterprises by transferring idle or underutilized resources. They also try to use the most efficient and profitable technology in extracting, refining, or manufacturing raw materials in foreign countries.

Inflation, tariff barriers, fluctuating exchange rates, trade barriers and restrictions, balance of payments disequilibrium, and restrictions of foreign trade policies are the most significant economic factors affecting international performance evaluation systems.

Inflation

Inflation is the decline in the general purchasing power of the monetary unit. Wide variations and rapid changes in inflation rates from one country to another are an important factor when MNCs are designing their international performance evaluation systems. In the absence of inflation, performance evaluation systems can be based on traditional domestic measures of performance with confidence in accounting information. However, when prices change, this confidence in accounting information is weakened. Subsidiary managers also find historical cost accounting data inadequate for many managerial decisions.

Higher inflation rates in a country cause prices of goods transferred to another country where lower inflation rates exist to rise, and subsidiaries in the latter country become less competitive. The subsidiary managers in that country find it more difficult to sell their products in the local market, and consequently their competitive position is impaired. Generally, relative inflation rates have an impact on the international business of MNCs.

There is a direct relationship between inflation rates and interest rates. When a country has a lower interest rate, it has a lower inflation rate too than other countries, and vice versa. However, a high inflation rate combined with a higher interest rate in a country may discourage any new investment by MNCs and, consequently, affect the goods transferred to that country.

Tariffs and Duties

Tariffs and duties are another environmental factor that may affect international business activities in general, and especially the performance of foreign subsidiaries and their managers. A tariff is the tool most commonly used as a form of trade restriction by governments. A tariff is "a tax, or duty, levied on a commodity when it crosses the boundary of a customs area." A customs area usually coincides with national political boundaries (Robock and Simmonds 1983, 138).

Transfer pricing policies, as a tool of international performance evaluation measures, can be used to reduce tariffs imposed on imports into the country or exports outside the country, and, consequently, the cost for an MNC will be less. However, foreign countries may feel that they are losing their revenue because of the manipulations of the transfer pricing policies of MNCs, and they may not accept the transfer price set by the MNC if it is too far from reality.

Any country can use a tariff or duty as a tool to exercise control over goods transferred out of or into the country. If the country imposes the tariff on outgoing goods, it is called an export duty; if imposed on incoming goods, it is called an import duty.

Foreign governments impose tariffs on imports and exports for three main purposes: to raise revenue for the government, to control the direction of foreign trade, and to protect domestic production against foreign competition. In foreign countries, providing a source of revenue for the government is ranked as the most important purpose of imposing tariffs. In developed countries, such as the United States, tariffs are used to restrict and control the import of goods.

In general, foreign governments can affect the international trade of specific products through the differences of tariff rates. High tariffs can be imposed on products that a country does not want to import, and low tariffs or zero tariffs may be imposed on essential products that are badly needed for the national economy.

In international business, the effect of tariffs on MNCs' profitability varies depending upon the particular country. For countries that depend upon foreign materials or finished goods, import tariffs may be low, and consequently, MNCs may be encouraged to transfer more goods to their foreign subsidiaries domiciled in these countries. On the opposite side are countries whose national products must compete against foreign imports. Governments, under these circumstances, impose high tariffs on imports of certain products to protect their own national products. MNCs may try to overcome these additional costs of paying high tariffs by using low transfer prices on their goods transferred into these countries. Under these circumstances, performance of foreign subsidiary managers will not be a reflection or realistic indicator of the manager's actions.

Foreign Exchange Rates

The exchange rate of any country is the economic indicator of how strong or weak the economy of a foreign country is. It provides the link between the national economy and the rest of the world economy. Any economic event, such as bankruptcy of one of the major banks in the country or a large deficit in the balance of payments for the second or third year in a row, has a direct impact on the country's exchange rate. Foreign trade policies, for example, affect the exchange rate directly when the supply or the demand for a country's products moves up or down.

The country's budget is considered to be one of the key factors for MNCs to make their own predictions of the government's intentions regarding tax laws and regulations, foreign exchange control policy, cash movement restriction policy, and any other variables that may affect the country's currency in the short or long run. The budget of the country can show the direction in which the economy may move. It indicates tariff policy, foreign trade policy, tax policy, foreign defense policy, foreign government spending, and many other budget decisions that may have a direct impact on currency markets.

Inflation is one of the key indicators of internal currency depreciation of a country, a fact that may lead to external currency depreciation. There is no perfect direct relationship between inflation and currency devaluation; the relationship is usually indirect and takes time to become clearly evident.

MNCs must take all these factors into consideration when designing their international performance measurement systems to ensure that their objectives, in foreign countries, can be achieved within the appropriate management control systems.

Balance of Payments

Balance of payments summarizes all the economic transactions between the home country and the rest of the world. These transactions include goods and services, transfer payments, loans, and investments. Inflation and interest rates, national income growth, and changes in money supply have a significant impact on the country's currency and its present and future exchange rates. All these factors may affect the balance of payments.

The balance of payments shows the net effect of all currency transactions of a country over a given period of time. When the balance of payments shows a deficit over a period of several years, it is an indication of the likely weakening of the value of the country's currency. This will be a threat to the currency's stability, and it is more likely that the currency will be devalued.

Deficits and surpluses in the balance of payments affect a country's currency in different ways. National income, money supply, prices, employment, interest rates, and foreign exchange rates are among the most important variables that are usually affected by a deficit or surplus.

MNCs should be aware that when a foreign country's balance of payments shows deficits one year after the other, the government is probably considering one or more of its tools to correct or reduce its deficit. Therefore, MNCs should be alert for restrictive monetary or fiscal policies, such as currency or trade controls, for the purpose of currency devaluation or to control inflation (Ball and McCulloch 1985, 281). MNCs may change their international transfer pricing policies and their performance measurement system to alleviate the impact of the new national policy of a country on their cash movements, the value of goods or services transferred into or out of the country, and the foreign exchange risk.

Sociological Environmental Factors

Sociological environmental factors include cultural and religious mores, attitudes toward growth and stability, and other societal values. These international sociological constraints interact with international political, legal, and economic environmental factors. Emotional feelings, for example, of a country toward foreigners may lead to laws, rules, restrictions, or regulations that significantly affect business firms operating abroad (Farmer and Richman 1980, 167). The feelings and attitudes of people in a given country are reflected in the regulations and rules that that country has established with respect to foreign subsidiary operations.

Some of these variables may have an impact on the financial control systems of MNCs investing in different countries, and each may affect the nature and degree of success of MNC control systems required in each host-country environment. MNCs must, therefore, consider seriously all sociological variables and their impact on foreign operations when designing their internal evaluation systems. They need to direct their attention toward what events might change the underlying social feelings and attitudes of people, which in turn would lead the political groups to alter their current tax and tariff laws, foreign exchange controls, and many other regulations to new and different ones under different national policies. As a result of any change that might occur in the current laws and regulations, MNCs must alter their pricing policies and performance measurement systems to achieve their major objectives.

Political and Legal Evirnomental Factors

Political and legal environmental factors include price controls, government instability, changes of political groups or government, timing of elections, nature of elections, and confiscation of local operations. All these variables can create a high degree of risk or uncertainty, alter the investment climate, and have a significant effect on MNCs' performance evaluation measures.

It is important that MNCs know how legal constraints and political actions of a given country directly affect their international transfer pricing policies. Because each country is independent, "it is expected that each will have a somewhat different legal structure than others, and that politics of one country will also have different impacts than those of other countries" (Farmer and Richman 1980, 185).

Allocation of resources is a potential source of conflict. On the one hand, the home office of the MNC wishes to exercise control measures over the utilization of its resources in foreign countries in order to ensure that these resources are used efficiently and profitably. On the other hand, the foreign country seeks to control the resources of MNCs to make sure that they are used in the national interest. As a result, the government of the host country may interfere by imposing protective measures that can prevent a foreign subsidiary from managing its operations efficiently.

HOW MNCS SHOULD EVALUATE THE PERFORMANCE OF THEIR FOREIGN SUBSIDIARY MANAGERS

Unfortunately, all political, social, and legal environmental variables are beyond the subsidiary manager's control, so managers should not be held responsible for the effects of these variables on the results of their activities. The challenge is that the manager may have two choices: to change the environment in the country—including economic, political-legal, social, and educational conditions—to be appropriate for the manager's system; or to change the internal accountability or performance measurement techniques to fit the country's environment.

Now, what can a manager do to change the environment in Canada, Japan, Mexico, Singapore, or the United Kingdom to fit the MNC's performance measurement system? Can the manager change the dominant cultural attitudes, for example, in Mexico or Japan? Can the manager change the economic system, for example, in North Korea from communism to capitalism? Can the manager change the political circumstances, for example, in Venezuela to a highly stable condition? Can the manager change the type of formal education and technical training, for example, in Argentina to be identical to the American educational and training programs?

Of course, the correct answer to these questions is no, the subsidiary manager cannot, because all these variables are far beyond any managers' control. It may be essential to distinguish between the performance of the foreign subsidiary and the performance of its manager because they seldom coincide, especially when foreign environmental conditions are distinctly different from domestic conditions. The manager's performance should be measured and evaluated on the basis of the activities or items that manager can control, such as direct materials, direct labor costs, the subsidiary's revenue. All activities or items that are not under the manager's control, such as income tax expense or interest rate on loans, should be excluded from the performance measurement report.

The foreign subsidiary's performance should be measured and evaluated on the basis of all activities and items needed for conducting the business so that MNC top management can decide whether the investment should be expanded, reduced, or terminated. All revenue and cost items that cannot be controlled by the foreign subsidiary manager should be allocated to the foreign subsidiary.

The Suggested Performance Evaluation Model for Foreign Subsidiaries

To look for the appropriate measures of performance evaluation systems to fit MNCs' operating activities into foreign countries, and the extent to which these measures have been designed to reflect environmental differences from one country to another, the author surveyed 178 MNCs. Replies from 56 MNCs' officers were received, for a total response rate of 31.5 percent.

Table 6.1 presents data of four of the selected samples of American MNCs that participated in the research and the nature of their business activities. Table 6.2 presents financial information of the same four American MNCs, included in Table 6.1. It is broken down into total

TABLE 6.1   Data of Four American MNCs and Their Foreign Subsidiaries

Company (assumed)	Industry	Countries
MNCA	Oil and Gas	Iran, Venezuela, Kuwait, Nigeria, and Saudi Arabia
MNCB	Steel	Canada, Egypt, China, Mexico, and Thailand
MNCC	Chemicals	Brazil, Malaysia, France, Japan, and the United Kingdom
MNCD	Electric and Electronic	Australia, South Korea, South Africa, Singapore, and Germany

TABLE 6.2 Financial Information of Foreign Subsidiaries (in millions of dollars)

Company	Country	Total Assets	Gross Revenue	Income after taxes	Actual ROI
MNCA	Iran	$100	$ 94	$19	19%
	Venezuela	$ 74	$ 88	$ 8.88	12%
	Kuwait	$140	$132	$22.4	16%
	Nigeria	$ 55	$ 60	$ 4.95	9%
	Saudi Arabia	$200	$220	$58	29%
MNCB	Canada	$ 60	$105	$10	16.7%
	Egypt	$ 28	$ 32	$ 5.09	18%
	China	$ 29	$ 22	$ 9.86	34%
	Mexico	$ 65	$ 74	$ 9.1	14%
	Thailand	$ 90	$110	$ 5.04	5.6%
MNCC	Brazil	$ 66	$ 80	$ 7.59	11.5%
	Malaysia	$ 98	$117	$22.54	23%
	France	$125	$140	$13.75	11%
	Japan	$240	$222	$48	20%
	United Kingdom	$190	$206	$36.48	11.8%
MNCD	Australia	$112	$140	$ 33.6	30%
	South Korea	$ 99	$109	$16.83	17%
	South Africa	$110	$ 99	$ 9.9	9%
	Singapore	$198	$250	$53.46	27%
	Germany	$180	$175	$34.56	19.2%

assets, gross revenues, and income after taxes. The ROI is included in the last column, and it is calculated by dividing income after taxes by the total assets of each foreign subsidiary.

For example, in the MNCA, the Saudi Arabian subsidiary realized the highest ROI (29 percent), which measures the profitability of a foreign subsidiary, among the five foreign subsidiaries, and the other subsidiary in Nigeria realized the lowest rate of return on investment ROI (9 percent).

Let's evaluate the performance of foreign subsidiary managers using the financial information presented in Table 6.2, assuming that the performance evaluation measure is the ROI. In MNCA, it would be concluded that the manager of the Saudi Arabian subsidiary did the best job in managing his subsidiary (with ROI of 29 percent), compared with the other four managers, and the manager of the Nigerian subsidiary of the same MNC did the worst job (ROI of 9 percent).

For MNCB, the Chinese subsidiary achieved the highest ROI of 34 percent. The subsidiary in Thailand came in with the lowest ROI of 5.6 percent, although its gross revenues are the highest of all the five foreign subsidiaries of MNCB. This comparison may be incorrect, however, because not all managers are working under the same environmental conditions. For example, Nigeria does not have the same social, political, economic, legal, or educational conditions as Saudi Arabia, and Thailand does not have the same environmental conditions as China.

How Should the Performance of Foreign Subsidiary Managers Be Measured?

What if you were the manager of a South Korean or South African subsidiary and worked for an Electric and Electronic MNC such as MNCD? Would you be evaluated on the basis of ROI of 17 percent or 9 percent, respectively, compared with a manager in Australia who realized ROI of 30 percent? Would you challenge the environmental conditions in South Korea or South Africa? Would the Australian subsidiary manager be promoted and rewarded on the basis of almost twice your ROI? Were the social, economic, or political conditions in South Korea or South Africa considered in evaluating the managers' performance?

Briefly, the performance evaluation systems now used by MNCs do not respond to these foreign environmental challenges and changes. Rather, the performance measure such as ROI, or any other measure, includes the effect of these environmental variables even though they are not and cannot be controlled by subsidiary managers. To consider the effect of one variable, management must examine all other foreign environmental variables and their interactions as they affect the performance of foreign subsidiaries.

For example, economic power has always been used for political stability, or social attitude or movement may cause government intervention. To implement a control system that is adequate and appropriate for MNC operations, foreign environmental variables should be measured in a manner that helps the MNC measure how well the foreign subsidiary manager has done his or her job on the basis of controllable factors only. It seems appropriate, therefore, for American and non-American MNCs to adopt a more relevant performance evaluation system that estimates the relative managerial contributions among foreign subsidiary managers, after considering the effects of noncontrollable foreign environmental factors, for a particular period of time (Abdallah 1984).

HOW DOES THE PERFORMANCE EVALUATION SYSTEM WORK IN MULTINATIONAL COMPANIES?

The measure performance of a foreign subsidiary can be described as the sum of

1. the effect of the levels of foreign noncontrollable environmental factors under which the subsidiary is operated,

2. the effect of the foreign subsidiary manager's actions after considering the effects of the noncontrollable environmental factors, and
3. other factors not explained by this model.

The objective of this model is to estimate the relative managerial performance of foreign managers after considering the effects of foreign noncontrollable environmental factors. Table 6.3 lists the 16 noncontrollable environmental factors for an American or non-American subsidiary. To show how the foreign subsidiary manager's actual contribution can be measured, let's look at MNCA's oil and gas subsidiary operating in Venezuela (refer to Table 6.2). The statistical tool for analyzing the data is step-wise multiple regression and correlation.

In order to measure, or assign a value to, the noncontrollable environmental factors, each international division officer was asked to rate the level of each of the 16 environmental variables in terms of their effect on subsidiary performance in particular countries. These factors were measured by using rank order measures. Each factor was rated separately on a scale from 0 to 100; 0 means there was no effect of the factor on the overall subsidiary performance, and 100 means the impact of the factor was very important.

The environmental model of the Venezuelan foreign subsidiary can be computed as follows, when Y is the total measured performance of the foreign subsidiary as ROI, M_s is the managerial contribution of the Venezuelan subsidiary manager, and X is a Venezuelan environmental factor (from Table 6.3).

$$Y = .7227^* - [0.0089^{**} X_{10} - 0.0175X_{14} - 0.0046X_{16}] + M_s$$

When the levels of noncontrollable Venezuelan environmental variables are $X_{10} = 35$, $X_{14} = 90$, and $X_{16} = 85$, and Y (ROI) = 12% (refer to Table 6.2).

Then,

$.12 = .7227 - [0.0089 (35) - 0.0175 (90) - 0.0046 (85)] + M_s^{***}$
$.12 = .7227 + [0.3115 - 1.575 + .391] + M_s$
$.12 = .7227 [-0.8725] + M_s$
$M_s = .12 - [.7227 - 0.8725]$
$\quad = .12 - [-0.1498]$
$M_s = .12 + .1498$
$\quad = 0.2698$ or 26.98%

*This number represents the regression constant; it indicates ROI when the noncontrollable Venezuelan environmental factors are equal to zero.
**These are the regression coefficients that express the relationship between the noncontrollable Venezuelan environmental factors and the measured performance of the foreign subsidiary.
***This is the managerial contribution by the Venezuelan subsidiary manager.

TABLE 6.3　The Foreign Environmental Variables

The Environmental Groups		The Noncontrollable Environmental Variables
Economic Variables	X_1	The general economic framework including the overall economic organizations of the country
	X_2	The organization and operation of the central banking system including controls over commercial banks and money supply
	X_3	Economic stability including the vulnerability of the country to economic fluctuations
	X_4	Capital markets and their honesty, effectiveness, and efficiency
Political-Legal Variables	X_5	Effectiveness and efficiency of the legal system
	X_6	The effect of the defense policy on business
	X_7	The effect of the foreign policy on business
	X_8	The degree of political stability and its effect on business (political risk)
Educational Variables	X_9	The quality of the formal education and the fitness to the needs of the country
	X_{10}	The extent and degree of technical training and the skills of persons obtaining such training and the qualification of trainers
	X_{11}	The management training programs to improve the skills and ability of managers
	X_{12}	The percentage of the total population and those employed in the industry with post-high school education
Social Variables	X_{13}	The dominant social attitude toward domestic and foreign business managers
	X_{14}	The dominant social attitude toward authority, power, and accountability of supervisors and managers
	X_{15}	The dominant cultural attitude toward teamwork and collective achievement and productivity
	X_{16}	The social attitude and values toward wealth and material gain

As you can see, the Venezuelan environmental factors—the extent and degree of technical training and the skills of persons obtaining such training and the qualification of trainers (X_{10}); the dominant social attitude toward authority, power, and accountability of supervisors and managers (X_{14}); and the social attitude and values toward wealth and material gain (X_{16})—significantly had affected the measured performance (in terms of ROI) of the Venezuelan subsidiary of the American MNCA Oil and Gas company operating in Venezuela. As a result, the managerial contribution of the Venezuelan subsidiary manager is 0.2698 or 26.98 percent.

Because managers in foreign countries operate under different environmental conditions, they face different economic, social, political, legal, and educational issues or problems. In setting foreign subsidiaries' goals, these differences should be taken into consideration by top management. In our example of the Venezuelan subsidiary, insomuch as all variations in the performance of the foreign subsidiaries related to the oil and gas industry and in oil and gas countries, the average foreign subsidiary manager achieves zero as a result of his or her managerial contribution. The better-than-average foreign subsidiary manager achieves a positive rating for his or her managerial contribution, and the below average manager achieves a negative rating for his or her managerial contribution.

With respect to the Venezuelan subsidiary, the measured performance (in terms of ROI) was 12 percent, and after extracting the effect of noncontrollable Venezuelan environmental factors (0.1498 or 14.98 percent), the managerial contribution attributable to the Venezuelan subsidiary manager's actions became 0.2698 (or 26.98). Thus, an appropriate target ROI for an oil and gas industry subsidiary in the Venezuelan environment should be at least 0.1490. The current manager's contribution was .2698. Because the estimated managerial contribution of a foreign subsidiary does not depend on the levels of the noncontrollable Venezuelan environmental factors, the managerial contribution can be comparable among managers of different foreign subsidiaries of the same company, which is MNCA in our example.

From the viewpoint of MNCA's top management, both managerial contribution and noncontrollable environmental factors are important because top-management can, in the long run, control both these components of the measured performance. Because the measured performance of the foreign subsidiary depends primarily on a particular location within the same industry, top-management should devote more attention to location selection in investment decision making especially in the oil and gas countries.

Using actual data on the level of foreign environmental factors rather than opinions would help make the model much more realistic. Because MNCs have their own resources—financial and human—there will not be any difficulty in applying this model.

The adoption of such a performance evaluation system requires no major adjustments of a traditional management accounting system to evaluate the performance of foreign subsidiary managers. The only added factors are the actual levels of noncontrollable foreign environmental factors under which the Venezuelan or any other oil and gas subsidiary operates. Those foreign environmental factors can be identified, assessed, and incorporated into the present system as a basis for making the MNC performance evaluation system objective, operational, and practical.

Performance Evaluation of Foreign Subsidiary with Fluctuations in Currency Values

MNCs set up their international transfer pricing policies at the central-management (or top-management) level to facilitate cash movements in the foreign country where currency restrictions exist and to minimize taxes. A conflict between international transfer pricing techniques and performance evaluation measurement of a foreign subsidiary manager is to be expected, and, in general, transfer pricing policies are not complementary to the profit center concept.

At the second quarter (1996) meeting of the Consortium for Advanced Manufacturing-International (CAM-I), it was emphasized that performance measurement consists of an integrated, comprehensive set of measures that flow from management's vision and strategy. It was also suggested that firms should try to understand investors' nonfinancial performance concerns. One presentation focused on Caterpillar, Inc.'s performance measurement system, which utilizes a market-based transfer pricing system and a balanced scorecard of nine top-tier performance measurements (Daly 1996).

Unfortunately, the traditional profit center concept for performance evaluation of a foreign subsidiary manager is inappropriate for MNCs because there is no clear distinction between operating subdivisions of MNCs. With integrated, centrally coordinated operations, foreign subsidiary management does not have authority for major decisions that affect its reported profits. Differences between foreign countries, such as social, economic, political, legal, and educational differences, have a considerable effect on a foreign subsidiary manager's performance. There is an urgent need for further research to introduce additional elements into traditional management accounting evaluation techniques.

In evaluating the performance of a foreign subsidiary, it is appropriate to evaluate its contribution to the objectives and goals of the whole MNC. It is also important to evaluate the contribution of foreign subsidiary managers to the performance of the MNC. David Solomons has stated, "In the absence of evidence to the contrary, the presumption is that the success of one implies the success of the other. But circumstances outside a manager's control may dictate success or failure of the venture" (Solomons 1965, 59).

Headquarters enforces a specific transfer price to be used by its own foreign subsidiaries to achieve certain corporate goals such as reducing domestic and foreign income tax liabilities, foreign exchange risk reduction, and foreign exchange control avoidance, among others. To achieve these goals, international transfer pricing may result in some foreign subsidiaries showing higher artificial profits, while others may show much lower artificial profits.

A foreign subsidiary manager may have the operations of his or her area being evaluated as if it were a completely autonomous and independent subsidiary. Foreign subsidiary managers may have the greatest degree of freedom in making decisions related to the short run. However, they have a lesser degree of freedom in making decisions directly affecting other foreign subsidiaries and the globe.

With the frequent fluctuations of currency values combined with the floating exchange rates system, MNCs face the problem of distorted performance measurements of their domestic and foreign subsidiaries as profit centers. (Malmstrom 1977, 25). Performance of foreign subsidiaries in U.S.-based MNCs is usually adjusted for any fluctuations in currency exchange rates (Benke and Edwards 1980, 118).

At Honeywell, Inc., Duane Malmstrom (1977) implemented a simple solution for this problem. His technique is called "dollar indexing." This technique is used to have the same impact as local currency invoicing, including two basic objectives: to allow realistic performance evaluation, and to reflect the real economic cost of the product transferred. Malmstrom used an indexed formula for U.S.-dollar transfer prices:

$$NTP = OTP \times \frac{CER}{PER}$$

where

OTP = new transfer price

OTP = old transfer price

CER = current exchange rate

PER = planned exchange rate

Using this formula results in applying a uniform transfer price for all goods transferred out of the same subsidiary.

For illustration, let us assume that a Singaporean subsidiary of an American MNC transferred 20,000 units of its products at a transfer price established by the parent U.S.-based MNC at $20.00 per unit to another foreign subsidiary located in Japan owned by the same MNC. The foreign exchange rates on July 24, 2002, were the Japanese yen (JPY)

1.00 = US$0.008506 or US$1.00 = JPY117.57, and Singaporean dollar (SGD) = US$0.5727 or US$1.00 = SGD1.7461. As can be seen in Table 6.4, the Singaporean subsidiary achieves a net income of US$165,000 or SGD288,107, while the Japanese subsidiary achieves a net income of $320,000, or JPY37,622,400.

If we assume that the U.S. dollar was depreciated equally against both the Singaporean and the Japanese currencies to US$1.00 = SGD1.4842 and US$1.00 = JPY99.9345, respectively, the income statements for both subsidiaries and the MNC measured in U.S. dollars and local currencies would be as shown in Table 6.5. Because the transfer price ($20.00 per unit) was set centrally by the U.S.-based MNC, the operating results of the Singaporean subsidiary would show a lower net income of $123,529 or SGD193,340, while the Japanese subsidiary would achieve a higher net income of $447,059 or JPY44,676,600 because of the devaluation of the U.S. dollar in the global market.

The effect of using the $20.00 as a transfer price for international operations when there was devaluation in the parent's currency resulted in switching the operating results of the selling subsidiary from net income of 41.3 percent of sales to a lower net income of 30.9 percent of sales. On the other hand, the operating results of the buying subsidiary would be in the opposite direction, switching from a net income of 32 percent to a higher net income of 38 percent. That is, this transaction not only transferred goods from the Singaporean subsidiary to the Japanese subsidiary but also transferred $41,471 ($165,000 − $123,529) of profits and a translation gain of $85,588 (for the MNC from $485,000 to $570,588), a total of $127,059. In this case, the MNC as a whole should show a profit of $570,588 higher than before by $85,588 because of the translation gains resulting from the devaluation of the U.S. dollar. For

TABLE 6.4   The Effect of Transfer Pricing on Performance Evaluation

Transfer Price	Singaporean Subsidiary		Japanese Subsidiary		The MNC in
@ $20	USD	SGD	USD	JPY	USD
Sales (@ $20 & $50)	$400,000	698,440	$1,000,000	117,570,000	$1,000,000
Less CGS	$150,000	261,915	$ 400,000	47,028,000	$ 150,000
Gross profit	$250,000	436,525	$ 600,000	70,542,000	$ 850,000
Less operating expenses	$ 85,000	148,419	$ 280,000	32,919,600	$ 365,000
Net operating income	$165,000	288,107	$ 320,000	37,622,400	$ 485,000
Net income as a % of sales	0.413	0.413	0.32	0.32	0.485
US$1=SGD1.7461					
US$1=JPY117.57					

TABLE 6.5 The Effect of Transfer Pricing with Changes in Foreign Exchange Rates on Performance Evaluation

Transfer Price	Singaporean Subsidiary		Japanese Subsidiary		The MNC
@ $20	USD	SGD	USD	JPY	(in USD)
Sales (@ $20 & $50)	$400,000	593,674	$1,176,471	117,570,000	$1,176,471
Less CGS	$176,471	261,915	$ 400,000	39,973,800	$ 176,471
Gross profit	$223,529	331,759	$ 776,471	77,596,200	$1,000,000
Less operating expenses	$100,000	148,419	$ 329,412	32,919,600	$ 429,412
Net operating income	$123,529	183,340	$ 447,059	44,676,600	$ 570,588
Net income as a % of sales	0.3088	0.3088	0.38	0.38	0.485
US$1=SGD1.4842					
US$1=JPY99.9345					

performance evaluation purposes, the manager of the Singaporean subsidiary was affected negatively by the change in the exchange rate and the imposed transfer price, while the Japanese subsidiary's manager did nothing more than before but showed a 38 percent net income percentage (6 points higher than before the change occurred).

Using the indexed formula for U.S.-dollar transfer prices suggested by Malmstrom, the adjusted transfer price would be

$$NTP = OTP \times \frac{CER}{PER}$$

$$NTP = \$20.00 \times \frac{SGD1.7461}{SGD1.4842} = \$23.53$$

$$NTP = \$20.00 \times \frac{JPY117.57}{JPY99.9345} = \$23.53$$

Table 6.6 shows the effect of transfer prices adjusted for changes in exchange rates. The new transfer price is $23.53, which is higher than the old one. For the Singaporean and the Japanese subsidiaries, the net income percentage as related to sales is the same as before any changes in the exchange rate, and both of them had the same measured performance as before. The MNC had higher global profits with the dollar devaluation by $85,588, which is a translation gain. However, the translation gains were divided in such a way that the Japanese subsidiary received $56,474 (66 percent out of total translation gains of $85,588), whereas the Singaporean subsidiary received only $29,148 (34 percent out of $85,588, which is the increase in the transfer price) due to how

TABLE 6.6   The Effect of Transfer Pricing Adjusted for Changes in Exchange Rates

Transfer Price	Singaporean Subsidiary		Japanese Subsidiary		The MNC
@ $20	USD	SGD	USD	JPY	(in USD)
Sales (@ $23.53 & $50)	$470,585	698,435	$1,176,471	117,570,000	$1,176,471
Less CGS	$176,471	261,915	$ 470,585	47,027,672	$ 176,471
Gross profit	$294,114	436,520	$ 705,886	70,542,328	$1,000,000
Less operating expenses	$100,000	148,419	$ 329,412	32,919,600	$ 429,412
Net operating income	$194,114	228,101	$ 376,474	37,622,728	$ 570,588
Net income as a % of sales	0.4125	0.4125	0.32	0.32	0.485
US$1=SGD1.4842					
US$1=JPY99.9345					

much the U.S. dollar was devalued in relation to the local currency. Therefore, the adjusted transfer price helps to avoid any distortion in the financial results and ratios and reflects the effect of the exchange rate fluctuations.

SUMMARY AND CONCLUSIONS

This chapter introduced, discussed, and analyzed the performance evaluation problem of MNCs in evaluating their foreign subsidiaries and their managers. First, the traditional performance evaluation measures were discussed. For most MNCs, the objective and practical way in which to treat the effects of environmental factors on foreign operations has not been reached. A foreign subsidiary manager's performance should not reflect how well the manager has done without regard to foreign environmental variables, but how well the manager has performed his or her job within those environmental factors.

Traditional management accounting techniques are inadequate to appropriately solve these problems, and MNCs are unable to achieve satisfactory and desired levels of performance evaluation. Management accounting techniques has not adequately considered the distinct characteristics of the environment within which MNCs operate and manage their businesses.

Second, a suggested performance evaluation system for foreign countries was presented. The proposed system estimates foreign subsidiary managers' relative performance after considering the effects of noncontrollable foreign environmental factors on the measured performance of foreign subsidiaries. Third, the suggested environmental model was applied to one of the foreign subsidiaries of an American MNC [name was omitted] to illustrate how MNCs can implement it in practice, some guidelines on the important issues in managerial, financial reporting, and taxation of American joint ventures in the foreign countries. Countries' rules, regulations, facts, and experiences that uniquely affect management and financial reporting of American-foreign joint ventures were also discussed.

There are many implications of this proposed model for performance evaluation for foreign subsidiary managers and decision making in allocating the limited resources (human and financial) of MNCs. One possible implication is that new advanced management accounting techniques should be developed and used to facilitate measurement and evaluation of the performance of foreign subsidiary managers of MNCs. Certainly, the proposed foreign environmental model is useful for MNCs in designing a system of performance evaluation of subsidiary managers combined with transfer pricing system. The proposed system incorporates the distinction of each foreign environmental factor into its design. Definitely, this new system will lead to improved systems, improved planning, and improved decision-making processes and outcomes.

REFERENCES

Abdallah, Wagdy M. 1984. Research for Business Decisions, No. 68. *Internal accountability: An international emphasis.* Mich.: UMI Research Press.
———. 2002. Global transfer pricing of multinationals and e-commerce in the twenty-first century. *Multinational Business Review* 10, no. 2 (Fall): 62–71.
———. 2001. *Managing multinationals in the Middle Ease: Accounting and tax issues.* Westport, Conn.: Greenwood Press, Inc.
———. 1986. Change the environment or change the system. *Management Accounting* (October): 33–37.
Abdallah, Wagdy, M., and Donald Keller. 1985. Measuring the multinational's performance. *Management Accounting* (October): 26–30.
Abdel-Khalik, A. Rashad, and Edward J. Lusk. 1974. Transfer pricing: A synthesis. *Accounting Review* 69: 3–23.
American Accounting Association. 1973. Report of the Committee on International Accounting. *The Accounting Review,* Supplement 48: 121–68.
Anctil, Regina M., and Sunil Dutta. 1999. Negotiated transfer pricing and divisional vs. firm-wide performance evaluation. *Accounting Review* 24, no. 1 (January): 87–104.
Ball, Donald A., and Wendell H. McCulloch, Jr. 1985. *International Business.* 2nd edition. Plano, Texas: Business Publications.
Benke, Ralph L., Jr., and James Don Edwards. 1980. *Transfer pricing techniques and uses.* New York: National Association of Accountants.
Bierman, Harold. 1978. ROI as a measure of managerial performance. In *Accounting for Managerial Decision-making,* 2nd Edition, edited by Don T. Decoster, Kansser V. Ramathan, and G. Sundem. Santa Barbara, Calif.: Wiley/Hamilton.

Borkowski, Susan C. 1999. International managerial performance evaluation: A five country comparison." *Journal of International Business Studies* 30, no.3 (3rd Quarter): 533–55.

Bursk, Edward C., and others. 1971. *Financial control of multinational operations.* New York: Financial Executive Research Foundation.

Choi, Frederick D. S., Carol Ann Frost, and Gary K. Meek. 2002. *International accounting,* 4th Edition. Upper Saddle River, N.J.: Prentice-Hall.

Daly, Dennis C. 1996. Performance measurement and management. *Management Accounting* 78, no. 3 (September): 65.

Eccles, R. G. 1985. *The transfer pricing problem.* Lexington, Mass.: Lexington Books.

Emmanuel, C. R., and M. Mehafdi. 1994. *Transfer pricing.* London: Academic Press.

Farmer, Richard N., and Barry M. Richman. 1980. *International business,* 3rd Edition. Bloomington, Ind.: Cedarwood Press.

Grabski, S. V. 1985. Transfer pricing in complex organization: A review and integration of recent empirical and analytical research. *Journal of Accounting Literature* 4: 33–75.

Leitch, R. A., and K. S. Barrett. 1992. Multinational enterprise transfer-pricing: Objectives and constraints. *Journal of Accounting Literature* 11: 47–92.

Malmstrom, Duane. 1977. Accommodating exchange rate fluctuations in inter-company pricing and invoicing. *Management Accounting* (September): 25.

Mauriel, John J. 1969. Evaluating and control of overseas operations. *Management Accounting* (May): 36.

Morsicato, Helen G., and Lee H. Radebaugh. 1979. Internal performance evaluation of multinational enterprise operations. *The International Journal of Accounting* 51 (fall): 77–94.

Persen, William, and Van Lessig. 1978. *Evaluating the financial performance of overseas operations.* New York: Financial Executive Research Foundation.

Robbins, Sidney M., and Robert B. Stobaugh. 1973. *Money in the multinational enterprise.* New York: Basic Books.

Robock, Stefan H., and Kenneth Simmonds. 1983. *International business and multinational enterprises,* 3rd Edition. Chicago, Ill.: Richard D. Irwin.

Solomons, David. 1965. *Divisional performance: Measurement and control.* Chicago, Ill.: Richard D. Irwin.

III

E-Commerce and Intangible Assets

7

E-Commerce and International Transfer Pricing in the Twenty-first Century

This chapter examines the e-commerce activities of multinational companies and its impact on designing transfer pricing techniques and strategies. First, the traditional framework of transfer pricing techniques and tax regulations that are used in e-commerce cross-border business transactions of MNCs are analyzed. Second, the right transfer pricing method that fits the nature of transfer pricing cross-border e-commerce activities is investigated. Third, taxation of tangible goods or digitized tangible products transferred through the Internet is discussed. Fourth, the challenges of e-commerce activities of multinationals in designing the appropriate transfer pricing systems are covered. Finally, several recommendations are given for financial executive officers to use in planning and designing their transfer pricing strategies to successfully combine changes in their operating environment with tax efficient strategies to realize several advantages.

INTRODUCTION

Worldwide use of the Internet is now a significant part of global business life. Very soon, e-commerce will be the driver of future developments in cross-border business transactions in the twenty-first century. However, current international tax regulations were written within the framework of national sovereignty in tax systems before the discovery of e-commerce. The rapid changes thrust upon the global business world through e-commerce are pushing every government, including the United States, to ensure its tax system integrity by closing the loopholes for either tax avoidance or tax evasion through the use of e-commerce transactions. E-commerce is considered by many tax authorities as a threat to revenues from traditional income and consumption tax systems (Merrill 2001). The main concern of tax authorities is that the highly mobile nature of e-commerce will lead to the significant increase of tax haven transactions that will further erode their tax base (Maguire 1999). Reports of several tax authorities, including the United States, Canada, the United Kingdom, the OECD, and many other foreign tax authorities, identified the major tax issues of e-commerce as jurisdiction, identification, information, and collection mechanisms (Boyle et al. 1999).

On the other hand, corporate financial officers (CFOs) and accountants who work for MNCs should ensure that that their transfer pricing policies reduce the risk of audits. To protect their tax bases, tax authorities must ensure that they collect a fair amount of corporate income tax from multinational corporations (MNCs) operating in their jurisdictions and thus have become more alert in enforcing the rules of transfer pricing. MNCs could face inconsistent and unfair treatment of cross-border transactions, double taxation, and penalties for noncompliance with different tax regulations of different countries.

Transfer pricing of e-commerce transactions that cross the border of any country have not been discussed to the same extent as other important strategic business and tax issues. International transfer pricing is a subject that no MNC, regardless of size or location, can afford to ignore. The complexity of the issue might require MNCs to redefine and update their transfer pricing strategies to go with the new challenge of information technology in the new millennium. Until now, the literature on the impact of e-commerce on international transfer pricing has not been discussed to the same extent as other tax and global issues. Most research efforts of management and accounting scholars have addressed either the issue of international transfer pricing or e-commerce in the United States and different countries around the world (Abdallah 1989; Boyle et al. 1999; Burns 2000; Eccles 1985; OECD 1995 and 1997; and Tang 1997). In recent years, extended research has not been undertaken on international transfer pricing strategies that are founded on e-commerce and international taxation of the United States and foreign countries. In MNCs, however, international taxation complicates transfer pricing and e-commerce problems. These problems have been addressed using traditional transfer pricing techniques. Although this has attracted a tremendous research and legislative effort to solve the technical issues, the equally pertinent e-commerce issues have been overlooked.

In 1997, the OECD identified several issues affecting the transfer pricing of global e-commerce transactions and suggested that the use of the profit split method (OECD 1995) as currently applied to the global trading of financial instruments, might be appropriate for e-commerce activity (OECD 1997). Difficulties in applying existing transfer pricing guidelines to e-commerce transactions include applying the transactional approach, establishing comparability and carrying out a functional analysis, applying traditional transaction methods, the tax treatment of integrated businesses, and determining and complying with appropriate documentation and information reporting requirements (OECD 1998).

Usually associated with large decentralized multinational companies and widely discussed in the management accounting and finance literature, transfer pricing issues now occupy center stage in international tax litigation and court cases over tax avoidance and evasion through manipulated transfer prices. In 1999 Ernst & Young conducted a survey of several MNCs, and it showed that 75 percent of MNCs believed that they would be hit with a transfer-pricing audit within the next two years (Hamilton 2000). On the other hand, in the same year, the U.S Tax Court decided on three major transfer pricing cases—GAC Produce, Inc., Compaq Computer Corp and H Group Holding (Burns 2000). The IRS won the H Group Holding and GAC cases, and lost the case against Compaq (Ibid.). Therefore, MNCs should pay close attention to transfer pricing issues and think wisely about going into the Advance Pricing Agreement program with the IRS.

All these studies have broadened our understanding of international transfer pricing techniques and strategies from a multinational's point of view. Much remains to be learned, however, about the impact of e-commerce on international transfer pricing strategies.

Maguire (1999) argued that e-commerce may not present new transfer pricing problems, it only magnifies existing issues such as the valuation of intangibles and services, and compliance with documentation and information reporting requirements. Moreover, the Organization of Economic and Cooperation Development (OECD) still thinks that existing principles in dealing with e-transfer pricing transactions are adequate, and that e-commerce has not presented any fundamentally new problems for transfer pricing. However, due to rapid development in communications resulting in instantaneous transmission of information, tax administrations are concerned that it may become more difficult to identify, trace, quantify, and verify cross-border transactions, and there are difficulties in applying internationally accepted transfer pricing methods to e-commerce.

MNCs, tax authorities, and international organizations are at the crossroads of not being able to solve the complicated problems created by e-commerce and transfer pricing. As MNCs manage their cross-border business transactions, transfer pricing methods and strategies for e-commerce transactions may be more difficult to apply in reducing their tax liabilities and integrate their production and marketing strategies on a worldwide basis.

TRADITIONAL FRAMEWORK OF TRANSFER PRICING TAX REGULATIONS

The impact of e-commerce on transfer pricing has not been discussed, either by tax authorities or by international organizations, to the same extent as other tax and global issues. The traditional framework of transfer pricing tax regulations is not appropriate for dealing with global e-commerce and both tangible goods and intangible services that occur in cyberspace. For e-commerce transactions conducted within an MNC, tax authorities may have difficulties in obtaining the required information and documentation and in finding the appropriate transfer pricing method because of the lack of data on uncontrolled comparable third-party transactions. The current approach of identifying transfer prices requires identification of the transaction and its analysis under the arm's length principle (Eicker 1999). And that is because tax regulations for transfer pricing issues were designed for the nondigital world.

The pace of cross-border activities is accelerating, due in large part to e-commerce, as customers search market places around the globe for the best price, quality, and service. The acceleration of e-commerce activities may put pressure on the traditional transfer pricing rules because it will be easier for affiliated companies within a single MNC to be involved in reciprocal transactions of tangible goods, digitized tangible products, or intangible services transferred through the use of their intranets. Moreover, where a successfully offshore e-commerce subsidiary uses intangible services acquired from related entities of the same MNC, it may be subject to painstaking transfer pricing scrutiny from the relevant tax authorities on the right price of the intercompany management fees or royalties (Maguire 1999).

The significant growth of the global market means that both MNCs and tax authorities should consider e-commerce cross-border business transactions and their effect on transfer pricing policies carefully. MNCs should ensure that their transfer pricing policies and strategies using e-commerce can be supported and that they are considered fair and acceptable. Foreign tax authorities should also ensure that they collect a fair and reasonable amount of corporate tax revenue from MNCs investing, operating, and conducting e-commerce in their countries.

SECTION 482 OF IRC

Section 482 of the U.S. Internal Revenue Code provides that the Internal Revenue Service (IRS) may allocate gross income, deductions, credits, or allowances among related entities to prevent the evasion of taxes and to reflect clearly the income of each entity of a corporate group. The purpose of Section 482 is to prevent shifting of income or profits from one commonly controlled entity to another by an MNC.

The application of Section 482 has tended to focus on the concept of comparing intragroup transfer prices with arm's-length third-party prices. The arm's-length standard is defined by the Code as the amount that would have been charged in independent transactions with unrelated parties under the same or similar circumstances. The main question now is whether e-commerce will require major changes in Section 482 in allocating income among jurisdictions or whether the traditional framework of transfer pricing tax regulations is appropriate for dealing with global e-commerce and not in need of any significant modifications.

Many problems may arise in translating Section 482 into practice with e-commerce of MNCs, because the tax regulations are ambiguous and vague. Consequently, facts and circumstances of what constitute the appropriate arm's-length price for e-commerce transactions to be used among related entities can give plenty of scope for debate and negotiations. Therefore, most of the cases between the IRS and MNCs require the courts to settle the disputes, and there is no one general rule arrived at among courts. Moreover, the provision of services to related parties via the Internet is a more complex issue. Fast exchanges and increased reliance on private MNC networks will bring pressure to bear on the traditional approach, and the traditional approach may even be impossible in the case of the reciprocal exchange of services through e-commerce (Eicker 1999).

In 1996, the U.S. Treasury Department issued a policy study, "Selected Tax Policy Implications of Global Electronic Commerce," which suggested that e-commerce makes it more difficult to identify the source of income, and, therefore, priority should be given to taxation in the jurisdiction of residence. It proposed a substance-over-form approach to determining the character of income (Merrill 2001). Therefore, income from the sale of copyrighted material, such as music CDs or computer software, should be treated in the same way whether the CD is delivered digitally or via a physical shipping medim. The only e-commerce-related tax regulations adopted by the U.S. Congress is the Internet Tax Freedom Act of 1998, which keeps Internet access free of sales tax in most states, and put off through October 31, 2001, on state and local taxation and multiple discriminatory taxes on e-commerce

(Merrill 2001). On November 28, 2001, President Bush signed a bill to extend the Internet Tax Freedom Act for two more years.

Currently, there is evidence of tax-motivated transfer pricing that comes in several forms. Though it is possible that high tax rates are correlated with other location attributes that depress the profitability of foreign investment, competitive conditions typically imply that after-tax rates of return should be equal in the absence of tax-motivated income shifting. It is true that before-tax profitability is negatively correlated with local tax rates, which is strongly suggestive of active tax avoidance (Hines 1999).

THE RIGHT TRANSFER PRICING METHODS FOR E-COMMERCE TRANSACTIONS OF MNCS

It is presumed that the use of nontraditional business practices such as the Web by online retailers should not theoretically result in generated income being treated differently for tax purposes. However, the nature of e-commerce business tends to mix up national borders and the source of income. Under Section 482 of IRC, the permissible methods for determining an arm's-length price are: comparable un-controlled price (CUP) method, resale price method (RPM), and cost-plus method (CPM). The three methods are required to be used in order, and a fourth alternative method may be used for all other situations in which none of the first three is considered appropriate and reasonable. The fourth can be based on profit-split approaches such as the comparable profits method and several profit-split methods (PSM).

For e-commerce transactions, there are several reasons to prefer traditional transactional transfer pricing such as the comparable uncontrolled price (CUP) method over profit split methods (PSM). CUP includes direct comparison of transaction prices between related party transactions and comparable unrelated party transaction and is, therefore, the most direct method for testing related transactions if information on sufficiently similar unrelated transactions is available (Shah et al. 2000). Another reason to prefer the traditional methods is that they are easier for MNCs to use and follow on a day-to-day basis, and it is the one more preferable under the U.S. regulations (Ibid.).

To choose the best transfer pricing method, the rule requires that the arm's-length result of related party transactions be determined under the method that, given the facts and circumstances, provides the most reliable indicator of an arm's-length result. If traditional methods are not applicable for e-commerce transactions or for such a high level of integration between related parties, the OECD guidelines permit the transactional profit method. Using this method, the overall profit of the group is divided between entities engaged like third parties would have been agreed upon. The PSM has already been established in some countries in the area of innovative financial transactions—for example, global trading. Revenue Canada recognizes transactional profit methods, such as the PSM and the transactional net margin method (TNMM) (Rolph and Niederhoffer 1999). The OECD has examined PSM and concluded that both the PSM and the TNMM are becoming more widespread.

A lack of available transactional comparables and the existence of intangible property may lead to the use of the PSM. The PSM assigns residual profit from intangible property and nonroutine risks borne, once routing profits are allocated using one of the standard methodologies prescribed by either the U.S. regulations or the OECD guidelines (Shah et al. 2000). However, the development of e-commerce business models has triggered a fundamental reconsideration of the rules that should guide the split of profits between a home office and a permanent establishment (PE) (Merrill 2001).

Spreading the ownership of intangibles and the risk through the MNC is another technique for transfer pricing of e-commerce transactions. Two different ways are suggested: central and distributed ownership (Stanley 2001). Under the central ownership approach, all the intangibles would be owned centrally and then, for example, licensed out. Under distributed ownership, the value of intangibles and their future developments would be split throughout the subsidiaries. This could be achieved by means of a cost sharing or cost contribution arrangement (Stanley 2001).

Many groups put more pressure for change in the traditional techniques to fit business transactions that occur in cyberspace. Companies need simultaneously to access and compete in an ever-growing number of geographically dispersed markets. At the same time, new and emerging technologies are increasing information flow and accessibility. This in turn is irritating geographic price transparency, raising the sophistication and expectations of consumers, and significantly reducing business startup costs (Durst et al. 1999).

E-commerce also puts pressure on the traditional principles of transfer pricing. Standardized rules apply to attribute the appropriate amount of income to each entity in an MNC. However, finding the appropriate transfer pricing method with e-commerce transactions may be difficult—especially if no comparable transaction is readily available. The challenge is therefore to develop acceptable profit allocations that can motivate foreign subsidiary managers in performing their jobs and satisfy the tax authorities of various countries.

TAXATION OF DIGITIZED TANGIBLE PRODUCTS AND INTANGIBLES TRANSFERRED THROUGH THE INTERNET

Tax authorities around the world are ever watchful for manipulation of transfer prices of digitized tangible products and intangible services between related entities that result in income distortions. For instance, tax authorities are on the lookout for transfer prices that result in income from the sale of products or services being allocated disproportionately to tax haven countries. Transfer pricing in e-commerce is an issue that is being looked at; though so far there is little progress. Current transfer pricing rules, which emphasize a transactional or functional approach, are difficult to apply to e-commerce.

However, the significant increase in the volume and complexity of e-commerce business transactions has tax authorities concerned that the existing tax systems with respect to taxable presence or permanent establishment (PE), character and source of income, and transfer pricing may be inappropriate to protect their respective tax bases from a virtual tax haven. In some cases, e-commerce alters not only the conventional business pattern but also the product itself. E-commerce cross-border transactions have also placed significant pressure on the conventional approach adopted by tax authorities to address non–arm's-length transfer pricing (Rolph and Niederhoffer 1999). Most of the disputes between MNCs and tax authorities may be caused by "failure to use OECD methods, failure to have any transfer pricing method at all, being driven by tax rather than by business reasons, and finally, as a result of badly worked out supply chain restructuring" (Stanley 2001, 28).

Historically, OECD member countries have entered into income tax treaties that have a fairly high threshold of taxable presence for foreign vendors and suppliers, as expressed in the PE provision of the model convention. OECD treaties also eliminate withholding taxes on imports of intangibles. Along with this trend, one would expect the OECD to recommend guidelines that would exempt the mere existence of Web sites and computer servers from treatment as a PE, and preclude the application of withholding tax on deliveries of most forms of digitized material (Maguire 1999).

Since 1999, the OECD has been discussing the application of the PE definition as related to e-commerce cross-border transactions. Application of the concepts of PE and character of income will determine which country—that of the seller or the buyer—will be able to tax a specific cross-border business transaction. Implicit in this is an allocation of revenue between the country of residence and the country of source.

The main issues in digital products or services transferred through e-commerce are threefold: Web-based services that are unique to e-commerce, the ability to deliver products electronically, and the ability to operate a Web-based business remotely. Services and digitized products, such as software, can be delivered over the Internet to customers around the world. Tax rules and regulations governing e-commerce transactions and electronic delivery of products are, however, virtually nonexistent.

One of the most compelling issues raised by e-commerce is whether a traditional PE concept retains its vitality when business is conducted in cyberspace. To impose tax on e-commerce tangible and intangible transactions, it is important to know whether or not an MNC has created a taxable presence in a country. This requires understanding of the three issues—the Web server (hardware), the Web site (software), and the Internet service provider (ISP)—to decide which one will be an indicator of the PE and determine the taxability of the income generated by e-commerce.

The Web Servers (Hardware)

Web servers, or hosts, are individual (hardware) computers running software that allows them to access and to be accessed by other computers over telephone lines. Servers act as hosts for individual Web sites (Hardesty 1999). The main issue is the effect of a Web server in a country on a foreign company's taxability in that country. A Web server could create a PE if it meets the usual requirement of having a fixed location in a country from which business is transacted. If it is established that a Web server has created a PE, the next issue is what income should be allocated to that server. In general, the bilateral tax treaties between the member countries of the OECD state that a foreign-owned company is not subject to tax on business profits in a country unless that company has a PE in that country.

However, the OECD model allows jurisdictions to impose net income tax on a business only if its activities in the jurisdiction rise to the level of a PE. The use of stand-alone Web servers to conduct business within a jurisdiction has raised the question about the PE rules; some tax authorities have suggested lowering the existing PE concept to allow taxation of MNCs that do business in a jurisdiction even though they have no physical presence (Merrill 2001).

The Web Site

A Web site is defined as "a collection of programs, data, and images which may be accessed over the Internet using a browser or some other form of access" (Hardesty 1999). A Web site that is accessible to customers in foreign countries by itself is not a fixed place of business and so cannot create a taxable presence or PE in those countries. However, if the server is loaded with a digitized product and is programmed to process and deliver orders, some countries might view it as a PE. Moreover, there might be a PE where the business that owns the Web site also owns the server; and the activities carried on through the web site are not within the normal exclusions for preparatory or auxiliary activities. Accordingly, server locations will have to be selected with care (Maguire 1999).

A commentary of OECD states that a Web site (software) should be distinguished from the server (hardware) that hosts the site. A Web site owner often makes a contract with an ISP to host the site, and ISPs usually do not provide Web site owners with control over hosting equipment. A Web-hosting arrangement with an ISP, except in very unusual circumstances, will not create a PE for the Web site owner because an ISP will not be considered an agent of the Web site owner (Merrill 2001). The Web server that is located for a sufficient period of time within a country and is used to carry on part or all of a business may constitute a PE even if no employees are at that location.

The Internet Service Provider (ISP)

An ISP is a commercial company that sells access to the Internet for a fee. The term ISP is used to represent a wide range of services that may be provided by a bandwidth provider of Internet connectivity, such as Web hosting, Internet firewall configuration, maintenance, and monitoring (Greenstein and Vasarhelyi 2002). The services of an ISP would not normally create an agency relationship between the ISP and its clients, and so the clients would not meet the requirement for a PE solely through the use of an ISP.

An important question in applying national income tax systems is whether a legal entity has enough presence in a foreign jurisdiction to justify income taxation by that country. The OECD model allows a jurisdiction to impose net income tax on a business only if its activities in that jurisdiction rise to the level of a PE.

Given this lack of clear understanding and discussion on transfer pricing of e-commerce business transactions, it is not surprising that tax authorities of different countries cannot reach an agreement on how to tax e-transfer pricing cross-border business transactions. Therefore, e-commerce will require major adjustments in the transitional means of allocating revenue among jurisdictions and in the current systems of tax administration. Moreover, e-commerce transactions could result in the disappearance of traditional audit trails (through creation of electronic books), in greater accessibility of tax havens and offshore transactions (Asher and Rajan 2001).

MNCs cannot wait for the tax authorities to sort out the international tax rules as e-business is changing the way we all operate now. The commercial imperatives demand immediate action, and it is therefore disappointing to see the relatively slow progress of the OECD and other bodies. In a time of manic and rapid change, MNCs face arguably greater uncertainty over taxation than at any previous point (Durst et al. 1999; Burns 2002; "Finance and Economics" 2004).

For intangible assets, MNCs have used a common policy by creating a hub in a tax haven country and shift the ownership of these intangibles over to this hub by using the other locations as quasi service providers to the hub, accepting minimal risk and profit, with the hub owning all the technology (Stanley 2001). This process requires a buy-in for the existing technology, and it is the understatement of the buy-in that forms the biggest source of income tax savings for the MNC. In response, the IRS has changed its policy and is now looking hard at such structures intending to set the value of the buy-ins (Ibid.).

For MNCs starting global Web operations, they should perform a country-by-country review of the tax issues, which will vary by type of business. Legitimate opportunities for basing e-commerce in tax-haven jurisdictions exist, but economic and tax hurdles as well as infrastructure risks that must be overcome to justify such a move should be thoroughly understood and taken into account (Maguire 1999).

The fast growth of e-commerce activities may increase the significance of transfer pricing rules because it will be easier for related companies to engage in reciprocal transactions in products and services through intranets. As far as marketing systems are concerned, no material changes in the calculation of transfer prices would take place in a related company e-commerce transaction. The changes in the structure of costs and calculated risks are the only issues that need to be accounted for (Eicker 1999).

DESIGNING THE GLOBAL TRANSFER PRICING SYSTEM OF E-COMMERCE FOR MULTINATIONALS

It is up to the CFOs and accountants to avoid the belief that one system of transfer pricing fits all countries. Transfer pricing disputes with different tax authorities produce winners and losers. Becoming a winner depends very much on the way a company designs and implements an effective transfer pricing system (TPS) of e-commerce before and during a tax audit, with particular emphasis on *before* (Bale 2001).

In the twenty-first century, tax management of transfer pricing of e-commerce, as the number one issue for MNCs, has become the most difficult area of international taxation. We repeat here that MNCs should pay close attention to transfer pricing issues of e-commerce and think wisely about going into an Advance Pricing Agreement (APA) program with IRS and foreign tax authorities.

MNCs should avoid any transfer pricing misstatement for tax reporting with the tax authorities. Otherwise, IRS and/or foreign tax authorities might intervene and impose tax penalties on MNCs for any over- or underreported transfer prices of e-commerce for the sake of tax evasion. Some companies have experienced the pain of not getting their transfer prices right in the eyes of the IRS. Remember the example of the DHL court case. DHL lost a hefty transfer pricing battle with the IRS because of the misstatement of the transfer price of the trade name (Shapland and Major 1999). As a result, DHL got slapped with a 40 percent penalty for this intentional pricing error.

Accountants and CFOs need to prepare an effective TPS supported by documents and need to be ready to meet the IRS or go to the court, if needed, to successfully present, defend, and win the game of transfer pricing against tax authorities. Seven strategic steps that accountants and CFOs should consider in winning the game of transfer pricing audit, or helping their companies to prepare and get ready to go to court for the tax audits, if needed, are discussed in detail next.

Design an Effective Transfer Pricing System of E-Commerce

Today, some financial executives of MNCs might believe that Section 482 of the IRC is designed to ensure technically perfect results when applying the appropriate TPM of e-commerce that satisfies the arm's-length standard. In fact recent cases and regulations focus more on what may be considered correct from the standpoint of economic valuation of e-commerce. Unfortunately, the IRS may intervene if it believes that an MNC took advantage of tax haven countries and did not allocate income between its cross-border transactions correctly.

Success in designing an effective transfer pricing system of e-commerce depends on determining the right goals of the system, seeking an APA with tax authorities, and having sufficient data of profitability of all joint ventures to use in supporting the system with facts and documents. If there is a high probability the IRS will scrutinize your company, it is crucial to ensure that your company's TPS is based on facts and supported by documents on industry practices and market conditions (Lubkin 2000).

As we start to investigate and redesign the TPS of e-commerce, four important key questions may open the door for strategic issues to be considered:

1. Has the company determined its goals of TPS of e-commerce (such as tax minimization with certainty of fair tax treatment, reduction of tariffs on imports and exports, minimization of foreign exchange risks, and time and compliance cost savings)?
2. Does the company need to adopt different tax structures of their TPS of e-commerce in different countries?
3. Have you considered the variations of e-commerce among different tax years of e-commerce involved in the analysis?
4. Is there a lack of data of profitability of every one of the company's e-commerce joint ventures and on all joint ventures as a whole?

Use a Global Transfer Pricing Method of E-Commerce

From an MNC's point of view, transfer prices of e-commerce are used to allocate net income among different subsidiaries in different countries under different legal, social, tax, and economic regulations. From the viewpoint of U.S. tax or foreign tax authorities, transfer pricing policies of e-commerce create problems because they do not reflect open market prices. All tax authorities insist on using the arm's-length standard for cross-border e-commerce transactions. For accountants and CFOs, deciding on what price of e-commerce may have been struck had the parties been unaffiliated—when they are not—engenders in the United States as much controversy, uncertainty, and potential for dispute as in any other country to be used with tax authorities. However, Section 482 allows MNCs to use the CUP, RPM, CPM, or an alternative method of e-commerce. Now, which TPM is the most acceptable and convincing of e-commerce for IRS and foreign tax authorities?

Accountants and CFOs may decide to use one of the three methods prescribed by the IRS in Section 482 that may be the best fitted for their e-commerce. In 1999, in the Compaq case, there was an obvious methodological preference for the CUP (Lubkin 2000). Compaq was able to prove that the transfer prices, after adjustment for minor physical differences, were comparable to those paid by Compaq to unrelated subcontractors in the United States (Ibid.). Accountants and CFOs, especially in the service industry, should consider the CPM. It is now the most widely used method for determining arm's-length transfer price under Section 482. It deals better than the CUP with the allocations related to the value of services or intangible assets. However, when using the CPM, you have to make sure that you use the same markup percentage over costs for your foreign subsidiaries as the one used in unrelated comparable business transactions.

Generally, we should consider the degree of comparability between controlled and uncontrolled e-commerce transactions by analyzing all functions included, the risk associated, economic conditions of the industry, and the nature of the products or services (Misey 1999). You should also test the arm's-length standard under different TPMs of e-commerce to check whether there are significant differences among them, to specify the expected range resulting from applying different TPMs, and then decide which one will be most acceptable and most convincing for tax authorities.

Allocate Income and Management Fees of E-Commerce Equally between Related and Unrelated Parties

Section 482, like other tax regulations of foreign countries, allows tax authorities to adjust income, management services, fees, or royalties of e-commerce, and all other expenses to reflect clearly the correct taxable income of MNCs and their subsidiaries within their territories. Most court cases, regulations, and administrative rulings often focus less on close legal analysis and more on reaching equitable results of allocations among related parties.

Consider the example of the Hyatt Hotel case. The MNC neither tried to coordinate fully its positions nor relied on similar firms to develop a similar concept for the same issues regarding four strategic questions (Lubkin 2000):

1. Had it allocated expenses between the United States and international groups for shared chain services equally?
2. Did Hyatt International Corporation (HIC) owe the U.S. group an annual royalty for the use of tradenames and/or trademarks in foreign countries?
3. Should HIC receive additional royalty income from the lower-tier international subsidiaries for holding the licenses to the Hyatt tradenames and/or trademarks?
4. Was income properly allocated between HIC and the lower-tier international subsidiaries based on HIC's management activities?

Based on the analysis presented here, it is advisable for MNCs to use equitable allocation or charge rates of e-commerce for their foreign subsidiaries as they do for local subsidiaries.

Have Sufficient Global Transfer Pricing Documentation of E-Commerce

An MNC is expected to have sufficient transfer pricing documentation of e-commerce to support and prove compliance with the arm's-length standard. In addition, it has to maintain updated and convincing documents about their e-commerce or industry practice and current market conditions of all countries involved. Having sufficient transfer pricing documentation of e-commerce may help your company to avoid the risk of transfer pricing penalties. Moreover, to be efficient in generating transfer-pricing documentation, the arm's-length price is the firmly established standard under intercompany transfer pricing regulations. To prove a consistent compliance with multiple jurisdictions, a global transfer pricing documentation system may be the best choice for an MNC.

Make a Successful and Well-Communicated Presentation of E-Commerce

The successful and conceptually well-communicated coherent presentation of e-commerce for an audit of TPS before the IRS and foreign tax authorities is the key to winning the game. We must present a strong and clearly understood story to explain the facts that support and prove the MNC's compliance with the arm's-length standard. The presentation of e-commerce for an audit should include:

- a fully coherent transfer pricing analytical report of the MNC's TPM of e-commerce, including risk analysis, based on comparable profits of both related and unrelated entities for e-commerce.
- the variations among different tax years of e-commerce involved.
- a demonstration of the strategic change of methodology to develop and support the analyses. If the TPM of e-commerce was changed, show that a significant change of methodology and approach may be needed to develop and support analyses more likely to prove to be successful in the court, if needed (Lubkin 2000).
- an explanation why the results or outcome of using TPM of e-commerce is reasonable.

Ensure the Confidentiality of E-Commerce

Every MNC would like to ensure that tax authorities would not disclose confidential information of e-commerce acquired in the course of tax examination to outsiders, except when authorized. The IRS maintains confidentiality of APA data, whereas other foreign tax authorities state that information provided in the APA process can and will be used in other cases when appropriate (Borkowski 2000). Therefore, American MNCs will be reluctant to provide foreign tax authorities with confidential financial and production information that might deteriorate the competitive position of the company. In this case, a decision should be made on what information should be revealed to the IRS but not to foreign tax authorities. It is unlikely that foreign tax authorities will give some confidentiality guarantees at all times.

Review the Transfer Pricing System of E-Commerce

How often should a company review its systems to be ready for a transfer pricing audit by tax authorities? What are the pros and cons of the current transfer pricing system? One of the problems that might be encountered by MNCs in their review includes lack of comparable systems and concerns about the acceptability of their pricing systems by foreign tax authorities. Accountants and CFOs should review transfer pricing policies and supporting documentation on a continuous basis and determine whether both home and foreign tax authorities' requirements are being met. Check what assumptions your company used last time for an acceptable and convincing TPM, and whether the same assumptions are still valid. If there are any changes in the assumptions, the consequences for the company's tax liability should be considered and integrated into the TPS.

TRANSFER PRICING STRATEGIES FOR E-COMMERCE TRANSACTIONS OF MNCs

In the twenty-first century, rapid technological innovation is having a profound effect on the way MNCs conduct international business and compete in the global marketplace. Now, it is essential for MNCs to conduct fundamental changes in their business model with respect to the delivery of products and services, transfer pricing systems, communication with suppliers, business partners, and customers, the storage and use of information, and their interaction with governments and regulatory bodies (Durst et al. 1999).

MNCs are responding to these challenges by reconfiguring their business model to implement optimized structures and take advantage of new technologies. However, the new structures and technologies that change the internal business organization often introduce conflicts with the diverse tax and regulatory frameworks applicable in different jurisdictions. At the same time, if tax and transfer pricing are properly managed in conjunction with the business change, opportunities exist to implement significant tax savings while at the same time dramatically simplifying transfer pricing arrangements and compliance (Ibid.).

Borkowski (2002) conducted a survey of a sample of Fortune 500 MNCs about transfer pricing methods used for cross-border tangible and intangible assets for two groups of MNCs: those not having e-commerce transactions (39 MNCs) and those having e-commerce transactions (35 MNCs). The transfer pricing methods used by MNCs can be seen in Table 7.1. Almost one third (33 percent) of MNCs who do not have e-commerce transactions used the CUP (arm's-length) method, and 40 percent of MNCs who have e-commerce transactions used the CUP method. For intangible assets, almost two thirds (65 percent) of MNCs who do not have e- commerce transactions used the CPM, and the majority (70 percent) of MNCs who have e-commerce transactions used the CPM.

In the twenty-first century, the main issue for companies considering the introduction of e-commerce should be the opportunities that it presents for transforming the business. However, when a company changes the way it is run, this provides an ideal opportunity for reviewing and updating the transfer pricing system and the tax structure of the group. It will usually be possible to introduce a structure that will be tax efficient and probably reduce the group's overall tax rate. MNCs must be prepared in advance for any requests for documentation that they may receive from the IRS and foreign tax authorities. This means taking into account transfer pricing planning up front as a major part of their overall business planning.

Executive financial officers (EFOs) of MNCs will need to have a fresh look at transfer pricing issues in the new millennium. In addition to dealing with the growing trend of formal documentation requirements, the new world of e-commerce will create fresh challenges. MNCs that engage in transfer pricing strategy in an integrated way with supply chain re-engineering will be the winners in terms of tax savings and transfer pricing simplicity (Durst et al. 1999).

To help MNCs in rationalizing and simplifying their transfer pricing strategies and creating tax efficiencies in the process, four important issues are discussed next with some recommendations to be considered

TABLE 7.1   Transfer Pricing Method Used for Traditional and E-Commerce Transactions

Transfer Pricing	Tangible Assets		Intangible Assets	
Method	Traditional	E-Commerce	Traditional	E-Commerce
CUP	33%	40%	35%	30%
RPM	21%	25%		
CPM	25%	20%	65%	70%
Others	21%	15%		
Total	100%	100%	100%	100%

Source: Borkowski 2002.

by EFOs when designing and updating their transfer pricing systems. First, a good way to facilitate the use of transfer pricing by MNCs is to do business-to-business e-commerce transactions and make them increasingly difficult for governments to detect.

However, the communications revolution presents no new problems, no fundamentally or categorically different dimensions, for transfer pricing. It just requires new strategy to match the new technology more quickly. The inability to tax Internet-based transactions on the one hand and non-zero tariffs on physical cross-border business on the other may hasten the pace of substitution of the mode of transactions to virtual commerce, as it gets technically feasible to do so. This in turn will further erode the tax base on tradable goods. Moreover, global agreements and standards will be needed before e-commerce can be taxed effectively. The communications revolution, which has led to the rapid growth of the Internet, could also offer some benefits to tax administration (Asher et al. 2001).

Second, the current general agreement among business accounting professionals is that existing transfer pricing tax rules can accommodate e-commerce and therefore the compliance challenges will be resolved and planning opportunities will be pursued in the normal course of business. Although tax authorities also tend to agree that existing transfer pricing tax rules can be applied to e-commerce, they are not yet convinced that they have identified all potential gaps in their system and counted the related potential loss of tax revenue. This uncertainty continues to increase a significant policy debate on the taxation of e-commerce at the international, national and state levels (Boyle et al. 1999; Burns 2002).

Third, given the uncertainty involved in transacting in this virtual economy from a tax perspective, the potential for an advance pricing agreement (APA) to resolve taxpayer uncertainty arising from transfer pricing issues in such a rapidly evolving environment may be the best choice for MNCs. An APA will help MNCs to avoid the risks of litigation, arbitration, and the consequences of economic double taxation (Stanley 2001). However, in the digital world, reaching an agreement on how to harmonize the taxation on cross-border e-commerce activities of MNCs is mission impossible.

Finally, the last operating structure that may be implemented will determine the company's local and global tax profiles. Many optimized business models are likely to increase the number and possibly the complexity of cross-border transfer pricing transactions within affiliated groups at a time when a growing number of governments are defining their transfer pricing regulations, stepping up their enforcement efforts, and imposing burdensome documentation requirements. Consequently, companies that successfully combine changes in their operating environment with tax efficient strategies can realize several potential advantages.

SUMMARY AND CONCLUDING REMARKS

International transfer pricing activities using e-commerce have not been discussed to the same extent as other important strategic business and tax issues. The complexity of the issue might require MNCs to redefine and update their transfer pricing strategies to meet the fast growth of information technology in the new millennium. The traditional framework of transfer pricing strategies and tax regulations may not be appropriate in dealing with global e-commerce activities. However, finding the appropriate transfer pricing method to deal with e-commerce transactions may be difficult with no availability of comparable uncontrolled transactions.

Accountants and CFOs are responsible for designing and implementing effective transfer pricing systems of e-commerce based on facts supported by documents to help their companies reduce or eliminate the risk of transfer pricing tax audits. This chapter provides accountants and CFOs with effective, practical, and the most convenient tools for developing effective transfer pricing systems of e-commerce.

To choose the best transfer pricing method, the rule requires that the arm's-length result of related party transactions be determined under the method that, given the facts and circumstances, provides the most reliable indicator of an arm's-length result. In the case of lack of available transactional comparables and the existence of intangible property may lead to the use of the profit split method (PSM).

One of the most important issues of e-commerce is whether a traditional permanent establishment (PE) concept retains its vitality when business is conducted in cyberspace. To impose tax on e-commerce tangible and intangible transactions, it is important to know whether or not an MNC has created a taxable presence in a country. In deciding which one will be an indicator of the permanent establishment and determining the taxability of the income generated by e-commerce transactions, three important issues were discussed: the Web server (hardware), the Web site (software), and the Internet service provider (ISP). A Web site should be distinguished from the server that hosts the site. A Web-hosting arrangement with an ISP will not create a PE for the Web site owner because an ISP will not be considered an agent of the Web site owner (Merrill 2001). The Web server that is located for a sufficient period of time within a country and is used to carry on part or all of a business may constitute a PE even if no personnel are at that location.

Given a lack of clear understanding and agreement of tax authorities on taxation of electronic transfer pricing activities, it is not surprising that MNCs will continue facilitating the use of transfer pricing for business-to-business e-commerce transactions and make them increasingly difficult for governments to detect. Moreover, executive financial officers of MNCs need to deal with the growing trend of formal documentation requirements; the new world of e-commerce will create fresh challenges. Given the uncertainty involved in transacting in this virtual economy from a tax perspective, the potential for an advance pricing agreement to resolve taxpayer uncertainty arising from electronic transfer pricing issues in such a rapidly evolving environment may be the best choice for MNCs.

In brief, two important steps should be taken: Considering the degree of comparability between controlled and uncontrolled e-commerce transactions, and testing the arm's-length standard of e-commerce under different transfer pricing methods to check whether there are significant differences among them and then decide which one will be the most convincing and acceptable for most tax authorities that are involved. There are two keys for MNCs to win the game. The first is to go for an advanced pricing agreement program with the tax authorities of the countries in which they have income tax liability. The second is to make a successful and conceptually coherent presentation of their transfer pricing method of e-commerce to prove compliance with the arm's-length standard. However, MNCs should be aware of the confidentiality issue. In most countries, all information disclosed to tax authorities under the advance pricing agreement program might be available to the public.

REFERENCES

Abdallah, Wagdy M. 1989. How to motivate and evaluate manager with international transfer pricing systems. *Management International Review,* 29, no. 1: 65–71.

Asher, M. G, and R. S. Rajan. 2001. Globalization and tax systems: Implications for developing countries with particular reference to Southeast Asia. *ASEAN Economic Bulletin* (Singapore) 18: 119–39.

Bale, D. 2001. One size does not fit all. *CA Magazine* (October): 51–52.

Borkowski, Susan C. 2000. Transfer pricing advance pricing agreements: Current status by country. *The International Tax Journal* 26 (spring): 1–16.

Borkowski, Susan C. 2002. Electronic commerce, transnational taxation, and transfer pricing: Issues and practices. *The International Tax Journal* 28, no. 2 (spring): 1–36.

Boyle, M. P., J. M. Peterson, Jr., W. J. Sample, T. L. Schottenstein, and G. D. Sprague. 1999. The emerging international tax environment for electronic commerce. *Tax Management International Journal* (June 11): 357–82.

Burns, P. 2000. United States. *International Tax Review,* Supplement, Transfer Pricing, no. 1: 131–37.

Durst, Michael C. 1999. United States. *International Tax Review* (February): 56–62.

Durst, M., G. Stone, C. Rolfe, and M. Happell. 1999. The new world of transfer pricing. *International Tax Review* (December): 4–6.

Eccles, R. G. 1985. *The Transfer Pricing Problem*. Lexington, Mass.: Lexington Books.

Eicker, K. 1999. Germany. *International Tax Review,* Supplement, E-commerce taxation: A guide (September): 54–56.

Finance and economics: A taxing battle: Corporate tax. 2004. *The Economist,* London, 370, no. 8360: 68–71.

Greenstein, M., and M. Vasarhelyi. 2002. *Electronic commerce–security, risk management, and control*. New York: McGraw-Hill/Irwin, 2nd Edition.

Hamilton, D. 2000. A heavy price to pay. *CA Magazine* 133 (May): 14–15.

Hardesty, D. E. 1999. *Electronic commerce–taxation and planning*. Boston: Warren, Gorham & Larmont of the RIA Group.

Hines, James R., Jr. 1999. Lessons from behavioral responses to international taxation. *National Tax Journal* (June): 305–22.

Klinger, F., and C. Kuhlmann. 2000. Germany. *International Financial Law Review,* Supplement, Banking Yearbook 2000, pp. 36–39.

Lubkin, G. P. 2000. Section 482: Major developments in 1999. *Tax Management Memorandum* 41 (March 27): 103–12.

Maguire, N. 1999. Taxation of e-commerce: An overview. *International Tax Review* (September): 3–12.

Merrill, P. R. 2001. International tax of e-commerce. *The CPA Journal* 3, no. 11 (November): 30–45.

Misey, R. J., Jr. 1999. A primer of transfer pricing. *Taxes* 77 (August): 43–46.

Organization for Economic Cooperation and Development Committee (OECD). 1995. *Transfer pricing guidelines for multinational enterprises and tax administrations*. Paris: OECD.

———. 1997. *Electronic commerce: The challenges to tax authorities and taxpayers* (An informal roundtable discussion between business and government), November 18, Turku, Finland. http://www.oecd.org/dataoecd/46/0/1923232.pdf

———. 1998. *A borderless world: realizing the potential of electronic commerce* (A Report by the Committee on Fiscal Affairs). Paris: OECD.

Rolph, B. and J. Niederhoffer. 1999. Transfer pricing and e-commerce. *International Tax Review* (September): 34–39.

Shah, Niles, L. Olsen, T. Rudd, M. Collardin, and B. Smith. 2000. Taxing the Internet goldrush. *International Tax Review* 11 (March): 13–19.

Shapland, Rick, and Bill Major. 1999. 40% transfer pricing penalty upheld. *The Tax Advisor* (April): 224–25.

Stanley, G. 2001. Transfer pricing takes center stage. *International Tax Review* 12, no. 9 (October): 25–31.

Tang, Roger Y. W. 1997. Intrafirm trade and global transfer pricing regulations (Westport, Conn.: Quorum Books).

8

Intangible Assets and International Taxation

In the twenty-first century, multinational companies (MNCs) have changed their ways of conducting global business from the traditional way on a country-by-country basis to the adoption of new global business models, such as e-commerce and shared services or intangible assets. Globalization of MNCs is always accompanied by more and more cross-border business transactions of goods, services, and technology. For MNCs, transfer pricing systems, of both tangible and intangible assets, should be designed to meet the new challenges more effectively than before.

An international transfer pricing is a source of conflict of objectives within MNCs. CEOs and corporate controllers do not agree on the use of transfer pricing techniques for cost allocation of resource decisions, economic business decisions, performance incentives, performance evaluation of foreign and domestic subsidiaries, and overall tax strategies. However, for all MNCs, one common objective of strategic tax planning for intellectual property is to reduce their worldwide long-term tax liabilities. This can only be achieved if three conditions are met (Walsh 2001):

1. The net earnings or profits generated by the intellectual property must be sheltered from income tax in the country or tax jurisdiction in which these profits arise.
2. The low-tax profits must be sheltered from current taxation in the home country or tax jurisdiction where the headquarters of an MNC is established.

3. To the extent that it is necessary to repatriate low-tax profits to the home country in a subsequent period, it must be possible to manage the tax burden that arises on repatriated earnings or profits.

This chapter investigates and discusses the issues most related to international transfer pricing of intangible assets and e-commerce including: general understanding of the characteristics and the nature of intangible assets of multinational companies and the related transfer pricing issues, the new trends in transfer pricing of intangible assets, multinationals' strategies of intangible assets ownership, transfer pricing methods for intangible assets, and designing the right transfer pricing system of intangible assets.

GENERAL UNDERSTANDING OF INTANGIBLE ASSETS

Intangible assets vary widely and include intellectual property such as brands, customer lists, technical designs, databases, and content-related intellectual property, such as patents or software, patented and unpatented technology in addition to the more traditional product and process formulations (Walsh 2001). All intellectual property is characterized as, to some extent, unique and legally protected, such as patents, trademarks, royalties, and copyrights. A trademark is any word, symbol, name, device, or combination thereof used to distinguish the goods or services of one manufacturer from those of another. For many retail businesses, brands are the most valuable assets. It is often said that brands become a testament to the reputation and goodwill of the customer base (Emmer and Henshall 2002). All intangible assets must be protected by nondisclosure, such as know-how and market research. Intangible assets, especially intellectual property, play a central role in new economy companies, and high-value intellectual property may negatively affect the market value of several MNCs (Walsh 2001).

Understanding the nature and the characteristics of intangible assets of MNCs and the related issues of transfer pricing systems is considered an essential step in designing the right and most appropriate pricing systems for MNCs. Intangible assets need different analysis than what is required for tangible assets, because they are the key to commercial success, especially in the hi-tech industry. Moreover, it may be difficult to use the traditional comparative analyses that are used with tangible assets, and under no circumstances that an MNC would be willing to risk allowing unrelated parties to exploit their intellectual property (Adams and Godshaw 2002). Therefore, it would be a big mistake for CEOs and financial executives of MNCs to believe that one system fits all.

Today, technology-based businesses form what has been called the new economy. The new economy has created an increase in new technology-based intellectual property, such as databases, information, organizational structures, know-how, and problem-solving techniques. The real measure of a company's value is now seen to rest in its people and technology/software ideas rather than in its hardware equipments and real estate. Tax planners who recognize and adapt to this can make valuable tax savings for their companies (Collardin and Vogele 2002).

NEW TRENDS AFFECTING TRANSFER PRICING OF INTANGIBLE ASSETS

MNCs and tax authorities have been facing great challenges in dealing with transfer pricing of intangible assets. The challenges include the globalization of MNCs and rapid expansion in the cross-border business transactions of services and technology, the shift from a predominantly manufacturing economy to a service economy spurred by innovative technology, and the increasing importance of intangibles in the production of income.

Tax authorities around the world have been addressing transfer pricing problems with increasing scrutiny and sophistication.

1. Section 482 of the IRC was revised in 1994.
2. Complementary measures such as the penalties in Code Section 6662 were set forth in 1994.
3. Similar initiatives by foreign tax authorities and the Organization for Economic Cooperation and Development (OECD) since 1995 have considerably increased the burden and complexity of transfer pricing problems, requiring MNCs to design their transfer pricing systems carefully.

On the other side, MNCs have been puzzled over how to resolve long troublesome income tax transfer pricing issues of intangible assets.

Several important trends have increased the importance of transfer pricing of intangible assets for MNCs. First, the growing globalization of markets and a consolidation of market structure, such as the restructuring of the telecommunications, electronics, pharmaceutical, aerospace, and other industries in Europe, are the outcome of the elimination of trade barriers through a unified European Union marketplace (Miesel, Higinbotham, and Yi 2002).

Second, in 1986, Section 482 of the IRC of the United States was amended to promulgate the "super royalty" provisions through the statutory commensurate-with-income standard. That was a response to the assumption that MNCs are not paying their fair share of tax to the U.S. tax authority and to the tax court decisions where MNCs were alleged to be directing income to related groups in tax haven countries (Levey 2001). Then, U.S. and foreign tax regulations started to define this standard in terms of an arm's-length result, the OECD members used the same rules in their respective tax regulations, documentation rules became the global tradition, and transfer pricing tax audits of MNCs dominated tax disputes among most foreign tax authorities (Ibid.). Finally, the DHL court case has become a landmark case and a good alert for MNCs' transfer pricing adjustments of intangible assets.

Third, an increasing concern is the ever-growing alertness and sophistication of national tax authorities concerned with protecting their country's share of the taxable income earned by multinationals (Ibid.). At the beginning, the tax regulations focused on an analysis of the transfer pricing methods of intangible assets that were deemed most appropriate under certain circumstances for the MNCs of the 1990s. (Levey 2001) Then, new transfer pricing methods, such as the basic arm's-length rate of return technique, were initially considered, with the comparable profits method/transactional net margin method (TNMM) a consequence of this thinking (Ibid.).

Recently, every MNC has become aware of its responsibility and obligation to establish and document a sound and practical transfer pricing system. These documents have become the focal point in all transfer pricing tax audits, and the MNC's success in audit and its ability to maintain reasonable reserves for financial reporting purposes are directly proportional to the quality of the analyses. These benchmarks are also the key to success in any strategic tax planning program pursued by an MNC. Further, more tax authorities around the world are opening their doors to considering advance pricing agreements (Levey 2001).

Finally, in the twenty-first century, the significant and fast development of the e-commerce era and service companies' paradigms in proportion to the old bricks-and-mortar business activities pushes the tax authorities to continue their attack on the transfer pricing practices of MNCs. Many countries continue to issue new transfer pricing regulations and adjust old ones to meet these e-commerce challenges (Levey 2001). E-commerce technology has encouraged MNCs to integrate their businesses with their suppliers and customers, regardless of the geographic locations concerned with the activity. E-commerce also facilitates the increasing globalization of business operations so that companies that have until now been confined to their national markets are now in a position to trade across borders. In the past, it used to take years or even decades to build up either name brand or market value on the basis of organic growth. Now, businesses with e-commerce activities have seen large increases in brand and other intellectual property values over a much shorter timescale (Walsh 2001).

MULTINATIONALS' STRATEGIES OF INTANGIBLE ASSETS OWNERSHIP

Strategic tax planning of MNCs for intangible assets may have a significant effect on the worldwide tax rate, without requiring major movement of the operating activities. The OECD transfer pricing model attributes profits not to the actual physical location where the research activities are undertaken, but rather to the business entity that is responsible for the economic risk of the relevant activities (Walsh 2001). Therefore, in selecting the country or the region in which the intellectual property, such as trademarks, name brands, and patents, is to be situated or owned, the capital gains tax rules, transaction taxes, and the facility for tax free asset will be vital (Ibid.).

However, in the case of brand intangibles, the unique nature of what constitutes a brand requires MNCs to consider a number of issues that do not commonly exist with other types of intangible assets. A brand comprises tangible and intangible benefits perceived by customers in the product/service offering. At the beginning, MNCs' tax planning for brands requires identification of each of the elements that contribute to brand recognition because these constitute property capable of being transferred (Emmer and Henshall 2002). Dividing intangible assets into elements permits the newly developed elements to be cost-shared by a tax-advantaged subsidiary so that economic ownership can be transferred to that entity, leaving economic ownership of the preexisting intangibles in the hands of the entity that invented them. If the preexisting elements' value declines over time while the value of the new elements rises comparatively, an increasing share of overall profits from brand intangibles can be transferred to the tax haven country (Ibid.).

The business transaction whereby a U.S. subsidiary of a foreign company (FC) obtains the right to use the FC intellectual property would, of course, be recognized for U.S. income tax purposes because the subsidiary would be a separate taxpayer. The outcome of the transaction would depend on how the U.S. subsidiary's use of the intangible asset is characterized. In the strategic planning stage, an MNC may choose one of three approaches for an intangible asset ownership: a centralized intangible asset ownership, a distributed intangible asset ownership, or geographic or regional distributed ownership. These three approaches involve increasing levels of operational change by the multinational group and the relocation of increasing levels of commercial risks and activities to the low-tax country or location (Walsh 2001).

Each one of the three approaches is discussed in detail in the following sections; however, the most important question for an MNC is: Which approach may be the most preferable? Three important variables should be the drivers for an MNC decision:

1. What are the historical circumstances or conditions of how the group or related parties subsidiaries were created or the way that the intangible asset was developed?
2. What is the management philosophy of the group (centralized or decentralized with more delegation of authority to foreign subsidiary managers)?
3. Most important, what is the tax strategy, including the effect on transfer pricing method used, of the MNC's perspective?

Centralized Ownership of Intangible Assets

Under centralized ownership, each intangible asset is legally and beneficially owned by an MNC, and its own foreign subsidiaries may use the intangible asset for their own business activities through a license agreement with the MNC and pay an appropriate royalty fee. This approach is called a licensing model, and the key transfer pricing problem is how to determine an arm's-length royalty fee for the right to use a specific intangible asset. An MNC does not have to use the same strategy for all of its owned intangible assets; it may use a different strategy for a different intangible asset.

One advantage of this approach is that MNCs may achieve cost efficiency by centralizing support functions to serve several locations in several countries. These centralized functions can relate to internal business functions, such as human resources administration or centralized accounting service, or to external, customer-facing functions such as call centers for technical queries. Examples of centralized manufacturing functions include software development in a low-cost or tax haven country and the research campus facilities that are common in the technology area (Walsh 2001).

Moreover, centralization of ownership may achieve a reduction in the cost base and a tax advantage through careful strategic tax planning to reduce the overall tax liability of the MNC by taking advantage of tax rate differences between the licensor and the licensee subsidiaries (Adam and Godshaw 2002). However, the tax cost of a transfer of intangible asset (especially if it is an intellectual property of a new sophisticated technology for multipurpose civilian and military uses) outside the borders of the home country territory may generally be substantial and often prohibited by some federal policies or regulations.

In the case of the trademark, if the subsidiary's use of the asset is by the same token a sale of branded goods, then the appropriate transfer price for the goods would have to take into account the fact that the goods themselves might be worth more than physically and functionally similar goods that are unbranded (Warner 2002). How much of a difference the surrounded trademark would have on the transfer price would depend, on the one hand, on how valuable the asset was in the U.S. market and, on the other hand, how much promotional and marketing support the subsidiary had to provide to support the MNC's brand (Ibid.). Moreover, the IRS may insist on the position that, if the U.S. subsidiary spends significantly larger than normal advertising and marketing expenditures in relation to those made by otherwise similar independent distributors, the U.S. subsidiary should be allocated compensation for assisting the parent company in developing the trademark (Ibid.).

Distributed Ownership of Intangible Assets

Under distributed intangible asset ownership, related parties of the MNC enter into a qualified cost-sharing agreement (CSA). In a typical arrangement, the members enter into a CSA under which each member agrees to pay a portion of the intangible development costs based on their respective anticipated benefits of the development of the new technology. It provides an alternative to licensing or selling intangible assets to related parties, because the participants of the agreement own the outcome of technology jointly. As part of such an agreement, some participants are often required to buy into certain preexisting intangible assets contributed to the CSA by other participants (Doonan and Tien 2002).

In the CSA, if the intangible asset transferred by a U.S. corporation, a sale or contribution of the intangible requires consideration of the commensurate-with-income standard, which generally holds that the intangible's transferor must recognize income over time that is commensurate with the income to be generated by the intangible. However, CSAs represent the escape hatch from this standard. Buy-in payments should reflect an arm's-length charge for the use of the preexisting intangible asset and should be based on the fair market value of the used intangible asset. Deciding on the arm's-length price or fair market value of the preexisting intangible asset is very difficult, because most highly developed intangibles tend to be unique and the issue becomes a source of controversy between the taxpayers and the IRS (Doonan and Tien).

If the CSA is property implemented, the IRS's ability to allocate income is limited to adjusting the relative development costs each participant should bear. Each participant is treated as the economic owner of the intangible asset and is entitled to receive income derived from the intangible in its local market (Emmer and Henshall 2003). To achieve the benefits offered by CSA, several issues should be considered before the commencement of the CSA, including the timing and valuation of future benefits and costs of using the intangible assets and the ownership of the resulting technology. Moreover, this necessitates an in-depth analysis of the benefits of the intangible property from past experience, know-how, and other prior knowledge on which the current research and development activities are founded (Miesel, Higinbotham, and Yi 2002).

Additionally, although moving an intangible outside the border of the United States in a tax-efficient manner is important, the real impact on the MNC's structural rate depends on how the intangible is deployed once it is outside the United States. Little savings will have been achieved if the income attributable to the intangible asset is subject to an effective rate similar to that of the United States. In general, intangibles assets can be deployed in either of two approaches: an operating company, such as a retail subsidiary, can exploit the brand intangible itself; or a holding company can license the intangible to operating companies within the group (Emmer and Henshall 2002). The latter strategy often provides greater tax savings for MNCs because the holding company can be located in a tax-haven country. However, withholding taxes on royalties paid by the operating companies can significantly lessen the effectiveness of this strategy. Most tax-haven countries may not have any tax treaties with the United States. Thus, royalties for the use of intangible assets will be subject to huge withholding tax rates imposed under local tax rule. American MNCs also must fight with subpart F rules in transferring intangible assets. The foreign personal holding company rules subject royalty income to U.S. income tax whenever an intangible is licensed from one controlled foreign corporation to another located in another country. This result can be limited by having the licensee make an entity classification election to be treated as a branch of the licensor for U.S. tax purposes (Ibid.).

If the subsidiary's use of the intangible asset were attributable to either a license or a transfer of U.S. rights, the subsidiary would have the right to pay a royalty to a foreign company that was commensurate-with-the income that was generated through use of the intangible asset. Under the commensurate-with-income rule—which governs the amount that U.S. taxpayers may deduct as consideration paid to related foreign parties as well as to income earned by U.S. taxpayers from transfers of intangible rights to related foreign parties—the U.S. subsidiary would be able to deduct an estimated royalty each year equal to the income generated that year attributable to the transfer. Because the intangible transferred would be the U.S. rights to the foreign party's intangible asset, the income attributable to the asset itself—as opposed to the income attributable to the U.S. subsidiary's ongoing marketing and promotional efforts—may not be great (Warner 2002).

If income generated by an asset is generally taxable to the asset's owner, it follows that a significant factor in reducing a global tax liability of an MNC is placement of the ownership of valuable assets in entities located in a tax-haven country. Several issues must be addressed in attempting this strategy, including to which jurisdiction ownership of the asset should be transferred, how ownership should be transferred, and how the asset will earn tax-advantaged income (Emmer and Henshall 2002).

However, this approach does not entail a joint legal ownership of the intangible asset. It may be more helpful and beneficial to register the intangible asset in the name of a single foreign subsidiary; however, it is important to maintain a central unit to police trademark or patent registrations of the intellectual property (Adams and Godshaw 2002). This approach does not of itself result in any tax savings, but facilitates the development by the low-tax location of enhanced versions of the intangible asset right that will rise in value while original property gradually declines toward the end of its economic life (Walsh 2002).

Geographic or Regional Ownership of Intangible Assets

Under this approach, a group of foreign subsidiaries of an MNC may organize itself by geographic regions (or by product applicability) and choose to have one operating subsidiary in each region own the intangible asset for that region. The regional subsidiaries themselves may achieve this by entering into a cost-sharing agreement (CSA). Each subsidiary would then in turn need to license the intangible asset to the separate country operating subsidiaries within their region (Adams and Godshaw 2002).

For example, when an American subsidiary carries on U.S. distribution activities of a foreign company, then any cross-border transaction whereby foreign companies provided services to the American subsidiary or even where foreign companies performed services that benefited both themselves and the American subsidiary will be taken into account in determining the American subsidiary's taxable income. According to Section 482 of the IRC, in applying the arm's-length transfer pricing standard, the American subsidiary is allowed to deduct at least the direct and indirect costs incurred by foreign companies in providing services, to the extent the services benefited the American subsidiary in more than an incidental way. Moreover, any post-sale support services provided to customers by foreign companies could be considered in determining the arm's-length price charged to the American subsidiary (Warner 2002).

How to Decide

For an MNC to decide which one of these three approaches should be used to achieve its strategic objectives, several factors need to be considered:

- The commercial characteristics of the location and its suitability as a location for intellectual property
- The internal fiscal regime of the location including the tax basis and tax rate
- The tax treatment that will apply to transactions with the low-tax country
- Any anticipated changes in local legislation, treaty negotiations in progress, and the impact of supranational proposals for tax harmonization, including OECD and EU tax competition proposals
- The tax treatment of the income in the low-tax location by the fiscal authority of the home country (Walsh 2001)

Selecting the ideal approach and location will depend on the analysis and comparison of the available candidate locations by reference to the needs of MNCs and the careful analysis of the previous factors and their impact on transfer pricing method used by the MNC.

TRANSFER PRICING METHODS FOR INTANGIBLE ASSETS

Most, if not all, countries use arm's length as the international transfer pricing standard for both tangible and intangible assets. Both the U.S. tax regulations on transfer pricing and the OECD Transfer Pricing Guidelines have expanded the consensus that the income tax consequences of related-party transactions should be determined based on the application of the arm's-length standard. The arm's-length standard is defined as the price that would have been charged in independent transactions with unrelated parties under the same or similar circumstances. From these situations, tax authorities have developed several specified methods for determining an arm's-length price.

The standard for applying arm's-length transfer pricing principles is the situation where U.S. operations are carried on through an American subsidiary of a foreign corporation. The IRS-U.S. regulations tax American subsidiaries of foreign corporations on their worldwide income. In determining the taxable income of an American subsidiary with respect to cross-border transactions with its foreign parent company, the IRS applies an arm's-length standard of Section 482 of the IRC. According to the arm's-length standard, intercompany transfer prices are tested by reference to prices charged in comparable uncontrolled business transactions between unrelated parties under similar circumstances.

All cross-border business transactions between an American subsidiary and its foreign parent should be evaluated for transfer pricing purposes based on the contractual terms made by the two related parties on condition that such terms are consistent with the two parties' behavior and the economic substance of the related business transaction. The key player of whether uncontrolled transactions are really comparable to the related-party transaction being tested is the extent to which the functions performed, assets used, and risks borne by the related parties are sufficiently similar so that the profits realized in the uncontrolled transactions are a reliable indicator of the transfer prices that would be realized if the related parties were dealing at true arm's length (Warner 2002).

Traditional techniques of valuating intangible assets for tax purposes, such as comparable uncontrolled price or resale price methods, might apply in situations where comparable transactions are available or stable knowledge-induced cash flows can be identified. Normally, however, tax planners will not have access to such data, and traditional valuation methods fall short (Collardin and Vogele 2002). Even if the stand-alone value of a subsidiary's intangible property can be ascertained, such value is likely to be minimal compared to the value of the global intangible because knowledge or technology is usually arranged in networks. Consequently, tax planners need to consider different valuation methods to work out the value of technology knowledge (Ibid.).

In practice, there are many difficulties and complications in applying the arm's-length standard, especially when an MNC conducts business transactions that independent companies would not undertake, such as highly specialized intangible assets and/or e-commerce cross-border business transactions that allow an MNC business to be highly integrated.

In the United States, Section 482 of Internal Revenue Code prescribes three specific transactions-based methods for determining arm's-length prices, to be used, and a fourth method that may be used for all other situations in which none of the first three are considered appropriate and reasonable. The three methods set forth in the regulations, to be used in order, are comparable uncontrolled price method, resale price method, and cost-plus method. However, the revised Section 482 of IRC has added two specified profit-based methods—the comparable profits method and the profit split method—to the existing transactions-based methods. Further, the hierarchy of methods has been eliminated, and the "best method rule" concept was adopted to optimize method selection according to the facts and circumstances of each case. Moreover, periodic adjustments of intangible prices are also required under the commensurate-with-income principle mandated by the U.S. Congress.

In all likelihood, the current arm's-length international transfer pricing methods used by tax authorities for intangible assets, including services provided by a foreign company to an American subsidiary or an American MNC to its foreign subsidiary, would be evaluated under one of six transfer pricing methods: the comparable uncontrolled price (CUP) method, the resale price method (RPM), cost-plus method (CPM), comparable profit method (CPrM), transactional net margin method (TNMM), or profit split method (PSM). The first three are viewed as traditional transaction-oriented methods, and the last three are profit-based methods. These methods are generally accepted by most tax authorities, satisfy the documentation requirements set forth by tax authorities, and represent the rules under which most transfer pricing controversies are to be resolved. For MNCs, it is important to examine these methods to understand the extent to which they respond fully to global business needs and form the foundation to defend MNCs' transfer pricing systems if they will be subject to transfer pricing tax audits in the near future.

Comparable Uncontrolled Price Method

Under the comparable uncontrolled price (CUP) method, the actual price of an intangible property charged by an MNC would be compared to prices charged for similar services performed or sold in comparable uncontrolled transactions including any sales by MNCs of the same goods or services to uncontrolled distributors in similar markets. In practice, unless the MNC sold the same product or performed the same service to uncontrolled customers in the United States or in a comparable market, it is not likely to use the CUP method. Even if an MNC sold its intangible property to an unrelated party in the United States or in a comparable market, fees or prices charged in those cross-border business transactions would not be reliable indicators of an arm's-length standard for sales to its American subsidiary unless such third-party transactions were similar to sales to the American subsidiary in terms of functions performed including research and development and product design; allocation of risks including market risk, R&D risk, and financial and currency risk; and contractual terms or reliable modifications that could be made to reconcile for the differences (Warner 2002).

In many countries, tax authorities employ a large number of examiners, or auditors, to address proper transfer prices of intangible assets under their own transfer pricing legislation and/or the Organization for Economic Cooperation and Development Transfer Pricing Guidelines. These local examiners tend to adopt nationalistic attitudes toward foreign-owned corporations. Each tax authority attempts to apply its own interpretation of the arm's-length standard of intangible assets in order to ensure that MNCs report at least the same amount of income as independent and uncontrolled comparable companies operating in their respective countries. In making assessments and the corresponding income adjustments, often they do not consider the MNC's overall global profitability, economic factors, ownership of intangible assets, or other factors that may differentiate the situation of the taxpayer from the comparable local companies or comparable local transactions of intangible assets (Raby et al. 2002).

When MNCs or other foreign subsidiaries exchange or trade services or intangible assets in uncontrolled transactions that are similar to the transactions of a given MNC, the arm's-length price is the market price prevailed in the business transactions. Intangible asset prices determined by the CUP method may require adjustment for minor or major differences in intellectual property or circumstances of sale, but they are essentially alternative prices at which the intangible asset in the sale to a related party could have been bought on the open market (Miesel, Higinbotham, and Yi 2003).

However, for intangible assets, it is seldom that open markets are found to trade MNCs' intermediate services or intangible assets, or when such markets are found, the services or assets are differentiated by significant variations in design, functionality, performance, or other factors such as brand names or trademarks. These intermediate services or intangible products should not be subject to pricing under the CUP method, and indeed the markets (if any) in which they are transacted are not realistic choices for buying and selling affiliates of a given MNC that is trading the service internally. In these cases, other prescribed arm's-length methods are based on comparisons of markups, with markups of independents performing similar functions, such as the RPM or CPM (Ibid.).

Resale Price Method

If an arm's-length price cannot be determined through the use of a CUP method, the tax regulations specify that the resale price method

(RPM) must be used. The arm's-length price of an intangible asset is computed by looking at the gross margin earned by the American subsidiary from resales from goods purchased from or services performed by a foreign company as compared to the gross margins earned by uncontrolled distributors from transactions in which they carried on similar functions. The RPM, as an alternative method, focuses on one side of the transaction, either the manufacturer or the distributor, and to estimate the transfer price using a functional approach. Unfortunately, gross profit information for comparable uncontrolled distributors may be neither available nor reliable as a benchmark for an arm's-length standard (Warner 2002).

Under the RPM, it is assumed that competition among independent wholesalers or distributors in the external market leads to similar margins being earned on sales by wholesalers or distributors that are offering similar services or performing similar functions. The RPM establishes the price a buyer should pay to allow it to earn a gross margin similar to that earned by companies performing similar functions. All excess profit on the transaction is assigned to the seller. As with the CUP method, minor or major adjustments are made to account for differences in the economic circumstances of the transaction and in the conditions of sale. Adjustments are also made for differences in the mix of functions performed by the independent resellers vis-à-vis the affiliated distributor (Miesel et al. 2003).

Different guidelines as to the appropriateness of any markup on the cost of intellectual property may be used. However, the appropriate markup percentage can be determined from uncontrolled sales made by other resellers under similar economic conditions and similar circumstances. Two methods are suggested to compute the markup percentage: the gross profit percentage and the net profit percentage. U.S. tax regulations prescribe the gross profit percentage method to be used in allocating the income of subsidiaries.

In applying the RPM effectively, comparability of functions and design of intellectual property is essential. Comparability is required under this method when there are similarities of the functions performed, risks assumed, and level of intangible assets to those of the related party whose transfer prices are being determined; and when the intangible assets are generally similar to the related party's assets. Comparability adjustments are made for some or all of the differences in the mix and intensity of functions performed, for economic conditions of the transaction, and for the conditions of the sale. These factors may include volume, payment or credit terms, contractual contemplations, customs duties, taxes, warranty conditions, testing costs, advertising power, and other related trade provisions (Miesel et al. 2003).

Cost-Plus Method

The transfer price is computed by multiplying the cost of producing or designing the intellectual property by an appropriate gross profit percentage to cover the functions it carries out. The appropriate gross profit percentage can be determined from comparable uncontrolled sales of the seller, another party of the uncontrolled sale, or unrelated parties. The implicit assumption underlying the CPM is that the competition in a large number of manufacturing firms will lead to similar prices and profit margins.

The CPM also requires comparables when the functions performed, risks assumed, and level of intangibles are the same as or similar to those of the related party. Adjustments are made for differences in sales and purchase terms, freight terms, inventory turnover, and other factors. Similarly, the production costs of the controlled (or related-party) manufacturer or the uncontrolled comparables may also have to be restated to reflect cost levels that are consistent with different life cycles of the intangible assets. Markups on comparable products, for example, may be fairly different depending on the channeled service dealers, drop-shippers, or manufacturers' sales branches (Miesel et al. 2003).

In order to use the CPM for intangible assets, both the tax authority and the MNC must know the accounting approach adopted by unrelated parties. For example, what costs are included in the cost base before the markup over costs is computed? Is it actual cost or standard cost? Are only manufacturing costs or is the cost base the sum of manufacturing costs plus some portion of operating expenses? The larger the cost base, the smaller should be the profit markup, or gross margin, over costs. As a one-sided method, the CPM focuses only on the profit markup of the seller and insists that the seller should earn only what arm's-length sellers engaging in similar transactions would earn in a competitive market. Therefore the CPM method tends to underestimate the transfer price because it gives all unallocated profits from the transaction to the buyer.

In concluding the three transactional transfer pricing methods, it is important to note that as the global business market expands with the use of Internet and e-commerce cross-border transactions, traditional transactional transfer pricing approaches have become irrelevant to the allocation of global income of MNCs. Comparable transactional pricing methods have been proved to be difficult to apply in globally integrated businesses, especially for those involving intangible assets, and formulary apportionment has been suggested as another option (Li 2002).

Comparable Profits Method

According to Section 482 of the IRC of the U.S. Tax Regulations, the comparable profit method (CPrM) is defined as a profit-based transfer pricing method that compares the operating profits of a controlled entity with the operating profits of a set of uncontrolled entities performing similar functions and incurring similar risks. To be consistent with the arm's-length standard, the operating profits of these uncontrolled companies define an arm's-length range of results, and the comparable profit method requires that this range be comprised of companies that demonstrate a similar level of comparability. Therefore, in applying the comparable profit method, the analyst should provide evidence that those companies comprising the arm's-length range have a similar level of comparability in terms of their respective functions performed, risks assumed, and ownership of intangible assets (Johnson 2001).

Under the comparable profits method, the American subsidiary's operating profits from its distribution activities would be compared with the operating profit of similarly uncontrolled distributors in terms of the rate of return on assets or capital employed, sales, operating expenses, or other benchmarks. The key factor in determining whether an uncontrolled distributor's business activities are comparable to those of a controlled party for purposes of applying the comparable profits method are functional and resource or asset similarity.

Theoretically, the resale price and cost-plus methods, when correctly applied, might be expected to produce economically valid results in terms of an arm's-length price determination. However, in practice, the vertically integrated MNCs may achieve profits that significantly exceed the joint profits of nonintegrated companies performing similar functions. In other cases, the existence of significant product, manufacturing, or marketing intangibles at the value-added stages may exclude comparisons with independent companies. In such cases, the taxpayer may rely on the CPM or the profit split method (Miesel et al. 2003). Moreover, because the transfer pricing is determined based on the analyst's comparable set, a great deal of argument in transfer pricing practice concerns factors of comparability, such as whether the functions performed, risks assumed, and ownership of intangible assets are really similar in the controlled and uncontrolled entities or transactions being compared (Johnson 2001).

Generally, the CPrM is used to compare the tested subsidiary's return on invested capital (ROI) or some other operating profit indicator (OPI) such as return on sales, with the ROI of companies using similar resources. The CPrM may be used to value routine manufacturing, distribution, or other functions of the tested subsidiary, and it is applied to price the transfer of intangible assets by reference to the operating profit properly attributable to the routine functions performed by the tested subsidiary (Miesel et al. 2003).

The CPrM may include different variations based on different rate-of-return indicators or OPIs. The primary variation is ROI. It follows from an economic principle that in competitive product and capital markets, companies with similar risk characteristics should earn the same ROI. Thus, the CPrM based on ROI applies the comparables' ROI (i.e., operating income divided by invested capital) to the affiliated entity's invested capital to obtain a measure of arm's-length operating profits.

Moreover, the U.S. tax regulations allow for the use of other OPIs if they provide a closer approximation of arm's-length standards. For example, return on sales (ROS) and return on assets (ROA) may be used. The use of these financial ratios or any others, however, typically requires closer functional comparability than the CPrM based on ROI, because they do not rely directly on the competitive product and capital markets (Ibid.).

When compared with the first three methods, the CPrM is different in three aspects. First, it relies more on comparability in factor and capital markets than on firm equivalency in functional or product matter. Second, it does not require the same degree of functional or product similarity that is required to apply the first three methods. Reasonable similarities in functions and product markets are acceptable, however, because factor market comparables should have similar levels of employed assets and intangible capital and similar risk characteristics relative to the related-party subsidiary being priced. Third, the CUP method generally provides more reliable estimates of arm's-length standard than the CPrM when data on next-to-product-market comparables are available; the resale price and cost-plus methods will generally provide more reliable estimates of arm's-length prices than the CPrM when close functional market comparables exist and adequate accounting information are available for the comparable assets (Ibid.).

Transactional Net Margin Method

The OECD Transfer Pricing guidelines adopted the transactional net margin method (TNMM) to be used in valuating tangible and intangible assets. There are some similarities and differences between the TNMM and the traditional transactional methods. First, the TNMM is similar to traditional transactional methods in that data on similar arm's-length companies is used at a micro level. Second, there is a key difference in that TNMM provides the appropriate markup on total costs (such as cost of goods sold, selling and general administrative costs) as opposed to the appropriate markup on cost of sales. Third, TNMM is less direct and accurate relative to traditional transactional methods because operating costs include fixed overheads that may be assigned on an arbitrary basis. Fourth, TNMM is often used on a companywide macro level rather than the micro level stipulated by both the CCRA and the OECD (Swaneveld, Nagaraian, and Przysuski 2002).

Moreover, the TNMM analysis is more popular due to the fact it is easily identifiable in terms of its simplicity, efficiency, and cost. The TNMM requires much less information and is more tolerant of transactional and functional differences than any of the more direct transactional methods. Furthermore, because the TNMM uses the net margin as its operating profit indicator, a positive result suggests that all the transactions undertaken by the tested subsidiary produce an aggregate result that is in accordance with the arm's-length standard.

The TNMM has become the transfer pricing method of choice because it requires less detailed information, does the work of what would otherwise take several analyses, and therefore produces a finished transfer pricing report in a fraction of the time it would take to analyze each related-party transaction independently. Although the aforementioned tendency is a distinct possibility, this reform still does not address the best method rule, thus leaving the possibility for a legal loophole. In this respect, it is important to point out a few facts (Narvaez-Hasfura and Torrey 2002).

However, the TNMM and the CPrM are very close to each other. Under the TNMM, U.S. or foreign tax authorities compare the net profit margin on an appropriate base earned by comparable outside parties on comparable uncontrolled transactions with the net profit on the same base earned by the related parties. The key issue is that TNMM is to be applied on a transactional rather than on a firm basis. The two methods are economically the same when applied appropriately (Miesel et al. 2003).

Profit Split Method

Two important issues have led MNCs and many consulting and CPA professional practitioners to choose a profit split method (PSM). First, intangible assets are more difficult to quantify using traditional transactions methods, and much of the residual profit of integrated business entities may be derived from intangible assets; most tax authorities may have difficulties in identifying the intangible assets as a separate factor (Li 2002). Second, traditional transactions methods, in some cases, fail to provide an economically sound basis of intangible assets for the arm's-length standard (Miesel et al. 2003). If the PSM is applied properly, it may be a significant alternative to the traditional transactional or profit-oriented methods, and it addresses the uniquely bilateral features of certain transactions while adhering to the arm's-length standard (Ibid.).

Whereas transactional methods use data at a specific intangible asset level by focusing on specific business lines and a narrow cost base, the PSM uses data on overall profit margins across all intangible assets and services performed to check whether the profit allocated to each entity is in line with that earned by similar arm's-length parties. In practice, both the PSM and TNMM are easier and less costly to implement than the three transactional methods. Moreover, PSM is typically used in complicated cases when other methods are not adequate to price the functions performed.

However, the use of the PSM is considered only as a last resort by the OECD guidelines. In practice, several countries either do not accept PSMs at all, or they base their acceptance on extreme transfer pricing scrutiny, which means that tax authorities almost always detect aspects they can criticize (Vogele and Brem 2003). In Canada, although the CCRA remains unenthusiastic to allow profit-based methods, it does refer to them because of their widespread use in the United States and in recognition of the complexities of conducting international business. Still, the Canadian tax authority considers profit-based methods to be last resorts for when transactional methods fail to be used (Swaneveld, Nagaraian and Przysuski 2002).

There are two steps to apply the PSM. The first step requires determining what portion of overall profit (or loss) can be readily attributed to individual subsidiaries. In the second step, the balance, which is an indistinguishable profit, is split among the various participants by employing a methodology consistent with the arm's-length standard, either by a market-based or non–market-based method (Ibid.). However, Miesel and colleagues (2002) identified two different techniques to apply PSM: the comparable profit split method (CPSM) and the residual profit split method (RPSM). The CPSM requires determining the shares of overall or residual profit (or loss) based on third-party information of an uncontrolled transaction in which the combined return on intangible assets is similar to that in the related-party situation and there is a similar division of intangible assets between the independent parties in the uncontrolled situation and the related parties in the controlled situation (Ibid.).

The RPSM requires only a slice (the residual) of the consolidated operating profit to be attributed to the joined parties based on the profit split principle. The RPSM proceeds in two steps: functional profit is provided by a return derived from data for functional comparables; and the remaining operating profit or loss is allocated based on residual capital to match the rate of return on capital, adjusted for market differences (Ibid.).

In practice, MNCs must follow the U.S. transfer pricing tax rules to determine the amount of the buy-in to be paid by the foreign company to the American subsidiary. The foreign company could utilize the PSM for valuation of the transferred intangible assets. Often, the residual PSM is used to value the buy-in. That method splits the intangible profit between legacy technology and new technology to be developed under the cost-sharing agreement (CSA). The split is based on the relative R&D costs incurred before and after the CSA. The buy-in amount is usually structured as a declining royalty over the life of the legacy technology (Ossi, Anolik, and Kilby 2001).

The profit split method, which attempts to distribute profits earned by various related parties, is typically used when one of the following two conditions applies: the related parties form an integrated whole making it difficult to evaluate separate units of the whole on an individual basis; or all related parties possess unique intangible assets. Because these entities are distinctive and complex, comparable arm's-length companies that do not vary materially in any respect may not be on hand.

A global profit split (GSP) method has been suggested for allocating global income (Li 2002). The GSP allocates the global profit of an integrated business to each subsidiary according to the economic contributions made by components of an MNC located in that country (Ibid.). This technique uses a formula that would reflect the economic factors that contribute to profit making. The GSP method may be consistent with the arm's-length standard, superior to traditional transactional transfer pricing methods, and considered as a fair and effective income allocation derived from globally integrated business operations (Ibid.).

DESIGNING THE RIGHT TRANSFER PRICING SYSTEM FOR INTANGIBLE ASSETS

Corporate executive officers of MNCs prompt several questions about the key elements in designing the most appropriate transfer pricing system for intangible assets. Is locating the enterprise intangibles in a certain jurisdiction strategically sound? In which jurisdiction should the legal vehicle for intangibles be formed? Which tax consequences are the intangibles going to trigger? How can MNCs apply the "best method rule" of transfer pricing? What is the expected impact of effective tax rates in both home and host countries? What are likely problem areas during a transfer pricing tax audit? How can the special purpose company's income be repatriated tax-efficiently? Answers to these questions can be found through an understanding of how MNCs can design effective transfer pricing systems of intangible assets.

In the planning stage, an MNC's transfer pricing system should be based on certain strategies to manage global earnings appearances throughout the value chain and the relevant management accounting needs. Rather than allow tax to drive the design of a business, this approach ensures that any change to the structure or process of a business is made with the full knowledge of the tax prospects and any administrative risks that they present. Management can then design strategies based on the true effect on earnings per share (Emmer and Henshall 2002).

The driving motivation behind developing an effective transfer pricing system for an intangible asset is to reinforce the integrated MNC's goal of maximizing total after-tax net income in order to focus on increasing the global value chain profit, rather than dividing the profit among foreign subsidiary units. In this case, the transfer pricing system serves multiple functions in that the MNC must provide sound economic bases for resource valuation and a performance measurement structure at each value-added stage (Miesel et al. 2002). Intranets and corporate portals are an example of the resources that can help companies to get more out of their existing knowledge. The knowledge supporting intranets and portals is valuable and can often be tax-optimized (Collardin and Vogele 2002).

Strategic planning for intangibles requires a strong understanding of the environmental conditions in which they will operate. Transfer pricing most often is concerned with the appropriate charge for the right to use an intangible rather than the intangible's absolute value. In the case of trademarks, such a charge can vary significantly among countries depending on whether the trademark is registered in the particular country and the relative importance of the local value as compared with international value. Trademarks that may carry well in certain countries or cultures may be unimpressive, or even inappropriate, in others (Emmer and Henshall 2002).

Another important aspect of designing an effective transfer pricing system is to incorporate short-run active features within the system for adjusting transfer prices as a function of marketplace environmental variables consistent with the MNC's allocation of resources for managing these variances or risks (Miesel et al. 2003). Rules for adjusting transfer prices in response to external marketplace risk factors are as critical to a successful transfer pricing system as the initial budgeted price leveles themselves, particularly when performance incentives and other management strategies for responding to external risks are interrelated with transfer pricing system (Ibid.).

When using intangible assets to reduce taxes, MNCs frequently assign income to special purpose subsidiaries in tax-haven countries. However, most tax regulations require that profit follows the underlying economic value drivers. Tax-induced special purpose subsidiaries are either risky (if they lack economic substance) or complicated to implement (if they require operational change). In a number of cases, moving conventional intangibles across the border does require prohibited high buy-in (transfer pricing) payments. Knowledge intangibles, on the other hand, derive their value from the pooling of fragmented preeminent intangibles that have little stand-alone value and thus require minimal transfer pricing payments. Therefore, financial executive officers or tax planners of MNCs should identify and pool fragmented knowledge assets tax efficiently (Collardin and Vogele 2002).

However, many MNCs' transfer pricing systems do not sufficiently respond to the applicable several tax regulations, and they impose indefensible tax compliance risks on MNCs. Internally based profit allocation formulas often conflict directly with the arm's-length principle. In practice, even when MNCs employ market-based methods for transfer pricing, the comparable prices are often based on simple industry averages or are not sufficiently analyzed to adjust for functional or economic differences.

Another important issue for MNCs contemplating global information special purpose companies is the potential income tax consequences of their operations in high tax rate market countries. The income tax consequences of local operations are usually discussed in terms of whether operation of the intangible or ownership of the computer equipment—server—will create a taxable presence. Where the Web site owner is fiscally resident in a country with a broad income tax treaty network, the issues are usually resolved with reference to the permanent establishment (PE) articles of applicable income tax treaties. Where an income tax treaty does not apply, the issues are resolved with reference to the domestic law of the host country, for example the less favorable U.S. business standard (Collardin and Vogele 2002).

The existing PE principles may be applied to information intangible activities in much the same manner as they are applied to more traditional activities. Thus, the existing fixed place of business rule, the dependent agent rule, and the preparatory and auxiliary exceptions to those rules of the permanent establishment article of income tax treaties will apply (Ibid.). To illustrate, if the special purpose company is organized, managed, and controlled in Paris, the domestic law of France would apply in determining whether placement of a fully localized French language version of its Web site on a server owned by a French subsidiary would expose the special purpose company to tax in France. In contrast, if the special purpose company is organized, managed, and controlled in Germany, the PE article of the applicable income tax treaty would apply, and because the French tax authority follows the lead of the OECD, such a Web hosting arrangement would not create a PE in France (Ibid.).

Another important issue of designing the transfer pricing system is how to select the best method. Under Section 482 of the U.S. IRC, the selection of an appropriate transfer pricing method is based on application of the "best method rule." The transfer pricing method that provides the most reliable and acceptable application of an arm's-length result, taking into account not only the comparability factors but also the availability of reliable information from comparable uncontrolled business transactions and parties, should be used (Warner 2002). In other words, the best method rule requires the MNC to analyze transfer prices in accordance with the most reliable estimate of arm's-length prices under the facts and circumstances of the case. In practice, application of the best method rule requires a careful balance in which an MNC selects the appropriate pricing methods, taking into account the business and economic circumstances of the controlled transaction, the availability and quality of potential comparable business transactions under each method, and the measures of comparable performance that can be used under the same circumstances (Miesel et al. 2003).

However, choosing the best pricing method can be difficult, particularly when the multinational group is a large and integrated enterprise competing with similar firms. In particular, Section 482 states that the two primary factors MNCs must take into consideration in selecting the best method are "[1] the degree of comparability between the controlled transaction (or taxpayer) and any uncontrolled comparables, and [2] the quality of the data and assumptions used in the analysis" (Ibid.).

Under the OECD guidelines (1995), the selection of the best method generally follows the same approach articulated in the U.S. Treasury regulations. In general, there will be one method that is suitable to provide the best estimates of arm's-length price. When no one method is conclusive, the method with "higher degrees of comparability and a more direct, closer relationship to the transaction" is preferable. Thus, the comparability and functional analysis are emphasized in the OECD guidelines. The OECD guidelines identify five factors that determine comparability with uncontrolled business transactions: characteristics of the properties or services, functions performed and risks assumed, contractual terms, economic circumstances, and business strategies.

Moreover, two methods are identified in the OECD guidelines to make intangible assets available to affiliates: the use of licensing agreements or the use of cost-sharing arrangements (CSA). Under the licensing agreements, the resulting intangibles will be owned by a single entity, which is the parent company, although the results of the project will actually be available to all the contributing members of the group.

Such arrangements will always be documented in advance with how costs are to be allocated, how the entry and exit of participants prior to completion of the project should be treated, and the outcomes of a local or foreign group member contributing intangibles to the agreement. The importance of each such issue will depend upon the national laws concerned.

The CSA may occur when two or more entities agree to share the actual cost and risk of a project to be undertaken by an existing or newly formed entity in return for the outcomes of the project, or when one entity undertakes to provide for the other parties to the agreement various services in return for contributions established in proportion to the expected benefits. It is important to note that there are major advantages in relation to such a CSA. In particular, from a practical point of view, these arrangements preclude the need to value the resulting intangible assets, and further, from a tax point of view, it may be the case that the payments pursuant to the arrangement may be made in lieu of a dividend and can, in certain cases, be tax deductible as well as permit the avoidance of withholding tax implications. However, different accounting and tax treatments and different restrictions prevailing in several countries on the transfer of the resulting intangible assets can put off the overall effectiveness of such a system (Mac 2001).

MNCs might encounter several difficulties in maintaining the effectiveness of their transfer pricing. One major difficulty is due to the fact that the arm's-length principle is based on the separate-entity approach, whereas MNCs are often globally integrated firms. Often, it is through integration that the MNC achieves economies of scale and scope in transaction costs, risk management, technological and other intangible assets, and other functions or risks (Miesel et al. 2003). Another difficulty that may obstruct the effective application of the arm's-length principle arises from situations in which MNCs engage in transactions that independent firms would not carry out, such as maintaining a new related business venture at a loss to create a bigger market share; transferring a valuable, closely held technology to a related party foreign subsidiary; or entering into specialized business contracts (Ibid.).

Another important issue that should be considered in designing an effective transfer pricing system for intangible assets is the effect of financial accounting standards 141 and 142 on the identification and usefulness of comparables in selecting the best transfer pricing method. On July 20, 2001, the Financial Accounting Standards Board (FASB) issued two standards: Statements of Financial Accounting Standards No. 141, Business Combinations, and No. 142, Goodwill and Other Intangible Assets. These standards introduced major accounting changes and also raise significant direct and indirect income tax issues for MNCs. One consequence of the accounting rule change includes a counterintuitive effective tax rate result under FAS 141 for cross-border acquisitions. U.S. acquirers of foreign objectives may experience higher effective tax rates in their U.S. GAAP financial statements if the objective of the acquisition is to minimize foreign income taxes (Hicks, Benson, and O'Connor 2001).

The implementation of FAS 142 opens the door for significant transfer pricing issues. Intercompany transfer prices may need to be reviewed and updated to ensure that they appropriately reflect impairments of indefinite lived intangible assets and that they reflect the carve-out of separately identifiable intangible assets from prior acquisitions, which were previously included in goodwill for financial reporting purposes. If these newly identified intangible assets are used by, or provided to, related entities for little or no transfer price, then the company may be exposed to transfer pricing allocation issues upon tax audit. Additionally, if the value of an intangible created from goodwill for financial reporting purposes is significantly lower than the value on which the intercompany transfer price is based, the taxpayer may find it difficult to convince the tax authorities of the appropriateness of a royalty charge for an asset that has been impaired for financial reporting purposes. Moreover, these new accounting rules may affect the identification and usefulness of comparables in the transfer pricing perspective (Ibid.).

Following are practical solutions that address strategic actions for MNCs. Their use will help in avoiding transfer pricing tax audits, adopting a practical approach to a transfer pricing system, and avoiding serious problems with tax authorities down the road (Swaneveld and Przysuski 2002).

1. A diagnostic transfer pricing audit should be performed to discover any problematic areas in an MNCs' transfer pricing system. It includes reviewing all the issues, questions, and documents the tax authority would request in a typical tax audit, thereby minimizing the risk that the examination will identify unexpected transfer pricing problems.
2. A risk assessment by analyzing current or planned cross-border business transactions should be conducted to identify transfer pricing issues and risks. This process includes three steps: Identify all cross-border business transactions subject to transfer pricing tax audit; review the reporting form to ensure that all related-party transactions and transfer pricing methodologies are properly disclosed; and identify any lack in transfer pricing policies, practices, or documentation.
3. A transfer pricing study should be prepared by developing and documenting the steps you follow to determine your transfer prices and contemporaneous documentation. This study, which

includes the following steps, not only ensures compliance with government requirements but also identifies opportunities to reduce taxes.

4. All key areas of the transfer pricing agreement with both parties (includes services, intangibles, research and development payments, etc.) should be identified to establish all the facts and circumstances regarding the activities, risks, and intangibles involved in the transaction and to select the best or the most appropriate transfer pricing methodology.
5. Arm's-length comparable companies should be identified to determine the appropriate price for similar circumstances and similar transactions.
6. Contemporaneous documentation should be prepared to serve as "insurance" to reduce the risk of assessment and penalties in case of a transfer pricing tax audit.
7. An Advance Pricing Agreement should be prepared for MNCs that anticipate transfer pricing problems with tax authorities.

Any of the above strategic actions would be a wise venture in the expansion of MNCs' global international business. They may assist in reducing global tax liabilities; determining how the functions, risks, and intangible assets of MNCs' global business impact profitability; identifying operational efficiencies and inefficiencies; and improving the structure of management accounting and costing systems.

SUMMARY AND CONCLUSIONS

This chapter introduced, discussed, and analyzed five issues most related to transfer pricing of intangible assets, e-commerce, and international taxation.

- General understanding of the characteristics and the nature of intangible assets of multinational companies and the related transfer pricing issue
- The new trends in transfer pricing of intangible assets
- MNCs' strategies of intangible assets ownership
- Transfer pricing methods for intangible assets
- Designing the right transfer pricing system of intangible assets

Understanding the nature and the characteristics of intangible assets of MNCs and the related issues of transfer pricing systems is considered an essential step in designing the right and most appropriate pricing systems for MNCs. Intangible assets need different analysis than what is required for tangible assets, because they are the key to commercial success, especially in the hi-tech industry.

MNCs and tax authorities have been facing great challenges in dealing with transfer pricing of intangible assets. The challenges include

- the globalization of MNCs and rapid expansion in the cross-border business transactions of services and technology
- the shift from a predominantly manufacturing economy to a service economy spurred by innovative technology
- the increasing importance of intangibles in the production of income.

In the twenty-first century, the significant and fast development of the e-commerce era and service companies' paradigms in proportion to the bricks-and-mortar business activities pushes the tax authorities around the world to continue their attack on transfer pricing practices of MNCs by issuing new transfer pricing regulations and adjusting old ones to meet these e-commerce challenges (Levey 2001).

In the strategic planning stage, an MNC may choose one of three approaches for an intangible asset ownership: a centralized intangible asset ownership, a distributed intangible asset ownership, or geographic or regional distributed ownership. Each of the three approaches was discussed in detail; however, the most important question for an MNC is: Which approach may be the most preferable? Three important variables should be the drivers for an MNC decision: the historical circumstances of how the group or related parties subsidiaries were created or the way that the intangible asset was developed; the management philosophy of the group; and the tax strategy, including the effect on transfer pricing method used, from the MNC's perspective.

To arrive at the arm's-length transfer pricing methods used by tax authorities for intangible assets, six transfer pricing methods were evaluated: the comparable uncontrolled price (CUP) method; the resale price method (RPM); cost-plus method (CPM); comparable profit method (CPrM); transactional net margin method (TNMM); and profit split method (PSM). The first three are viewed as traditional transaction-oriented methods, and the last three are profit-based methods.

Finally, the design of the right and effective transfer pricing system for intangible assets was discussed and analyzed. It included strategies to be used to manage global earnings appearances throughout the entire value chain; the driving motivation behind developing an effective transfer pricing system; understanding the environmental conditions in which intangible assets will operate; the incorporation of short-run active features within the system for adjusting transfer prices as a function of marketplace environmental variables; potential income tax consequences of MNCs' operations in high tax rate markets; how to select the best transfer pricing method under the U.S. tax code and the OECD Guidelines; and practical solutions that address strategic actions for MNCs to use in avoiding transfer pricing tax audits.

The increasing complexity and awareness of several tax authorities around the world and the requirements for truthful declarations of transfer pricing methods require a constructive response from MNCs with advance articulation and full documentation. Multinationals faced with pricing controversies must recognize early on the potential economic consequences of an inadequate defense: long, drawn-out litigation and negotiation in uncertain proceedings of several court cases. Therefore, MNCs should evaluate their transfer pricing policies and base international transfer prices more consistently on competitive and marketplace realties, thereby supporting profit as a meaningful, constructive objective for foreign subsidiaries and affiliates.

REFERENCES

Adams, Chris D., and Gerald M. Godshaw. 2002. Intellectual property and transfer pricing. *International Tax Review*, Supplement, Intellectual Property, pp. 74–81.

Collardin, Marcus, and Alexander Vogele. 2002. Knowledge intangibles—leveraging the tax advantages. *International Tax Review* 13, no. 7 (July/August): 59–61.

Doonan, Jacqueline, and Jessica Tien. 2002. The best method for determining cost-sharing payments. *International Tax Review* 13, no. 9 (October): 37–38.

Emmer, Maurice, and John Henshall. 2002. Building and maintaining brand value. *International Tax Review*, Supplement, Industry Guide: Financial Services (July): 41–46.

Hicks, Hal, David Benson, and Margaret O. Connor. 2001. U.S. revitalizes its treaty network. *International Journal Review* 12, no. 10 (November): 48–52.

Johnson, Robert E. 2001. The role of cluster analysis in assessing comparability under the U.S. transfer pricing regulations. *Business Economics* 36, no. 2 (April): 30–38.

Levey, Marc M. 2001. Transfer pricing—What is next. *International Tax Review*, Supplement, The Best of the Best (June): 91–92.

Li, Jinyang. 2002. Global profit split: An evolutionary approach to international income allocation. *Canadian Tax Journal* 50(3): 825–69.

Mac, Thessa. 2001. Exploiting intangibles the cost-effective way. *International Tax Review* 12, no. 9 (October): 15–17.

Miesel, Victor H., Harlow H. Higinbotham, and Chun W. Yi. 2002. International transfer pricing: Practical solutions for intercompany pricing. *The International Tax Journal* 28, no. 4 (fall): 1–22.

Miesel, Victor H., Harlow H. Higinbotham, and Chun W Yi. 2003. International transfer pricing: Practical solutions for intercompany pricing—part II. *The International Tax Journal* 29, no. 1 (winter): 1–40.

Narvaez-Hasfura, Jorg, and Eric Torrey. 2002. Mexican transfer pricing under the microscope. *International Tax Review* 13, no. 7 (July/August): 37–38.

Organization for Economic Cooperation and Development Committee (OECD). 1995. *Transfer Pricing Guidelines for Multinational Enterprises and Tax Administrations*, Paris: OECD.

Ossi, Greg, Stuart Anolik, and John Kilby. 2001. Offshore operations. *International Tax Review* (no. 4, Supplement, E-Commerce): 57–69.

Raby, Nick, Kirsten Blum, Katherine Treasure, and E. Miller Williams. 2002. US: Transfer pricing strategies. *International Tax Review,* Supplement, Regional Guides: North America, pp. 19–25.

Swaneveld, Hendrik, Venkat Nagaraian, and Martin Przysuski. 2002. Canada cracks down on profit split. *International Tax Review* 13, no. 5 (May): 35–36.

Swaneveld, Hendrik, and Martin Przysuski. 2002. Transfer pricing now a Canadian priority. *CMA Management* 76, no. 2 (April): 42–44.

Vogele, Alexander, and Markus Brem. 2002/2003. Do APAs prevent disputes? *International Tax Review* 14, no. 1 (December 2002/January 2003): 35.

Walsh, Mary. 2001. Get the best value from intangibles. *International Tax Review* 12, no. 2 (February): 23–36.

Warner, John P. 2002. Taxing interbranch dealings: Application of separate taxpayer arm's length principles to inbound interbranch distribution dealings. *Tax Management International Journal* 31, no. 3 (March 8): 155–70.

IV

Tax Regulations and Practices of Transfer Pricing in Selected Countries

Arm's-Length Price and Advance Pricing Agreement Programs in Selected Countries

Transfer pricing is considered one of the most important as well as complicated business issues in the world. This complexity is compounded when transfer pricing is combined with e-commerce cross-border business transactions. As globalization and Internet technology continue so quickly, all tax authorities worldwide are paying close attention to transfer pricing issues and trying to change their tax regulations and rules at a fast pace, which can mean headaches for corporate and financial executive officers of MNCs. However, the upside is that many countries are adopting a similar approach to eliminate or reduce tax abuses or evasion as a result of using non–arm's-length transfer pricing techniques.

This chapter and chapter 10 are concerned with recent international developments and changes in tax regulations and practices of transfer pricing legislation with respect to four different transfer pricing issues: transfer pricing in general, including arm's-length standards; advance pricing agreement programs; documentation; and penalties. This chapter covers the first two issues of transfer pricing systems: arm's-length price standard and the advance pricing agreement programs in selected countries. Chapter 10 covers documentation and penalties of transfer pricing in the same selected countries. Comparative analysis of selected countries in different areas of the world is presented. The two chapters also concentrate on the countries that are important to the executive officers of American multinational companies. The selected countries, in alphabetical order, are Canada, France, Germany,

Japan, Mexico, Netherlands, the United Kingdom, and the United States.

INTRODUCTION

All MNCs, without exception, try to achieve certain goals with their transfer pricing systems. Avoiding the risk of transfer pricing tax audits is one of them. According to the 2001 Ernst & Young fourth survey, transfer pricing was judged to be the single most important tax issue facing multinational companies (Lewis and Lim 2002). Interviews with various revenue authorities around the globe indicate that tax authorities also view transfer pricing as a top audit issue, scrutinizing MNCs' pricing for intercompany transactions to make sure that the arm's-length standard is applied (Ackerman and Hobster 2002).

On the other hand, tax authorities of different countries are at different stages of maturity in getting to grips with transfer pricing issues. In general, tax authorities strive to get a fair share of tax revenues for their own countries. Conflicts between transfer pricing practices of MNCs and the governmental transfer pricing regime in all countries have pushed tax authorities to require adoption of the arm's-length pricing principle, extensive documentation in support of the methods to determine transfer prices, and imposition of stringent penalties for noncompliance.

Both the U.S. Internal Revenue Code and the report of the Organization for Economic Cooperation and Development (OECD) offer the best explanation of an arm's-length standard. The OECD defines arm's-length prices as prices that would have been paid between unrelated parties for the same or similar goods or services under the same or similar conditions or circumstances (OECD 1995). The Internal Revenue Code defines arm's-length prices as prices that were charged or would have been charged in independent transactions with unrelated parties under the same or similar conditions or circumstances. Accordingly, the arm's-length pricing principle refers to the use of arm's-length prices for dealing with intracompany transactions.

In the following sections, two of the most important transfer pricing issues are analyzed and discussed. In the first section, the arm's-length standard of the selected countries and the OECD guidelines are analyzed and discussed. In the second section, Advance Pricing Agreement (APA) programs, as a solution for avoiding tax audits and litigation, of the selected countries, are examined.

ARM'S-LENGTH STANDARD

Tax authorities around the world require that prices charged for goods and services between related parties be consistent with the amount that would have been charged if uncontrolled taxpayers had engaged in the same transaction under the same conditions or circumstances. Recently, most industrialized countries have imposed new regulations that enforce strict transfer pricing requirements. Many foreign tax authorities, especially in most industrialized countries, have followed the lead of the IRS-U.S. as a model, adopting and enforcing similar arm's-length standards for transfer pricing by means of documentation requirements with penalties for noncompliance (Felgran and Yamada 2001). It should be noted that although all foreign tax authorities of the countries covered seek to adhere to the OECD Guidelines in implementing these, major differences in transfer pricing policies and regulations arise. A summary of current regulations and practices of the selected countries follows.

The Organization for Economic Cooperation and Development

The OECD Transfer Pricing Guidelines endorse the arm's-length standard as the international standard for the intracompany cross-border transfer pricing. Through its Committee on Fiscal Affairs, the OECD has been and is working to make a consensus among its member countries on international taxation principles, thereby avoiding unilateral responses to multilateral problems. The committee's goal is to increase awareness of the relevant transfer pricing issues, both for the taxpayers and the tax authorities in at least the OECD member countries.

In 1995, the OECD adopted parallel arm's-length transfer pricing principles in the first major update of its 1979 transfer pricing guidelines. These revised guidelines provide an internationally accepted statement of principles and methods that are broadly similar in scope and standards to the U.S. tax regulations (Miesel, Higinbotham, and Yi 2002). On July 27, 1995, the OECD released its final version, titled *Transfer Pricing Guidelines for Multinational Enterprises and Tax Administration*. These guidelines include the 1979 *Transfer Pricing and Multinational Enterprises* and the 1984 report *Transfer Pricing and Multinational Enterprises: Three Taxation Issues*. The guidelines are not law, and member countries are encouraged to follow them. Nonetheless, most member countries do not have their own detailed transfer pricing regulations and they have been following the OECD guidelines on transfer pricing.

Despite some differences, the guidelines are generally consistent with Section 482 of IRC on transfer pricing regulations. American MNCs that comply with Section 482 regulations should not be exposed to a significant risk of double taxation in OECD member countries. The guidelines emphasize the arm's-length standard and the use of transaction-based methods that rely on comparable uncontrolled transactions. Section 482 of IRC requires the taxpayer to select the "best method rule," that, under the facts and circumstances, will provide the "most reliable measure" of an arm's-length standard relative to the other potentially applicable methods. Under the guidelines, the MNC must select the method that provides the "best estimate" of an arm's-length standard (Greenhill and Bee 1996).

The guidelines discussed important issues related to transfer pricing policies: the arm's-length standard, transfer pricing methods, and transfer of intangible asset and services. They are discussed next as they relate to arm's-length price.

The Arm's-Length Standard

The 1995 OECD guidelines, the same as Section 482, provide that no adjustment should be made to an MNC's transfer pricing results if those results are within an arm's-length range derived from the use of two or more comparable uncontrolled transactions or more than one pricing method. However, if the MNC's transfer pricing results are outside the arm's-length range, those results may be adjusted to be within the range. Under Section 482, such an adjustment will normally be to the midpoint of the range; under the 1995 guidelines, the adjustment would be to the point that best reflects the facts and circumstances.

Transfer Pricing Methods

The 1995 guidelines explain the following transfer pricing methods in detail: the three traditional transaction methods that include comparable uncontrolled price (CUP) method, resale price method (RPM), and cost-plus method (CPLM); transactional profit methods that include profit split method (PSM) and transactional net margin method (TNMM); and global formulary apportionment method (GFA). In several cases, the three traditional transactions methods (CUP, RPM, CPLM) and the two transactional profit methods can be used as arm's-length standards. However, the GFA is considered as a non–arm's-length method and is rejected by the OECD.

The OECD guidelines, similar to Section 482, provide standards of comparability that emphasize functions performed, risks assumed, and assets used. Both permit the use of inexact comparables "similar" to the controlled transaction under review. The types of risks that must be taken into account under both sets of rules include market risks; risks of loss associated with the investment in and use of property, plant, and equipment; risks associated with the success or failure of research and developmental activities; and financial risks such as those caused by currency exchange rate and interest rate variability.

The 1995 guidelines express a strong preference for the use of transactional methods for testing the arm's-length character of transfer prices for transfers of tangible property. These methods include the comparable uncontrolled price method, the resale method and the cost-plus method. These are "specified methods" under Section 482 regulations.

There are no substantive differences between Section 482 regulations and the guidelines in the concepts underlying these methods, the manner in which these methods are to be applied, or the conditions under which these methods would likely be the best method. Section 482 regulations and the guidelines differ only in their evaluation of the probability that comparable uncontrolled transactions can be identified and that adequate and reliable data about the comparables can reasonably be obtained. The guidelines state that the inability to apply the transactional methods will be the exceptional, not the normal, case (Greenhill and Bee 1996).

Both the Section 482 regulations and the 1995 guidelines provide for the use of other methods when the transactional methods cannot be used. Under the Section 482 regulations, a taxpayer may use the comparable profits method (CPM) or the profit split method; under the guidelines, a taxpayer may use the profit split method or the TNMM. Unlike the Section 482 regulations, which limit the use of the profit split method, the guidelines express a strong preference for the use of the profit split method over the TNMM. It should be noted that the profit split method will produce a very different result than will be obtained under any of the other methods specified in either the Section 482 regulations or the guidelines.

The OECD 1995 guidelines would allow an MNC to base its profit split analysis on projected profits, seemingly without regard to actual profits realized; such an approach would not be permitted under the Section 482 regulations. The TNMM is substantially equivalent to the CPM under the Section 482 regulations. Some OECD members rejected the use of the CPM mainly because they could not understand the requirements in Section 482 of the IRC. Some OECD countries perceive the CPM as only the imposition of industrywide average returns to a taxpayer's entire business activity, without any regard to comparability and to factors other than transfer pricing that might ignore profit margins. However, the Section 482 regulations have explicit comparability standards that apply to all pricing methods. Thus, when properly used, the CPM and the TNMM should produce to a large extent the same result (Greenhill and Bee 1996).

Transfers of Intangible Property and Services
In 1995 guidelines, intangible property is divided into three groups as follows: the rights to use industrial assets such as patents, trade

names, trademarks, models, or designs; literary and artistic property rights; and intellectual property such as know-how and trade secrets.

These intangible assets may or may not have any book value on the MNC financial statements, but many of them may be very valuable to the company. On the contrary, some of them may be associated with high risks (such as product liability or environmental or air pollution). The 1995 guidelines do not address the arm's-length principle for either the transfer of intangible property or cost sharing, or the provision of intercompany services. On April 11, 1996, the OECD updated its guidelines for transfer of intangible property and services (Greenhill and Bee 1996).

Canada

In June 1998, the Canadian government amended its tax laws to align them with current international tax regulations and practices. The new transfer pricing regulations are outlined in Section 247 of the Income Tax Act. According to the Canadian transfer pricing rules, following the OECD guidelines, taxpayers are required to disclose all non–arm's-length business transactions with foreign affiliates and with confirmation that their transfer pricing systems are supported with all relevant documentation (Felgran and Yamada 2001). The Canadian legislation includes various provisions to ensure that businesses use the acceptable transfer pricing methods, including the definition of the arm's-length principle that forms the basis for determining the acceptable transfer prices; the methodologies that firms may use to arrive at transfer prices; the documentation the tax authority requires when it conducts an audit of a company's transfer prices; the reporting form, TI 06, that must be filed to report all nonresident related-party transactions; and the penalty that applies should an organization not comply with these requirements.

The main objectives of the 1998 amendments were put in place to blend Canada's transfer pricing legislation with the 1995 *Transfer Pricing Guidelines for Multinational Enterprises and Tax Administrations* developed by the OECD. However, the new legislation indicated that neither the OECD guidelines nor the transfer pricing methods that the OECD indicated could produce an arm's-length price. Rather, it left these tasks to information circular 87-2R, which provided guidance on the rules set out in the Canadian legislation (Swaneveld, Przysuski, and Nagaraian 2002a).

In 1999, Revenue Canada became the Canada Customs and Revenue Agency (CCRA) and initiated a transformation of its operating environment to more effectively protect Canada's tax base. Over the last three years, the CCRA has been rolling out a series of new policies and programs targeted directly at bringing to an end international profit manipulation.

European Countries

In an attempt to eliminate double taxation in connection with profit adjustments between related parties of the same group, the European Union in 1990 adopted a Transfer Pricing Convention that went into effect almost five years later. This convention applies when profits are included in the income of more than one contracting country by reason of allocations among related taxpayers in order to reflect arm's-length conditions. Competent authorities who fail to reach an agreement pursuant to their treaty's mutual agreement procedure must establish an "advisory commission" to deliver an opinion on elimination of the relevant double taxation. The obligation to arbitrate may not be disregarded without the taxpayers' consent. The convention allows tax authorities to ignore the commission's decision. Within six months after the commission's decision has been rendered, the competent authorities may decide to deviate from it. However, the decision is binding only if the competent authorities fail to agree otherwise, because both countries remain free to disregard the arbitrators' decision by deciding to settle the case in a completely different manner than the one stated in the Transfer Pricing Convention (Park 2002).

However, the European Union (EU) has several difficulties in translating transfer pricing standards to practice, because member countries' regimes differ on the question of what documentation is acceptable and on how to interpret the OECD transfer pricing guidelines. Moreover, significant double taxation, with the arbitration process, is seen as too expensive and time-consuming to be reliable. It is suggested that a Europe-wide Joint Forum on transfer pricing agree on a more coordinated approach on the OECD guidelines generally and documentation in particular (Hobster 2002).

France

In light of the recent transfer pricing trends that have taken place in several European countries and at the level of the OECD, since 1996 France has been carrying out a reform process that imposes new obligations on taxpayers and strengthens its tax authorities' power. In general, the French tax authorities tend to follow the OECD Guidelines when determining in which types of cases the transfer pricing rules are to be applied. They thus recognize the validity of the various methods of determining transfer prices endorsed by the OECD. In practice, the tax authorities often use comparative methods. However, the main issue is one of justifying the method used by the multinational companies.

In the French General Tax Code (FGTC), there are two articles considered as the foundation for the French transfer pricing regulations—article 57 and article 238 A. Furthermore, to enable the tax authorities to audit the transfer pricing systems used by French companies, the legislature has provided them with specific procedural regulations. Under article 57, profits indirectly transferred by a company established in France to affiliated companies established outside of France are to be added back into its results to determine the income tax it owes. To apply article 57, the French Tax Authorities must provide proof of three major issues combined (Sporken et al. 2001):

- Indirect transfer of profits abroad—either by increasing or decreasing sale or purchase prices, or by any other means
- A controlling link between the two companies
- De facto control, which can result from a contractual link or from the circumstances of the relationship between the two companies

Where all these criteria are met, article 57 of the FGTC provides that the profits transferred abroad are to be added back into the French company's taxable income (Ibid.).

Article 238 A of the FGTC shifts the burden of proof of the deductibility of certain sums that are owed or paid by individuals or business entities established in France to other individuals or business entities established outside of France, and that benefit from favorable tax treatment in the other country. The same rule applies to payments made to financial institutions established in a tax haven country (Ibid.). To implement article 238 A of the FGTC, the tax authorities must first establish that the beneficiary of the payments is subject to favorable tax treatment in the other country. Where the tax authorities provide proof of this, the deductibility of the sums paid by the French company in respect of financial costs, industrial property rights, or services provided is allowed only if the debtor proves by any means available that, on the one hand, the corresponding transactions really occurred and, on the other hand, the expenses were normal in nature (Ibid.).

Germany

In Germany, affiliated MNCs shall set transfer prices for goods delivered, intangibles transferred, and services provided as if the companies were not related to each other, which is the arm's-length standard. Unfortunately, OECD guidelines, as well as the administrative principles, are very general, and there is no juridical basis that explains how a required comparable search should be performed. Therefore, determining the appropriate transfer price is not easy in practice, and finding comparable data that reflects the specific business condition is a big challenge for MNCs.

For MNCs to compare their transfer pricing systems with others with similar unrelated party businesses, transactions among unrelated third parties have to be identified. Based on a functional and risk analysis, comparable prices are extracted from database searches, and comfort ranges of prices or profitability are established. Further, the comparable transactions may be adjusted to reflect the underlying conditions of the transaction in question. The used transfer pricing method determines the comparability factors; for example, the comparable uncontrolled price method requires strict product comparability, whereas the resale price method and cost-plus method focus instead on comparable functions and risks and are more tolerant of the product comparability requirement. Compared to other industrialized countries, the publication of detailed financial company data is still limited in Germany, especially on a transactional basis. However, there is a trend toward more data transparency in the course of European integration and an investor-driven market. As a result, more financial data about German companies is now publicly available than five years ago (Schmitz and Korner 2000).

An MNC should document comparable transactions that strongly support and confirm its chosen transfer pricing methodology. Such an approach enables the MNC to defend its transfer pricing in the face of a tax audit. The trend toward the use of comparable data or companies has been further strengthened by a landmark transfer-pricing court decision in 1999. The regional tax court in Düsseldorf disallowed the use of comparables unavailable to the public in Germany. These comparables were extracted from the files of the tax authorities, and the court ruled that their use violated the rights of the taxpayer and led to a breach of tax secrecy. The dispute centered around the appropriateness of the gross margin applied by a German distributor and the comparison with gross margins from undisclosed third-party distributors. The decision is not final and binding, though no appeal to the German Federal Tax Court was allowed. The tax authorities, however, have filed a complaint against this decision (Schmitz and Korner 2000).

During the 1990s, as MNCs started to integrate globally, the transfer of products, intangibles and services among group companies increased significantly. In Germany, intercompany transfer pricing became more and more a crucial factor in tax planning than before. Although transfer pricing is actively used by U.S. MNCs as a tax planning tool, the attention to transfer pricing in Germany is only just emerging (Ibid.).

In Germany, fiscal authorities also focus on transfer prices because pricing decisions influence a jurisdiction's tax collections. In various countries, authorities are adopting specific transfer pricing regulations, either following OECD guidelines or developing domestic solutions. German fiscal authorities have increased their focus on transfer pricing issues, not only when auditing loss-making companies but also when reviewing single transactions or operational segments, or even profitable companies. According to Ernst and Young's Transfer Pricing 1999 Global Survey, German multinationals regard administrative and management services as well as intercompany financing as the transactions most susceptible to transfer pricing audits and disputes (Ibid.).

German transfer pricing standard is based on the arm's-length principle of the OECD guidelines, and the three traditional standard methods of determining arm's-length prices: comparable uncontrolled price (CUP), resale price method (RPM), and cost-plus method (CPM.) Like the OECD, the German tax authorities are against the use of the methods of global formulary apportionment used in the United States by certain individual states. However, the official German position on profit-oriented methods such as the profit split method (PSM) and the transactional net margin method (TNMM) is that they should only be used for estimating, or verifying the results reached under the three traditional standard methods.

In Germany, the OECD Guidelines do not constitute tax law. A general statement of the arm's-length standard is found in section 1 of the Foreign Transactions Tax Act (AStG). This statute applies when German corporations transfer goods and services at very low prices to their foreign subsidiaries. Otherwise, most adjustments in the corporate area are based on the corporate tax law concept of constructive dividends and the corollary doctrine of constructive contributions (Vogele and Bader 2002).

The pace of German transfer pricing developments in the period from mid-August 1999 to mid-August 2001 was swift. In a ruling dated June 21, 2001, the Federal Tax Court affirmed the existence of "serious doubts" as to the compatibility of the arm's-length principle with the antidiscrimination provisions of EU law. The ruling grants the taxpayer a stay of tax collection pending a judgment on the merits (Sporken et al. 2001).

In October 2001, the Federal Tax Court concluded that German law does not require German taxpayers to generate special transfer pricing documentation. This decision complements a May 2001 decision holding that the lack of a transfer pricing documentation law precluded the German tax authorities from penalizing taxpayers that did not document their transfer pricing methods. Until new legislation is issued, taxpayers remain obliged only to provide oral responses, answer auditors' questions, and provide documentation only if the taxpayer has already prepared such documentation (Dodge and DiCenso 2002).

Japan

In general, the National Tax Administration (NTA) of Japan has adhered to the OECD guidelines in designing its transfer pricing tax regulations. Japanese taxpayers are not required to maintain documentation; however, a penalty may be imposed if an adjustment is made. The government is expected to review current transfer pricing tax regulation to make it more compatible with other industrialized countries' systems (Felgran and Yamada 2001).

In line with their general sense that transfer pricing is an issue, Japanese MNCs are also concerned over several dispute possibilities at both local and worldwide levels. Although the Japan National Tax Authority (NTA) does not conduct targeted campaigns, it has recently increased its interest in intragroup services related topics, probably with a view to issuing more specific rules within the next years (Lewis and Lim 2002). In 2001, more Japanese MNCs consider transfer pricing as their biggest issue in dealing with tax authorities. The high importance also accorded the issue by New Zealand companies probably reflects the relatively recent introduction of a transfer pricing regime and the even more recent publication of guidelines (Ibid.).

Mexico

The first Mexican transfer pricing legislation was enacted in 1995 in relation to companies operating under the inbound manufacturing regime. The transfer pricing rules provide a safe harbor for those business entities that report an amount that is equal to at least 5 percent of assets for Mexican income tax purposes. The base of the Mexican transfer pricing regulatory structure is that, without proof to the contrary, transactions between related parties are not at arm's-length standard. Therefore, the responsibility for demonstrating the use of arm's-length standard of the cross-border intercompany transactions lies with the taxpayer. Moreover, all transactions between Mexican residents and business entities located in low tax jurisdictions are deemed to be conducted between related parties and the transactions are not at arm's-length standard. The Mexican regulation also sets out norms of comparability to determine the scope of any differences existing between the independent and related-party cross-border transactions (Valdes, Hahn, and Muniz 1999).

As part of the Mexican government's aim of competing effectively in world markets, and especially within the framework of the North

American Free Trade Association, the Mexican government introduced new laws effective January 1, 1997, with regards to transfer pricing. These rules include the traditional and alternative methods as developed by the OECD *Transfer Pricing Guidelines for Multinational Enterprises and Tax Administrators* to determine the transfer prices with regard to the transfers of tangible products, transfer of intangible products or services, financing business transactions, or service transactions.

Recently, the Mexican government added transfer pricing rules to its tax laws, requiring taxpayers with related-party transactions to comply with the arm's-length standard. On December 31, 2000, the Official Gazette of the Federation included amendments to article 58, section 14 of the Mexican Income Tax Law, a section that deals with transfer pricing rules. These modifications have the potential to drastically change transfer pricing applications in Mexico and, more importantly, may uncover previous transfer pricing irregularities (Narvaez-Hasfura and Torrey 2002). However, unlike the United States, Mexican transfer pricing rules do not foresee the need to use the so-called "best method rule"; the best method rule essentially calls for the most reliable result under the arm's-length standard, based on quality of available data and assumptions, and the use of comparables. (Valdes, Hahn, and Muniz 1999).

In following the OECD guidelines, Mexico explicitly adheres to the arm's-length standard to regulate transfer prices, profit margins, or any other cross-border compensation set by related parties operating in different countries. Thus, the main purpose of the Mexican rules is to ensure that an appropriate allocation of profit is achieved taking into account the functions, risks, and intangibles, so that the income corresponding to the Mexican taxpayer will be accurately reflected.

However, in Mexico, experience has shown that the use of transfer pricing practices of the United States will generally allow the taxpayer to satisfy the Mexican documentation requirements. Nonetheless, care should be taken to make the appropriate adjustments and address such formalistic matters as providing the domicile and tax residence of the relevant foreign parties (Ibid.).

Netherlands

Until the year 2000, there were no specific transfer pricing tax rules in the Netherlands. However, the Netherlands has implemented the OECD guidelines. In the Netherlands, there is no detailed legislation to deal with transfer pricing. On March 30, 2001, the Dutch Ministry of Finance published the outline of the new Dutch tax ruling practice and introduced transfer pricing rules. Both were effective on April 1, 2001. The ministry has stated that their transfer pricing rule is based on the arm's-length principle and OECD guidelines. The guidelines apply, in principle, in the Netherlands, based on article 3.8 of the Dutch Income Tax Act, and the taxpayers have to demonstrate that their transfer pricing system is at arm's-length price.

The Dutch tax authorities tend to follow the OECD guidelines when determining which transfer pricing method is acceptable, although the new transfer pricing regulation does discuss ranges. The main issue in matters of determining the transfer pricing methods and ranges is justifying the method and result for the company (Sporken et al. 2001).

The United Kingdom

In 1998, the U.K. Corporation Tax Self Assessment (CTSA) fully incorporated the OECD guidelines into the U.K. legislation and applied them to accounting periods ending on or after July 1, 1999. Under the new regulations, taxpayers are required to apply the arm's-length principle in computing their income for tax purposes. Taxpayers must also prepare and maintain sufficient transfer pricing documentation as part of routine tax preparation to have a complete return.

The 1998 legislation represents a significant departure from the previous legislation in a number of respects, which can be summarized as follows (Sporken et al. 2001):

- The directional power of the Inland Revenue is abolished. Instead, taxpayers will be obliged to apply the arm's-length standard when submitting their tax returns.
- The legislation contains a new basic pricing rule, which is to be construed in accordance with article 9 (1) of OECD Model Tax Convention on Income and on Capital, and the OECD guidelines.
- The new legislation broadens the transactions and arrangements that will be subject to legislation.
- The self-assessment penalty regime will apply to transfer pricing with the possibility of penalties for negligent or fraudulent actions of up to 100 percent of the tax adjustment arising.

In the United Kingdom, basic transfer pricing rules lead to the adjustment of tax liabilities by reference to the application of the arm's-length standard. In the absence of appropriate compensating payments between parties to the relevant transactions, however, the economic position of those parties remains one that is distorted by the actual price at which those transactions have taken place. The amounts involved can, of course, be substantial, and this can mean that funds are recognized in one company that, on a proper application of the arm's-length principle, would have been those of a different company. The making of secondary adjustments is a possible remedy to this. Such adjustments attempt to return the economic positions of parties to transactions on which transfer pricing adjustments have been made to those that would have appertained had pricing been arm's length in the first place (Haigh 2002).

The United States

The United States has been the historic leader in establishing the arm's-length standard as the recognized principle for determining cross-border transfer prices and the allocation of profits between subsidiaries of MNCs. The keystone of the U.S. approach to transfer pricing regulations, Code Section 482, has been in place since 1917. Section 482 of the Internal Revenue Code gives the power to the Internal Revenue Service to allocate income and expenses among related parties to prevent tax evasion or to clearly reflect the income of each company.

Responding to increasing globalization, overwhelming use of e-commerce transactions and growing international trade in services and intangibles, transfer pricing regulations in the United States have changed several times over the past three decades. In 1994, the United States updated the transfer pricing regulations, and they enforce the arm's-length standard as the overreaching principle in setting transfer prices under Section 482 of the Internal Revenue Code. In 1995, Section 6662 imposed up to a 40 percent penalty on the additional taxes that result from income adjustments due to the failure to comply with Section 482 of the IRC.

As transfer pricing enforcement becomes an ever–higher priority for taxing authorities worldwide, failure to keep its rules and enforcement current is not a viable option for the IRS. The volume of new guidance from the IRS and the court cases seems certain to increase. However, these are also, undeniably, exciting times for transfer pricing consultants and professionals (Burns 2000).

ADVANCE PRICING AGREEMENT
PROGRAMS

The right and acceptable transfer price from a tax authority's perspective is the market or arm's-length price. MNCs may have difficulties to prove that the transfer price was equal to the market price; therefore, they often find themselves in disputes with tax authorities. But now there is a solution. The Advance Pricing Agreement (APA) program gives MNCs an opportunity to avoid costly audits and litigation by allowing them to negotiate in advance with tax authorities regarding the facts, the transfer pricing methodology, and an acceptable range of results. The United States was the first country to adopt substantial penalties relating to transfer pricing and to require that companies maintain detailed documentation of their transfer pricing systems. Many MNCs, fearful of penalties, responded by seeking to reduce risk exposures in the United States.

The benefits do not end with avoiding penalties and gaining certainty. The APA process can actually save MNCs time and money. How? Effective communication, narrowly defined information disclosure, and the nonadversarial nature of the APA process mean that an MNC will spend less time taking this approach versus an examination or litigation. Here are several examples of the benefits of the APA program:

1. For MNCs, they can avoid penalties and gain substantial certainty with respect to how the desired transfer pricing activities will be treated for tax purposes and, in the case of a bilateral APA, how U.S. transfer pricing activities will be treated by foreign tax authorities as well.

2. The APA process provides an environment in which the taxpayer and the competent authorities cooperate to determine which transfer pricing method should apply to transfer pricing activities. The APA process stimulates a free flow of information between all parties involved in the process so as to come to a legally correct and practical and workable result.

3. The APAs offer an opportunity for taxpayers and tax authorities to consider transfer pricing issues in a nonadversarial manner and perhaps be more flexible than in the more confrontational environment of a transfer pricing audit. An APA may be less costly, in time and money, than a full tax audit.

4. The APA can reduce the taxpayer's record-keeping burden. Taxpayers will have to keep records to substantiate only one reasonable methodology (the TPM agreed upon), and generally do not have the burden of keeping all documents potentially relevant to other methodologies that the IRS could consider in an examination.

5. The APA process may help taxpayers avoid extended litigation, subjects the TPM to extensive review, and retains legal merit. Clearly, an APA could assist taxpayers by providing some certainty about future tax treatment of international transactions and therefore aid tax planning.

6. Multilateral APAs should reduce the possibility of double taxation, although this is less likely with unilateral APAs. The APAs could provide tax authorities with a better understanding of an MNC's business and could allow the development of industry skills that would allow better handling of other cases by the tax authorities.

In summary, the advantages of APAs include friendly collaboration between the MNC and IRS, possible avoidance of costly and time-consuming audits and litigation, and the reduction of uncertainty about the tax treatment of international transfer pricing activities.

However, MNCs expose themselves to the following risks by applying for an APA:

1. Unilateral APAs may be a problem because they do not eliminate the possibility of double taxation between countries. For example, MNCs may be encouraged to overallocate income to the APA country and thus create a potential problem in the non-APA countries involved. Where compensating adjustments are used to provide the required result of a unilateral APA, this may cause difficulties with the foreign tax authority in allowing a corresponding adjustment if the arm's-length price is not preserved.
2. Tax authorities may scrutinize the industry and taxpayer-specific information submitted and the annual reports for each taxable year of a MNC covered by the APA.
3. An APA may not be flexible enough to reflect changes in the assumptions such as industry and/or market conditions. What was acceptable transfer pricing method at the time the APA was signed may be quite disadvantageous in later years.
4. An APA program would place a resource burden on tax authorities that may be impossible to handle without diversion of resources from other competing areas of priority. Matching the expected timescales of the taxpayers and the tax authorities would be difficult to achieve.
5. There is a danger that a tax administration will seek more information for an APA than they would under a normal tax audit, and this should be avoided. Other concerns include confidentiality of sensitive information, the misuse of data obtained through an APA, application of the data to earlier years, the effect on competitors, and the difficulties (and costs) of applying an APA program to small MNCs.

Tax authorities all over the world tend to consider transfer pricing as a soft target because of the difficulties involved and the fact that most MNCs are ready to pay. The simultaneous increase in scrutiny of transfer pricing by governments around the world places new pressure on the tax executive of the multinational company. More than ever before, effective management of an MNC's transfer pricing policies requires a global approach in which, perhaps, the greatest danger consists of focusing too closely on the enforcement risks in a single country, or small group of countries, while ignoring equally significant risks in others (Durst 1999).

The APA programs in Canada, France, Germany, Netherlands, Japan, Mexico, the United Kingdom, and the United States vary by degree of complexity and formality. APA programs are more popular with tax authorities than with MNCs. The principal reasons for nonparticipation of many MNCs in the APA include documentation, the costs involved, and confidentiality concerns with the information contained in the documentation.

The Organization for Economic Cooperation and Development (OECD)

An APA is based on article 25 of the OECD Model Tax Convention on Income and Capital, and is an advance agreement on transfer pricing to be applied on cross-border transactions in principle in the future. The OECD (1995) defines the Advance Pricing Agreement (APA) as

> an arrangement that determines, in advance of controlled transactions, an appropriate set of criteria (e.g. method, comparables and appropriate adjustments thereto) for the determination of the transfer pricing for those transactions over a fixed period of time. An APA is formally initiated by a taxpayer and requires negotiations between the taxpayer and one or more tax administrations.

An APA agreement provides the taxpayer not only with certainty on the subject matter in its country of residence but also in another country, regarding the arm's-length remuneration of the group companies involved. Another advantage of an APA is that double taxation issues may be avoided or resolved (Sporken et al. 2001).

Important issues in any APA are the predictions made about the future and the assumptions on which the predictions are based. The OECD suggests that although it may be possible to predict an appropriate method, a target for future transfer prices or profit levels would be less reliable, although ranges of results may be possible. The OECD suggests that APAs may be useful when traditional transfer pricing methods are difficult to apply, when the debate of an MNC arises for allocation of income or profit among related parties, for cost contribution arrangements and for dealing with permanent establishment issues. It is important to know that some countries may be prevented from entering into APAs due to domestic law. However, they may be able to conclude an APA under the mutual agreement procedure if a relevant tax treaty is in force.

Clearly, bilateral or multilateral APAs are to be preferred to unilateral arrangements. However, the OECD suggests that where unilateral arrangements are negotiated, the other affected tax authorities should be informed as early as possible to determine whether they are willing to consider a bilateral arrangement.

As part of the negotiation of an APA, an MNC would be required to provide its view of the most appropriate transfer pricing methodology supported by appropriate documents, which may include a functional analysis and examples of any appropriate comparables. The tax administration will still retain a transfer pricing audit responsibility to ensure that the material facts are unchanged and that APA conditions have been followed.

Due to the recent introduction of APA programs by many member countries, the OECD has had a number of discussions on the APA process and is proposing in the next months to work out guidelines on how to implement APAs. However, in the current Transfer Pricing Guidelines, the OECD reserves its recommendation and does not encourage the expansion of such programs. The OECD suggests that if programs are developed, then multilateral rather than unilateral APAs should be the priority and that countries using APAs should coordinate their procedures and that access should be available to all MNCs or taxpayers. Unfortunately, the OECD guidelines on the APA fall short of actively encouraging the expansion of APA program but intend to monitor their use by those countries who choose to use them.

Canada

In March 2001, the Canada Customs and Revenue Agency (CCRA) issued its Information Circular IC94-4R, which sets out the new international transfer pricing rules as they apply to APAs. The APA program is designed to help taxpayers confirm acceptable transfer pricing methodologies for transactions in which they participate with nonresidents with whom they do not deal at arm's length. The CCRA provides APAs as an administrative service; there is no legal requirement to enter into one. Given that most APAs are expected to involve the United States, it is not surprising that the Canadian APA process is very similar to that in the United States. Nearly all the APAs currently being pursued with CCRA involve Canadian–U.S. transactions.

The APA program was originally introduced in 1993 with the stated intent of avoiding double taxation, helping taxpayers determine appropriate transfer pricing methodologies for non–arm's-length transactions, and serving to resolve transfer pricing disputes. Since 1994, the Canadian Tax authority has been seeking input from taxpayers, tax practitioners, and other specialists regarding ways to improve the existing APA program. These inputs resulted in the release of last year's circular, which the contributing parties hoped would resolve a number of issues and present a more beneficial program.

However, the Revised Advance Pricing Arrangements outlined in the circular fall short of the Canadian government's promises to make APAs less expensive, less time-consuming, and generally more appealing to business. An APA remains an in-depth audit process rather than an instrument of negotiation or a critical analysis procedure. The process needs to become simpler, less expensive, and more practical for a much greater number of MNCs, so as to offer a level playing field across the board without consideration of size and sophistication (Swaneveld, Przysuski, and Nagaraian 2002a).

In the Canadian transfer pricing regulations, despite years of user and professional input, the process and documentation have not been modified to the extent where they address four overarching issues: cost, privacy, provincial audits, and double taxation. Let us examine these in turn. A fast-track APA process, similar to the one offered by the IRS-U.S. and that would not necessarily rely on an army of experts, would be extremely beneficial for smaller businesses. Unfortunately, this concept was not presented in the government's revised APA program (Ibid.).

Although the government's position is that the APA process is separate from the audit process, the reality is that if a taxpayer backs out of the APA process, an examination would likely be triggered. During this examination, the auditors will thoroughly scrutinize all available sources of information, including that gathered through the APA process. As a consequence, an aborted APA application invites at least the risk of a loss of privacy (Ibid.).

Tax disputes involving two or more treaty countries giving rise to an issue of double taxation are often resolved through discussions between the competent authorities under the mutual agreement procedure of most tax treaties. Canadian MNCs that have been reassessed have the choice of disputing the reassessments in the domestic appeals branch of Canada Custom and Revenue Agency (CCRA) and/or submitting the case to the competent authorities (*Canada* 2002). The good news is that more companies are doing more business in more countries every day. The bad news is that governments are finding it challenging to manage the compliance issues—and examinations are becoming increasingly arduous. MNCs are required to do more work, provide more information, and gather more documentation. The process is becoming longer, more complicated, and more expensive (Swaneveld, Przysuski, and Nagarian 2002b).

In October 1994, Revenue Canada reached agreement with Australia, Japan, and the United States on common procedures for Bilateral Advance Pricing Arrangements.

France

On September 7, 1999, the French tax authorities issued instructions establishing an APA procedures helping MNCs to obtain the agreement of tax authorities on the method of determining their transfer prices. The agreement is effective only for the future and for a limited period. During the examination stage of this procedure, the tax authorities can conduct a tax audit. Generally, the procedure is initiated by the taxpayer, which must submit all documentation that could substantiate the reasonableness of the method of transfer pricing used, as well as its consistency with the arm's-length standard. Negotiations then take place between the taxpayer and the French tax authorities.

Pursuant to the instruction of September 7, 1999, France offers the possibility of requesting a bilateral APA, provided that the other country has signed a treaty with France that contains a clause relating to article 25-3 of the OECD treaty. However, to date, the French tax authorities have not granted any APAs, although at least one multilateral APA request is pending (Sporken et al. 2001).

Germany

In August 2000, German tax authorities issued section 3 of the proposed regulations on transfer pricing documentation and procedures. The Ministry of Finance has released a first draft of the "Principles for the Examination of Income Allocation between Multinational Enterprises with Respect to the Treatment of Income Adjustments, Audit Procedures and Advance Pricing Agreements." Those regulations apply to tax audits covering fiscal year 1999 and subsequent years. The draft circular is intended to replace sections 8 and 9 of the present Administrative Principles (AP) of 1983. The draft circular focuses strongly on the procedural aspects of transfer pricing compliance and audits and covers advance pricing agreements. The final regulations under German law will not constitute binding law for taxpayers or courts, but will bind instead the tax administration (Borstell and Wellens 2000).

The draft circular contains three different sections. The first section on the proposed treatment of income adjustments is technical and only slightly updates the AP of 1983. The second section on audit procedures and taxpayer cooperation dramatically tightens German documentation requirements and compliance standards, and puts a very significant documentation burden on German MNCs. The third section on advance pricing agreements is very much restricted to basic observations on procedural matters and the legal basis for APAs (Borstell and Wellens 2000).

So far, most of the completed APA cases have been unilateral. Although a few bilateral APAs are known to have been commenced, it is unclear whether any ever proceeded to completion. By far, a considerable number of unilateral APAs have been finalized. Most situations lending themselves to resolution via an APA are multilateral in nature. Unfortunately, there are great practical difficulties of multilateral APAs that open the door to the question of whether a series of unilateral APAs is not the more realistic alternative.

Japan

Japan's APA system was introduced on April 24, 1987, by a separate circular "Concerning the Confirmation of the Method to Compute the Arm's Length Price Etc." It represented the first example anywhere in the world of an advance agreement system set up to determine arm's-length prices between tax authorities and taxpayers. The system is an administrative procedure under which the Japanese tax authorities may confirm that the prices of controlled intercompany cross-border transactions proposed by a taxpayer are established on an arm's-length standard. It is completely voluntary in nature and can be filed with regard to all or a portion of the taxpayer's business transactions. In Japan, there is an increasing trend of willingness of MNCs to make bilateral APA applications (Miyamoto, Yoast, and Noble 1999).

In general, a Japanese taxpayer may initiate APA system negotiations by submitting a request for confirmation of the transfer pricing method to be used in combination with a foreign related business transaction to the tax office with jurisdiction over the taxpayer. Under the 1987 circular, the APA system is limited to addressing the following two issues (Ibid.): the most reasonable method that the MNC might adopt to compute its transfer prices, and the documentation that would support that the taxpayer's proposed methodology is in fact the most reasonable transfer pricing method.

In practice, the majority of filled applications for the APA system by MNCs are bilateral in nature, even though the Japanese legislation has not been amended to include provisions for bilateral APA system agreements. Moreover, the Japanese tax authorities encourage bilateral discussions unless there is a good reason for using a unilateral request (Ibid.).

Mexico

Under Mexican tax law, companies with related-party transactions have the option of requesting an APA from the tax authorities, to mutually agree on several issues, including the transfer pricing method to be used and the profit margins to be obtained in all business transactions carried out with related parties. Given the significant tax penalties and adjustments that may result from a transfer pricing dispute, there is a substantial incentive to negotiate transfer prices with the Mexican tax authority (Narvaez-Hasfura and Torrey 2002).

In practice, the use of the APA mechanisms has been limited to MNCs engaged in specific manufacturing companies usually located along the border with the United States. However, as Mexican transfer pricing tax audits and controversies intensify, it is more likely that other MNCs will try to take advantage of using the APA system for their intracompany or related business transactions. The good news for MNCs is the strong advances made by the Mexican tax authority's APA program to improve the flexibility of the system to deal with a numerous of companies and industries, to improve the communication and negotiation with foreign tax authorities that will eventually result in an increase the likelihood that the APA program will extend to include many other companies (Narvaez-Hasfura and Torrey 2002).

Netherlands

In 1994, the Dutch secretary of finance had already introduced the APA process in the Netherlands under the APA regulations. However, effective April 1, 2001, a new APA decree was introduced. The APA decree is based on the OECD APA guidelines. The Dutch decree provides a detailed list of what should be included in the request and APA itself. The duration will be four to five years, unless another period is considered to be reasonable. APAs can also have a retroactive effect. APAs will be possible bilaterally, multilaterally (involving several countries), or unilaterally. An application for an APA must meet the requirements of the Dutch transfer pricing regulations (Sporken et al. 2001).

The United Kingdom

In 1999, the U.K. Inland Revenue introduced a statutory procedure for advance pricing agreements (APAs). It also published a Statement of Practice explaining how APAs are administered and providing detailed guidelines about how the Inland Revenue interprets the legislation and how it intends to apply the legislation in practice. The APA process will have four stages: an expression of interest, a formal submission of an application for clarification, an evaluation, and an agreement. In October 1999, the Inland Revenue published further guidance to provide an outline of what might be expected to happen generally in bilateral APA applications in order to assist U.K. taxpayers when considering making such an application (Sporken et al. 2001).

Following the OECD guidelines, bilateral and multilateral APAs are preferred to unilateral agreements. The term is three to five years, with renewals possible. Rollbacks will be considered, and, if an audit is ongoing, in appropriate circumstances APAs can be used to deal with those audit issues. In general, an APA can be unilateral or bilateral. However, the Inland Revenue has stated that it encourages bilateral APAs, as this avoids potential double taxation and provides assurance that the methods for dealing with cross-border transactions covered in the APA will be accepted by both tax authorities.

The major differences between U.K. and U.S. APAs (Borkowski 2000) are as follows:

1. The IRS-U.S. allows for MNCs only transactions between related taxpayers, whereas Inland Revenue also includes foreign branch transactions, attribution on income to a permanent establishment, and purely domestic APAs.
2. The United Kingdom limits APAs to large MNC cases, whereas the IRS encourages MNCs of any size and complexity to participate in the APA program.
3. The IRS-U.S. encourages rollbacks whenever feasible, whereas the Inland Revenue states that a rollback is an appropriate means of resolving a transfer pricing issue in earlier years.
4. The IRS-U.S. maintains confidentiality of MNC APA information, whereas Inland Revenue states clearly that information provided in the APA process can and will be public information and used in other cases when appropriate.

The United States

The United States was the first country to respond to domestic political pressures for tax enforcement of MNCs in the 1980s and early 1990s and adopted new regulations designed to make enforcement easier, to adopt substantial penalties relating to transfer pricing, and to require that companies maintain detailed documentation of their transfer pricing policies. Many MNCs, fearful of penalties, responded by seeking to reduce risk exposures in the United States (Durst 1999, 57).

In 1991, the IRS released the official procedures for obtaining an APA in Revenue Procedure 91-22. The IRS's APA Program is designed to provide MNCs an opportunity to avoid costly audits and litigation by allowing them to negotiate a prospective agreement with the IRS regarding the facts, the transfer pricing methodology, and an acceptable range of results. The program is aimed at MNCs interested in avoiding penalties, managing risk, and determining their tax liability with a high degree of certainty (Wrappe, Milani, and Joy 1999). In 1995, the IRS explained the general objectives of the APA program as follows:

1. Help MNCs to arrive at an understanding with the IRS on three basic issues: the factual nature of the intercompany transactions to which the APA applies, an appropriate transfer pricing methodology (TPM) applicable to those transactions and the expected range of results from applying the TPM to the transactions. However, in appropriate cases, the IRS will consider APAs that set forth a TPM without the specification of any range.
2. Encourage common understanding and cooperation between the taxpayers and the IRS and that harmonizes and incorporates the opinions and views of all the IRS functions involved with the taxpayer.
3. Agree in an expedited fashion, as compared with the traditional method, which entails separate and distinct dealings with the Examination, Appeals, and Competent Authority functions and/or possible subsequent litigation.
4. Agree in a cost-effective fashion for both the taxpayer and the IRS.

Therefore, the APA program's goal is to agree upon the best method to calculate arm's-length prices, which allows MNCs to determine the acceptable transfer price and, ultimately, their tax liability with certainty. An APA will result in no surprises for the MNC. Because the IRS has agreed prospectively, MNCs will not find themselves involved in transfer pricing disputes later as long as they comply with the agreement, which can cover as many as five years and can also be applied to prior years.

Another major time-saver is the fact that the taxpayer and the IRS agree in advance what information is relevant to the taxpayer's transfer pricing decision. Without an APA, taxpayers would have to maintain documentation sufficient to demonstrate that other transfer pricing methodologies are less appropriate (Wrappe, Milani, and Joy 1999).

If an MNC pursues an APA, they will be working with transfer pricing professionals trained in negotiation skills. The IRS APA team is committed to hearing the taxpayer's side of the story through this interactive process. They are motivated to settle cases because the IRS recognizes the need to resolve transfer pricing disputes more efficiently. Both the IRS and taxpayer APA teams have a team leader. In addition, an economist and an international examiner participate on the IRS's APA team. On the taxpayer's APA team are the lead negotiator, a transfer pricing specialist (typically the same person), an economist, and a director of tax who is responsible for factual content. As you can see, there are three disciplines at work—legal, accounting, and economics—and if you get these three to agree, most likely you have a good deal.

In 1996, the IRS revised the procedures involved in securing an APA. Here is our guide to the phases of the APA process.

1. Prefiling conference. Before you formally request an APA, you may want to participate in one or more prefiling conferences to explore whether the program is right for you. These conferences center on MNC business operations, past transfer pricing practices, and potential problems with the APA process.
2. Evaluation and negotiation. The IRS's APA team initially evaluates your request within 45 days of receiving it. Within 60 days of receipt, the two teams agree to a case plan and schedule. After the IRS team receives any additional information from you, it evaluates the information to determine the appropriate transfer pricing method and an acceptable range of market prices. The IRS team then attempts to reach an informal decision on your request, which is followed by a formal agreement.
3. Administration and renewal. Once you finalize the agreement, you must file an annual report, which demonstrates good faith compliance with the terms and conditions of the APA; calculate compensating adjustments, if any (tax reporting adjustments that are made to comply with the terms of the APA); and maintain books and records sufficient to help the IRS to examine your compliance with the APA.

SUMMARY AND CONCLUSIONS

This chapter has analyzed and discussed two important issues of transfer pricing: arm's-length standard and advance pricing agreement programs in selected countries. It covered comparative analysis of several selected countries of each continent; however, it concentrated on the countries that are important to the executive officers of American multinational companies. The Organization for Economic Cooperation and Development (OECD) guidelines on transfer pricing issues were used in the comparative analysis of the selected countries.

With respect to the arm's-length standard of transfer pricing, the United States has been the historic leader in establishing the standard as the recognized principle for determining cross-border transfer pricing and the allocation of profits between related subsidiaries of MNCs. Responding to the increasing globalization, overwhelming use of e-commerce transactions, and growing international trade in services and intangibles, transfer pricing regulations in the United States have changed several times over the past three decades. In 1994, the United States updated their transfer pricing regulations, and they enforce the arm's-length standard as the overreaching principle in setting transfer prices under Section 482 of the Internal Revenue Code. Many foreign tax authorities have followed the lead of IRS-U.S. as a model, adopting and enforcing similar arm's-length standards.

In 1995, the OECD adopted parallel arm's-length transfer pricing principles in the first major update of its 1979 transfer pricing guidelines. These revised guidelines provide an internationally accepted statement of principles and methods that are broadly similar in scope and standards to the U.S. tax regulations (Miesel, Higinbotham, and Yi 2002). Even though there are some differences, the guidelines are generally consistent with Section 482 of the IRC on transfer pricing regulations.

Canada, France, Germany, Japan, Mexico,, the Netherlands, Mexico and the United Kingdom all (seek to) adhere to the OECD guidelines. Until recently, these countries had worked largely within the existing statutory framework. However, in 1998, Canada tried to blend its transfer pricing legislation with the 1995 OECD guidelines. However, the new legislation indicates that neither the OECD guidelines nor the transfer pricing methods that the OECD indicated could produce an arm's-length standard.

France strengthened its tax authorities' powers in 1996 and imposed new obligations on taxpayers. The United Kingdom implemented specific transfer pricing legislation in 1998/1999 and fully incorporated OECD guidelines into the U.K. legislation. The Netherlands issued a transfer pricing decree in March 2001 based on the arm's-length principle and OECD guidelines. In Germany many transfer pricing regulations have and will be introduced. Whereas the U.K. legislation makes a specific reference to the OECD, and so will the Dutch legislation in the near future, France and Germany do not. France, Germany, and the United Kingdom in particular have chosen to make their own specific transfer pricing (related) legislation. The Netherlands at present still has the least in terms of transfer pricing rules, but this will change in the near future. The Dutch ministry would like to keep the transfer pricing system open and flexible, but it is still to be seen as to whether this will be the case in practice (Sporken et al. 2001).

The tax authorities in France, Germany, Japan, the Netherlands, Mexico, and the United Kingdom are all in the process of modernizing their countries transfer pricing machinery to adhere to the OECD guidelines and better defend their share of tax revenues in both a European and global economy. This process will not necessarily be for the benefit of the multinational companies, as they will face ever-increasing transfer pricing compliance burdens and difficulties to prove that the transfer price is equal to the market price; therefore, they often find themselves in disputes with tax authorities. In the near future, the number of transfer pricing disputes and cases before the courts will increase, but now there is a solution. The APA programs with tax authorities will give MNCs an opportunity to avoid costly tax audits and litigation by allowing them to negotiate in advance with tax authorities regarding the facts, the transfer pricing methodology, and the acceptance range of results, and, then, the number of APAs will further increase significantly.

REFERENCES

Ackerman, Robert E., and John Hobster. 2002. Managing transfer pricing audit risks. *The CPA Journal* 72, no. 2 (February): 57–59.

Borkowski, Susan C. 2000. Transfer pricing advance pricing agreements: Current status by country. *The International Tax Journal* 26, no. 2 (spring): 1–16.

Borstell, Thomas, and Ludger Wellens. 2000. Germany draft threatens heavy burden. *International Tax Review* 11, no. 4 (April): 11–14.

Burns, Paul. 2000. United States. *International Tax Review* (London): 131–37.

Canada: Resolving transfer pricing disputes. 2002. *International Tax Review* 13, no. 8 (September): 62.

Dodge, Bill, and Giovanni DiCenso. 2002. Global transfer pricing developments. *International Tax Review* 13, no. 5 (May): 49–51.

Durst, Michael C. 1999. United States. *International Tax Review* (February): 56–62.

Felgran, Steven D., and Mito Yamada. 2001. Transfer pricing: A truly global concern. *Financial Executive* (Morristown, N.J.) (November): 21–27.

Greenhill, Mitchell, and Charles W. Bee, Jr. 1996. Transfer pricing guidelines issued by the OECD. *The Tax Adviser* (May): 265–66.

Haigh, Ronald E. 2002. The operation of the mutual agreement procedure in the United Kingdom. *Tax Management International Journal* 13, no. 10 (October 11): 499–508.

Hobster, John. 2002. European transfer pricing: At the crossroads? *Journal of International Taxation* 13, no. 7 (July): 55–57.

Lewis, David, and Lisa Lim. 2002. How companies approach transfer pricing in the Asia-Pacific. *International Tax Review* 13, no. 8 (September): 37–40.

Miesel, Victor H., Harlow H. Higinbotham, and Chun W Yi. 2002. International transfer pricing: Practical solutions for intercompany pricing. *The International Tax Journal* 28, no. 4 (fall): 1–22.

Miyamoto, Akio, Dean Yoost, and Greg Noble. 1999. Japanese APAs hit their stride. *International Tax Review* 10, no. 4 (April): 39–43.

Narvaez-Hasfura, Jorge, and Eric Torrey. 2002. Mexican transfer pricing under the microscope. *International Tax Review* 13, no. 7 (July/August): 37–38.

Organization for Economic Cooperation and Development Committee (OECD). 1995. *Transfer Pricing Guidelines for Multinational Enterprises and Tax Administrations.* Paris: OECD.

Park, William W. 2002. Income tax treaty arbitration. *Tax Management International Journal* 13, no. 5 (May 10): 219–53.

Schmitz, Annette E., and Gesa Korner. 2000. Recent developments in transfer pricing. *Corporate Finance,* Supplement to Germany Meets the Challenges (London) (May): 41–43.

Sporken, Eduard, Alexander Vogele, William Bader, and Pascal Luquete. 2001. Transfer pricing in Europe: OECD versus local practice. *International Tax Review* 12, no.9 (October): 46–53.

Swaneveld, Hendrik, Martin Przysuski, and Venkat Nagaraian. 2002a. Canada's
    APA program falls short of promises. *International Tax Review* 13, no. 6
    (June): 42–44.
——. 2002b. Getting the most out of Canada's protocol regime. *International Tax
    Review* 13, no. 8 (September): 47–48.
Valdes, Miguel, William Hahn, and Nicolas Muniz. 1999. Mexico builds on
    promising start. *International Tax Review* 10, no. 7 (July/August): 53–57.
Vogele, Alexander, and William Bader. 2002. New deal for German transfer
    pricing. *International Tax Review* 13, no. 2 (February): 22–27.
Wrappe, Steven C., Ken Milani, and Julie Joy. 1999. The transfer price is right . . . or
    is it? *Strategic Finance* (July): 38–43.

10

Documentation and Penalties of Transfer Pricing in Selected Countries

Global transfer pricing for competitive advantage must achieve certain objectives for MNCs while adapting to local and international trade policies and tax regulations. Operating in the global environment makes the rules and strategies of the transfer pricing system dynamic. As many governments incorporate new tax rules and more rigorously enforce current transfer price regulations, the need to develop a responsive documented transfer pricing system becomes increasingly important. Decision-makers of MNCs must continually refine components of their transfer pricing systems to reflect current and potential environmental influences.

An MNC is expected to have sufficient transfer pricing documentation of intracompay transactions including e-commerce to support and prove compliance with the arm's-length standard and to avoid the risk of transfer pricing penalties. In addition, it has to maintain updated and convincing documents about its e-commerce or industry practice and current market conditions of all countries involved. To prove a consistent compliance with multiple jurisdictions, a global transfer pricing documentation system may be the best choice for an MNC (Abdallah 2002).

For governments, the common features of a transfer pricing regulation include adoption of the arm's-length pricing principle, requirement of extensive documentation in support of the transfer pricing methods to determine prices, and imposition of stringent penalties for noncompliance. Moreover, with the globalization of MNCs and rapid expansion in the cross-border flow of digitized goods, services, and technology, national tax authorities have been addressing transfer-pricing issues with increasing scrutiny, documentation, and penalties. Above all, three elements have drastically increased the burden and complexity of transfer pricing issues: the 1994 revision of the regulations under Section 482 of the IRC, complementary measures such as the penalties in Code Section 6662 set forth in 1994, and parallel initiatives by foreign tax authorities and the OECD since 1995. They also dramatically push MNCs to establish or declare their intercompany transfer pricing methods at the time a return is filed (contemporaneous documentation) (Miesel et al. 2002).

In June 2002, the Pacific Association of Tax Administrators (PATA), which includes Australia, Canada, Japan, and the United States as its members, issued a proposal to harmonize transfer pricing documentation requirements. The objectives of the proposal are

- to reduce transfer pricing compliance costs and burdens.
- to promote the efficient and equitable operation of the tax systems.
- to facilitate the efficient preparation and maintenance of transfer pricing documentation thereby enabling the timely production of such information upon request by tax auditors.
- to create and maintain a single package of transfer pricing records and documentation in order to satisfy the transfer pricing documentation of all PATA members (Lyons and Fernandez 2002).

In this chapter, two of the most important transfer pricing issues are analyzed and discussed. The first section focuses on documentation of transfer pricing of the selected countries and the Organization for Economic Cooperation and Development (OECD) as a basis for MNCs to justify that their transfer pricing strategies are consistent with the arm's-length standard. Section two covers penalties imposed by tax authorities for false information, underpayment attributable to a substantial valuation misstatement, failure to keep proper records, failure to file, late filing, and any other violation or tax abuse of transfer pricing regulations.

DOCUMENTATION OF TRANSFER PRICING

Documentation of transfer pricing has become an important issue, as MNCs need to justify that their transfer pricing methods are consistent with the arm's-length standard. At the same time documentation of transfer pricing is often considered as just an annoying aspect of tax compliance to be accomplished with as little effort and attention as possible. Tax authorities' requirements that taxpayers maintain documentation of their transfer pricing methods appear to be spreading fast. Moreover, the documentation should present a detailed description of the circumstances surrounding the intercompany business transactions and an analysis of their implication for each country or tax jurisdiction.

When a tax authority asks an MNC about its transfer pricing system, the taxpayer should be able to explain why the documentation it provided was appropriate, instead of having to begin by discrediting its own documentation. For MNCs, transfer pricing documentation is a significant issue. Four important questions should be answered, or at least highlighted, by MNCs' financial officers, accountants, and lawyers as they prepare transfer pricing documentation:

1. Can the MNCs' documentation satisfy the IRS without creating exposure with other foreign governments?
2. Do the MNCs have to produce separate documents for each country? If separate documents are necessary, are competent authority proceedings or treaty requests likely to mean that each government will see the documentation prepared for the other?
3. Can any government use any differences to reject the documentation produced for its use?
4. Does one set of documentation fit all or do specific facts and circumstances prevail for every country?

The Organization for Economic Cooperation and Development

The OECD (1995) guidelines provide extensive discussion on the documentation to be obtained from MNCs in connection with a transfer pricing system. The OECD (1995) guidelines suggest that MNCs should make reasonable efforts when establishing their transfer pricing policies to determine whether their transfer pricing results meet the arm's-length standard. The OECD (1995) also recognizes that tax authorities should have the right to obtain the documentation to verify compliance with the arm's-length price. The 1995 guidelines encourage member countries to administer penalty systems in a manner that is fair and not unduly onerous for MNCs.

Canada

The most significant change on the T106 of the Canadian regulations on transfer pricing is that taxpayers can no longer maintain a wait-and-see attitude concerning transfer pricing documentation. For the first time, they must specifically indicate whether up-to-date documentation has been prepared for non–arm's-length transactions with each nonresident. Obviously, a "No" response is likely to invite closer scrutiny by Revenue Canada (Zorzi 1999).

For MNCs, it is important to review their current transfer pricing methods and documentation to ensure that they are in line with the Canadian regulations. If there are gaps, certain tax planning strategies should be implemented to help them avoid lengthy tax audits, large reassessments, and costly penalties for their companies.

The new legislation introduced a requirement for contemporaneous documentation. Under the new rules, all taxpayers that conduct a minimum of $1 million in cross-border business transactions are required to have specified contemporaneous documentation. This documentation consists of six categories of information, including (Swaneveld et al. 2002):

1. Descriptions of the products or services sold.
2. Terms and conditions of the transaction, and how they relate to the terms and conditions of other transactions entered into between the business and the non–arm's-length nonresident.
3. All the organizations involved in the transaction and their relationships.
4. An assessment of the risks assumed by each party, the functions performed, any intangibles involved, and the capital employed in the transaction.
5. The organization must provide a description of the pricing policy established between the nonresident and the Canadian party. As well as describe the specific transfer pricing methodology used, the documentation must explain the rationale for selecting that method.
6. Assumptions, strategies, and policies that influenced the determination of the transfer price.

The specific amount and type of contemporaneous documentation expected depends on the size of the MNCs involved, the sizes and types of business transactions, and the transfer pricing methods selected. The documentation must be available at the same time when tax returns are due; for MNCs, this is six months after the end of the tax year (Ibid.).

France

The French tax authorities, in the context of a tax audit, have the right to ask the taxpayer for information on its transfer pricing policy. If the tax authorities have gathered the evidence giving rise to the presumption that the enterprise made an indirect transfer of profit, the audited taxpayer is obligated to keep substantial documentation, while at the same time the scope of the tax authorities' investigation is limited to the following specific list of issues (Sporken et al. 2001):

- The relations between the French and foreign MNCs.
- The method of determining the transfer prices between the companies—the company must be able to justify the method used and provide adequate documentation in support of its choice. The methods included in the OECD guidelines are recognized by the French tax authorities.
- The nature of the activities carried out by the associated foreign enterprise.
- The local tax treatment applied to the related or associated company, where the French company owns more than 50 percent of its stocks or runs it directly.

If the enterprise's replies are considered inadequate, it mainly runs the risk of the tax authorities evaluating the amount of the transfers on the basis of the information in its possession as well as imposing a fine per financial year covered by the request (Ibid.).

Germany

On October 17, 2003, the new regulations of the German Transfer Pricing Documentation Law were approved. The new documentation regulations follow the OECD guidelines and international standards; they were made effective retroactively to January 1, 2003. They may roll back in certain cases to pre-2003 years. According to the new regulations, the taxpayer is subject to documentation requirements if the taxpayer is engaged in cross-border business with related parties and shall produce evidence of having dealt with the related party under arm's-length conditions (Voegele and Brem 2003).

Under the current regulation, the taxpayer is required to prepare comprehensive documentation as to whether, and to what extent, the transactions between related parties are at arm's-length price. Moreover, the regulations enable the tax auditor to issue the rebuttable presumption that the transfer price in question is not at arm's length. If the taxpayer cannot rebut such a presumption, the tax administration is empowered to estimate the taxable income. If the documentation does not exist, a minimal penalty of $5,800 may be applied, and it may be increased to up to 10 percent of the adjusted income of the company (Ibid.).

In general, the documentation requirements are derived from the obligation of German taxpayers to cooperate with the tax authorities when determining the conditions that might be of importance for examining the case of income allocation. An important extended obligation is to provide appropriate documents in cases of business transactions with foreign related entities. The documentation should include information about group structure, products and services, markets, existing agreements, and transfer pricing method. As contemporaneous documentation is required, documents will have to be updated on a continual basis.

All documents should provide the tax authorities with an understanding of the mechanism and decision process for establishing transfer prices. If a company fails to provide adequate documentation, the tax authorities can make estimations of the profit of the German company (Schmitz and Korner 2000).

The new rules on transfer pricing documentation require taxpayers to maintain records for all transactions involving cross-border related parties, as well as cross-border profit allocations between headquarters and permanent establishments (Ernst and Young 2003). The regulations also include the economic and legal basis for agreements pertaining to prices and other business transactions with related parties based on the arm's-length price. It may be concluded that the German transfer pricing documentation rules comply, for the most part, with the OECD guidelines.

In general, the documentation requirements by the regulations are intended to assist the German tax authorities' understanding of the taxpayers' cross-border related party transactions and in deciding whether and to what extent income has been calculated according to the arm's-length standard. For MNCs to comply with the new German documentation requirements and to avoid penalties and double taxation, transfer pricing documentation must include description of the transaction, functional analysis, selection of most appropriate transfer pricing method, economic analysis and documentation of the arm's-length price, and appendices with all supporting information (Ibid.).

Japan

Generally, the National Tax Administration (NTA) has adhered to the OECD guidelines of documentation in creating its regulations. Although Japanese taxpayers are not required to maintain documentation, a penalty of 10 percent of the additional tax due may be imposed if an adjustment is made, and the penalty is increased to 15 percent if the additional tax due is more than 500,000 yen or more than the amount of tax paid on the original return, whichever is greater. Moreover, in fraud cases, a 35 percent penalty may be charged separately. It is expected that the regulations will become stricter in the next few years as the government reviews current regulations to possibly bring Japanese transfer pricing taxation in line with other countries' transfer pricing rules (Felgran and Yamada 2001).

In 2003, a new tax reform revised the Detailed Statement Regarding Foreign Related Companies. The new revision requires taxpayers to describe the transfer pricing methodologies used to calculate the arm's-length prices of each of their cross-border related party transactions and to furnish information used as the basis for deriving the arm's-length prices. The requirements apply to final returns for years beginning on and after April 1, 2003. In substance, the revised requirement may require taxpayers to provide detailed analysis and documentation of controlled transactions with their foreign affiliates. Therefore, for years beginning on and after April 1, 2003, this may mean the introduction of a transfer pricing documentation rule for taxpayers in Japan (Asian 2003).

Recently, the Pacific Association of Tax Administrators (PATA) developed proposed uniform transfer pricing documentation requirements (Pacific 2002). PATA members include Japan, the United States, Australia, and Canada. PATA members are seeking comments on the proposal. PATA members have agreed on principles under which taxpayers can create uniform transfer pricing documentation so that one set of documentation can meet their respective transfer pricing documentation provisions (PATA documentation package) and thus eliminate the need to prepare different documentation for each country. The PATA documentation package is a voluntary procedure that, if satisfied, will protect taxpayers in each of the four countries from otherwise applicable transfer pricing documentation penalties (Benson, O'Connor, and Hester 2002). Unfortunately, the proposal does not achieve its goal of reducing the compliance burden.

Mexico

At the time Mexican taxpayers file their tax return, they must have the transfer pricing documentation ready. Moreover, the MNC will need to conduct a transfer pricing study and provide an opinion by its certified public accountants that the taxpayer has complied with the formal requirements of the transfer pricing regulations. Unfortunately, Mexico's transfer pricing documentation requirements are among the most restricted in the world. Two important issues must be considered: which international intercompany transactions must be documented, and the potential conflict between taxpayers and their outside accountants that is caused by the documentation requirements (Valdes, Hahn, and Muniz 1999).

In general, the Mexican transfer pricing documentation rules have achieved their objective of providing tax authorities with effective ways to closely monitor those transactions undertaken by Mexican MNCs with their foreign related parties—provided the Mexican tax authorities take all necessary steps to make sure that their transfer pricing regulations cover most of the unpredictable needs of MNCs operating in Mexico. In contrast to the countries that have adopted formal transfer pricing rules, Mexico is one of the few countries in the world that requires taxpayers to satisfy certain documentation requirements with regard to transactions undertaken by their residents with foreign related parties. In other words, business intercompany transactions among Mexican residents do not have to be documented, although all transactions (whether with foreign or domestic related parties) are to be determined based on the arm's-length standard (Ibid.).

For income tax purposes, only large companies are required to document their transactions with foreign related parties. Taxpayers entitled to make quarterly income tax payments are generally not required to prepare the documentation, unless the transactions are with entities located in low income-tax countries. An MNC that fails to provide documentation with regard to its intracompany transactions will risk a tax audit during the five years following the filing of the corresponding tax return.

Mexican tax authorities should consider adopting certain rules that will make the transfer pricing rules in Mexico more flexible, such as eliminating the need for transfer pricing documentation for transactions with foreign related parties that are below a certain threshold amount, especially for smaller taxpayers. Furthermore, the tax authorities may provide taxpayers with further guidance as to other matters, including the method of determining an arm's-length standard for transactions involving intangible property, the use of non-Mexican databases in order to identify comparable entities, and the use of an unspecified method in cases where the use of any of the other specified methods does not result in an arm's-length standard (Valdes, Hahn, and Muniz 1999).

Netherlands

The Dutch Ministry of Finance published their transfer pricing regulations effective April 1, 2001, also with the objective of codifying the arm's-length principle later in 2001. Documentation requirements were expected to be introduced before the end of 2001. The latter wish is primarily driven by the fact that the Dutch tax authorities have lately not been too successful in the Dutch courts in winning most of the transfer pricing cases (Sporken et al. 2001).

Section 86 of the Corporate Income Tax Act requires taxpayers to have available sufficient information to show how the transfer prices were established and from which it can be determined whether the prices satisfy the arm's-length price. Part of the objective behind this provision is to ensure that information concerning the transfer pricing system will become available in Netherlands to enable the Dutch tax authorities to test the transactions by reference to the arm's-length standard (Rutges, Sporken, and Larking 2002).

If a transfer pricing correction is made, it is the taxable profit in Netherlands that will be primarily increased. Moreover, interest for late payment will always be due, albeit at a very low interest rate. Penalties may be charged on any additional tax due.

The United Kingdom

In the United Kingdom, supporting documentation for transfer pricing systems needs to be prepared and preserved in accordance with the OECD guidelines of prudent business management. The Inland Revenue has issued guidance as to the required level of documentation. In addition, the OECD guidelines documentation standard, as detailed in chapter 5 of the guidelines, is to be used in interpreting the U.K. documentation requirements for transfer pricing. Under the new regime, taxpayers are expected to keep a level of documentation commensurate with the requirement of prudent business management (Sporken et al. 2001).

The Inland Revenue issued guidance on documentation requirements stating that the extent of the documentation needs to be reasonable, given the complexity of the relevant transaction and should cover, at least, the following items:

- Information on relevant commercial or financial relations falling within the scope of the new regulations
- The nature and terms of relevant transactions (including transfer prices and related party transaction)
- The method(s) by which the nature and terms of relevant business intracompany transactions were arrived at, including any study of comparables and any functional analysis undertaken
- How the selected method has resulted in arm's-length prices

The new statutory arrangements do not require additional documentation to be prepared, provided the existing documentation is sufficient to enable the company to make a complete return under corporate tax self-assessment. Documentation should exist at the time that a tax return is made and should be retained for at least six years (Sporken et al. 2001).

The United States

Recent trends of tax authorities around the world have caused the tax executive to take an increasingly multinational approach to the problem of international transfer pricing. Gradually, countries around the world are developing more uniform approaches to transfer pricing documentation. However, there remains substantial variation in transfer pricing documentation and practices among countries. Therefore, MNCs must design their transfer pricing policies and documentation to fit the unique international operating structure and tax enforcement and the specific rules and enforcement practices of the countries in which they conduct business.

Under the provisions of Section 6662(e) applicable to 1990 through 1992, the years under consideration in DHL, a taxpayer could avoid the penalty if it showed that there was a reasonable cause for the taxpayer's determination of such price and that the taxpayer acted in good faith as to such price. Section 6662(e) was amended effective for tax years beginning after 1993, but only for transfer pricing cases. The amendments provide that a taxpayer can avoid the penalty only if it shows that it reasonably determined its transfer prices, contemporaneously documented its transfer pricing determinations, and provided that documentation to the IRS within 30 days of request. Outside of transfer pricing cases, the general reasonable cause or good faith rule still applies (Levey et al. 2002).

The need for globally designed transfer pricing policies and documentation places great demands on MNCs and their advisers to achieve the goal of simultaneously addressing transfer pricing needs in several countries, while at the same time keeping compliance costs within acceptable limits. Those who do will hold a large and justifiable competitive advantage. Development of core global documentation, coupled with tax planning suited to the substance of the MNC's operations, are the key tools that can allow MNCs to harness the new international environment to their advantage (Durst 1999).

In the United States, Section 482 of the IRC was amended in 1986 to promulgate the "super royalty" provisions through the statutory matching-with-income standard. This was in response to ideas that foreign MNCs were not paying their fair share of U.S. tax, and to certain U.S. Tax Court decisions where MNCs were perceived to be allocating most of their income to affiliates in tax haven countries. Since that time, regulatory projects started to define this standard in terms of an arm's-length result, member countries of the OECD simulated these rules in their respective tax regulations, documentation rules became the global norm, and tax audits of an MNC's transfer pricing policy dominated tax controversies among most foreign tax authorities worldwide (Levey 2001).

Recently, the IRS (news release IR-2002-77) and the Pacific Association of Tax Administrators (PATA) announced a joint proposal to simplify transfer pricing documentation. PATA members have agreed on principles under which taxpayers can create uniform transfer pricing documentation so that one set of documentation can meet their respective transfer pricing documentation provisions (PATA documentation package) and thus eliminate the need to prepare different documentation for each country. The PATA documentation package is a voluntary procedure that, if satisfied, will protect taxpayers in each of the four PATA jurisdictions from otherwise applicable transfer pricing documentation penalties. The Tax Executive Committee strongly supported the proposed harmonization changes and encouraged the Service to open dialogues with other international governmental entities to expand simplification efforts (Purcell 2002). A copy of the proposed multilateral transfer pricing documentation requirements may be obtained at the IRS Web site.

The IRS surveyed taxpayers regarding their compliance with the documentation rules of the IRC (Burns 2002). A large number of respondents document more than half of their intercompany business transactions. Only 17 percent of the respondents document fewer than 5 percent of their intracompany transactions. In all size categories except the smallest, a majority of respondents reported increasing the percentage of their tax compliance budgets devoted to transfer pricing issues since 1994. Moreover, larger MNCs were more likely than smaller ones to mention cost as a significant factor in decisions for the noncompliance. Of the respondents who had been subject to a transfer pricing tax audit, a majority timely provided their documentation upon request, but almost one third believed that documentation significantly reduced the time spent resolving transfer pricing issues. In a second survey, a small sample of large MNCs, subject to ongoing tax audit, were reviewed to assess the quality of documentation and its usefulness to auditors. Particularly, two key parts of any transfer pricing analysis— the functional analysis and the explanation of comparables selection— were often deficient in the documentation reviewed. However, the auditors questioned were "virtually unanimous" that documentation simplified the gathering of information needed for their tax audits. These findings may have an effect on tax administrators who are considering imposing new documentation requirements (Ibid.).

PENALTIES OF TRANSFER PRICING

Transfer pricing tax rules of most countries require MNCs to use the arm's-length principle, document all transfer pricing related-party transactions in compliance with tax authorities rules of all countries in which it has operations, and supply information with the documentation that is sufficient to explain completely the reported transfer prices on the tax returns. Otherwise, penalties can be imposed for tax under-payment or a substantial valuation misstatement.

However, if intercompany transfer prices are not according to the arm's-length principle, the taxable income of an MNC is to be adjusted by tax authorities to what it would have been had the parties of interest not been related. In adjusting the transfer prices and other related issues to be according to the arm's-length standard, there are no specific regulations of any tax authority on what transfer pricing method(s) should be used for tax assessment. However, two indicators of the arm's-length price can be used: a market price of the product or service in the open market, or a comparable uncontrolled price of a similar or identical product under similar or identical conditions. If neither such market price is available, nor a comparable uncontrolled price exists, different methods including resale price, cost-plus, or transactional profit methods will be applicable.

Moreover, it is critical that an MNC's documentation show compli-ance with tax authorities' rules of all countries in which it has opera-tions. Without a workable, acceptable, and documented transfer pricing system enabling MNCs to create and convince tax authorities by the right and acceptable transfer pricing method, there would be no way for an MNC to avoid penalties imposed by transfer pricing tax regulations.

Over the past decade, the United States and other countries have greatly increased enforcement efforts for transfer pricing tax regula-tions. For instance, Canada is nearly doubling its staff to increase transfer pricing examinations. Countries such as Australia, Brazil, Japan, France, and several others have put penalties for substantial valuation misstatement of taxable income in place. This enhanced en-forcement greatly increases the likelihood that more than one country will attempt to tax the same income—which means double taxation. In this environment of increased enforcement, MNCs should make all transfer pricing decisions by defending these decisions against the IRS and other tax authorities (Wrappe, Milani, and Joy 1999). None of the other countries specifies fines for transfer pricing adjustments, as such. However, the general penalties for a resulting underpayment of tax may be applicable, as discussed in the next sections.

At the international level, PATA members have agreed on principles under which taxpayers can create uniform transfer pricing documenta-tion so that one set of documentation can meet the need of different countries' transfer pricing documentation rules and thus eliminate the need to prepare different documentation for each country. The PATA documentation package is a voluntary procedure that, if satisfied, will protect taxpayers in each of the four PATA jurisdictions from otherwise applicable transfer pricing documentation penalties (Benson, O'Connor, and Hester 2002).

OECD

The 1995 guidelines provide extensive discussion on the documentation to be obtained from MNCs in connection with a transfer pricing inquiry. The OECD guidelines (1995) suggest that MNCs should make reasonable efforts when establishing their transfer pricing policies to determine whether their transfer pricing results meet the arm's-length standard. The OECD also recognizes that tax authorities should have the right to obtain the documentation to verify compliance with the arm's-length standard. The 1995 guidelines encourage member countries to administer penalty systems in a manner that is fair and not unduly onerous for MNCs (OECD 1995). Thus, U.S. MNCs are not relieved of the need for contemporaneous documentation required under Section 6662(e) to avoid the risk of U.S. transfer pricing penalties.

Canada

Canadian tax regulations may impose penalties of 10 percent of the full amount of the adjustments made in a tax year, but only when the adjustments exceed the lesser of 10 percent of the taxpayer's gross revenue for the year or $5 million Canadian (Felgran and Yamada 2001). According to the Canadian tax regulations, failure to file—or late filing of—the T106 and errors or omissions on it will result in significant penalties: $100 to $2,500 for late filing, depending on the number of days overdue; and $500 per month to a maximum of $12,000 per form for failure to file (this penalty is doubled for failure to comply with a Revenue Canada request) (Zorzi 1999). However, the penalty for a false statement or omission is $24,000. Authorized officers would be well advised to familiarize themselves with the new Canadian transfer pricing rules and requirements in order to ensure that appropriate measures have been taken (Ibid.).

France

In France, if tax authorities consider the MNC's replies on transfer pricing policy inadequate, there will be a risk of the tax authorities evaluating the amount of the transfers on the basis of the information in its possession, as well as imposing a fine of 50,000 French francs (which is equivalent to $6,963) per financial year covered by the tax return (Sporken et al. 2001). Following the OECD guidelines, MNCs are advised to prepare relevant documentation to show that transfer prices are according to the French tax regulations. Penalties between 40 and 80 percent of additional tax may be imposed if a taxpayer acted fraudulently or negligently. Fixed fines of 50,000 French francs may also be imposed just for not complying with regulations (Felgran and Yamada 2001).

Germany

Germany traditionally had the reputation of being an island with southern shores, no transfer pricing documentation penalties, and no clear-cut and aggressive application of profit-oriented approaches. It followed a new tendency at the Federal Tax Court that corporations have an implicit, legally effective requirement to document the adequacy of transfer prices: how far they are at arm's length, the functions and risks taken into account, and any comparables used (Stanley 2001).

In August 2000, the draft documentation rules required taxpayers to prepare a full-blown transfer pricing study in defense of the transfer prices used. A failure of timely compliance with documentation production requests would allegedly permit the tax authorities to invoke the estimation rules. Therefore, the August 2000 judgment stands for the proposition that a taxpayer must produce the relevant documents in its possession, whereas the May 2001 ruling holds that a taxpayer may not be penalized for failure to produce documents that it never created in the first place.

The proposed regulations—in draft form since August 2000—require that transfer pricing documentation following the OECD guidelines be provided at the request of the tax authorities at the time of audit. Although no specific penalties exist under the current legislation, severe penalties, including imprisonment, can be applied in a case of fraud.

The German tax authorities are in the process of revising their transfer pricing rules to better defend Germany's share of tax revenues in a global economy. So far, they have largely worked within the existing statutory framework and in particular have not sought transfer pricing penalty legislation. The volume of transfer pricing regulations recently enacted or proposed is indicative of the intensity of their efforts. The May 2001 interlocutory decision by the Federal Tax Court rejecting transfer pricing documentation requirements, at least outside of special situations such as cost-sharing arrangements, must be regarded as a major setback for the tax authorities. The decision of the Federal Tax Court on the merits in the same litigation will probably be Germany's most important transfer pricing decision in a decade. Depending on its tenor, the tax authorities may be compelled to seek new legislation (Vogele 2001).

If a taxpayer fails to submit the documentation required by the tax rules, German tax authorities may presume that the income derived from these cross-border related-party transactions are underdeclared. This presumption applies not only if the taxpayer fails to submit such information but also if the documents submitted are essentially unfit for the purpose or—as may occur int he case of extraordinary related-party business transactions—were not recorded in time. In these situations, the German tax authorities are entitled to estimate the income derived from such transactions. If income can be estimated only within a certain range, the statute can be fully exploited to the disadvantage of the taxpayer when estimating his income. The burden of proof that the declared income and not the income estimated by the tax authorities was correct will rest with the German resident taxpayer (Birkholz, Brodersen, Ransch, Klein, et al. 2003).

In an MNC or its German subsidiary fails to submit the documentation of it the documentation submitted turns out to be useless for the purpose, according to transfer pricing rules the tax authorities may assess a penalty of from 5 percent to as much as 10 percent of the increase of adjusted income according to the tax rules. In any event, the minimum penalty is 5,000 Euro. In addition, a penalty of up to one million Euro is to be assessed for a delay in submitting the requested documentation, and of at least Euro 100 for each day in excess of the time limit (Ibid.).

Japan

In general, the OECD guidelines have been followed by the National Tax Administration (NTA) in designing Japan's transfer pricing tax regulations. A penalty of 10 percent of the additional tax due may be charged if an adjustment is made, and an additional 5 percent if the additional tax due is more than 500,000 yen or more than the amount of tax paid on the original return, whichever is greater, and an additional 35 percent penalty if a taxpayer is considered to have acted fraudulently. However, Japanese taxpayers are not required to maintain documentation (Felgran and Yamada 2001).

Mexico

If there are disagreements on transfer pricing issues, Mexican tax rules impose considerable penalties. Failure to timely and correctly file the transfer pricing informative tax return creates the possibility that the tax authority will disallow all deductions for payments made to related parties resident outside Mexico. There is also an $8,000 penalty for failure to promptly and correctly file the informative tax return, although this fine is insignificant compared to the potential nondeductibility risk.

In general, Mexican tax rules set forth penalties for taxpayers of between 50 percent and 100 percent of the amount of tax determined to be underpaid by the tax authorities as a result of a tax audit examination. Also, if a determination is made by the tax authorities that the taxpayer's net operating loss as claimed on its corporate income tax return is overstated, the taxpayer will be subject to penalties of up to 30 or 40 percent of the overstated amount. Nevertheless, if a taxpayer has complied with the documentation requirements, the penalties may be reduced by 50 percent, and those penalties related to net operating losses are reduced to between 15 and 20 percent of the overstated amount.

As a result of the 1999 Tax Reform, penalties are no longer restricted to the taxpayer. Under certain circumstances, the auditor who issues the tax report may also be subject to penalties if he or she fails to disclose unpaid taxes resulting in an underpayment greater than 20 percent of taxes withheld or 30 percent of the taxpayer's overall tax liability. Under such circumstances, the auditor faces penalties equal to between 10 and 20 percent of the tax underpaid, but not greater than twice the amount of fees charged by the auditor to issue the tax report.

In addition to the penalties connected to the informative return, penalties are also associated with non–arm's-length pricing standard. If the Mexican tax authority considers that a particular related-party transaction was not carried out at arm's-length standard, thereby diminishing the Mexican company's taxable base, the tax authority would adjust the corresponding income or deductions to reflect its perception of the arm's-length price. Aside from that adjustment, which would be subject to inflation adjustments and surcharges, Mexican tax law contains provisions for an additional penalty of 50 to 100 percent of the omitted tax. However, the penalty would be reduced by half if the Mexican taxpayer maintained contemporaneous transfer pricing documentation (Narvaez-Hasfura and Torrey 2002).

Mexican law further imposes an obligation on taxpayers to prepare, keep, and file the evidentiary documentation with regard to transfer pricing, and that relates to transactions executed with nonresident related parties, to support compliance with the arm's-length standard in such transactions. As such, Mexican taxpayers must maintain contemporaneous transfer pricing documentation and must also file a transfer pricing summary informative return with the Mexican tax authority (Ibid.).

Netherlands

In general, the Dutch tax authorities take the position that a transfer pricing correction always requires a secondary adjustment, in addition to the primary profit adjustment, of at least a capital contribution if the correction was to the benefit of the Dutch company, which may give rise to Dutch capital tax (present rate is 0.55 percent); or a deemed dividend distribution if the correction was at the expense of the Dutch company, which may create a Dutch dividend withholding tax requirement (depending on the [applicability of a] tax treaty). However, the burden of proof in respect to secondary adjustments is on the Dutch tax authorities.

The penalties vary from 0 to 100 percent, depending on the degree of intent to avoid tax or gross negligence of the taxpayer. It should be noted that until today, penalties in respect to transfer pricing have been very rarely applied in respect to a transfer pricing correction. This may change in the future even without a change in the Dutch penalty rules.

The United Kingdom

Under the 1998 Corporation Tax Self-Assessment rules, the Inland Revenue may impose penalties if it determines that the tax return was not prepared in compliance with the arm's-length standard. In such cases, penalties of up to 100 percent of any additional tax can be imposed, and penalties of up to £3,000 can be charged for failure to keep proper records documenting transfer prices (Felgran and Yamada 2001). Due to the fact that MNCs must complete their self-assessment tax returns on the basis that their transfer prices are arm's length, penalties can be charged where a return is made that is not in accordance with the arm's-length principle; it can be shown that the return was submitted fraudulently or negligently by the taxpayer; and U.K. tax is lost as a result.

The Inland Revenue acknowledges that the arm's-length standard is a matter of judgment and there is not always one right answer. The Inland Revenue's guidance advises that where taxpayers show that they have made an honest and reasonable attempt to comply with the legislation, there will be no penalty even if there is an adjustment. The Inland Revenue also advises that there is an obligation on MNCs to do what a reasonable person would do to ensure that their income tax returns are made in accordance with the arm's-length principle. This includes (Sporken et al. 2001):

- using their commercial knowledge and judgment to make arrangements and set prices that comply with the arm's-length standard
- being able to show that they made an honest and reasonable attempt to comply with the arm's-length standard and with the legislation
- seeking professional help where they know they need it

In addition to the tax-geared penalties referred to earlier, penalties of up to £3,000 ($4,364) can be charged for failure to keep proper records. Moreover, the APA legislation provides that tax-geared penalties will apply if a company makes a return that is not in accordance with the terms of the APA, and where false or misleading information was submitted in the course of obtaining the APA. A penalty of up to £10,000 may also be applied where false or misleading information is supplied in connection with an application for an APA (Ibid.). The maximum penalty that may be charged is equal to the tax lost by reason of the offense.

The United States

At the end of the 1980s, the U.S. tax authorities began taking transfer pricing issues more seriously by imposing huge penalties (20 to 40 percent of the tax underpayment caused by transfer pricing issues) and strict record-keeping requirements. Other countries balked at this drastic move, saying that governments should not interfere that far into corporate decision-making. MNCs' decision makers in corporate tax departments quickly determined that if they underpaid the United States, they could be exposed to huge penalties, but if they underpaid other countries, they would not face these consequences.

In the United States, the transfer pricing regulations consider specific penalties for any underpayment attributable to a substantial valuation misstatement pertaining to either a transaction between related parties described in the transfer pricing regulations (the transactional penalty) or a net transfer price adjustment (the net adjustment penalty). The penalty is 20 percent of the underpayment for a substantial valuation misstatement and is increased to 40 percent in the case of a gross valuation misstatement. The transfer pricing penalty is not imposed, however, on any portion of the penalty base attributable to transactions for which the MNC or taxpayer shows reasonable cause and good faith in setting its transfer prices.

Unfortunately, the uncertainty created by the arm's-length standard often benefits a country that has a relatively sophisticated and more aggressive tax administration. In fact, aggressive U.S. transfer pricing practices often hurt opposing governments. The result is a troubling erosion of the tax base of weaker countries. In practice, MNCs would be more willing to enter into APAs with a dominant tax administration in order to avoid onerous penalties or adverse transfer pricing adjustments. The IRS-U.S. is perhaps the most aggressive tax administration in the world (Li 2002.)

SUMMARY AND CONCLUSIONS

This chapter examined, analyzed, and discussed two of the most important transfer pricing issues: documentation and penalties of selected countries. Documentation requirements are not limited to the United States. All selected eight countries require taxpayers to document related-party transfer pricing transactions; however, half of them—Canada, Mexico, the United Kingdom, and the United States—have formal specific documentation regulations of transfer pricing, as can be seen from Table 10.1. The other four countries either do not have formal rules for documentation or try to adhere to the OECD guidelines. In France, transfer pricing documentation is required only if the tax authorities have gathered evidence giving rise to a violation of transfer pricing tax rules. Germany has no legal basis for field tax officers to ask for special transfer pricing documentation. Japan has adhered generally to the OECD guidelines of documentation. The Dutch tax authorities require taxpayers to have available sufficient information in their administration to indicate how the transfer prices were established and from which it can be determined whether the prices satisfy the arm's-length standard.

It is critical that an MNC's documentation show compliance with both U.S. and foreign transfer pricing tax rules. Without a well-designed and workable transfer pricing system enabling MNCs to create and receive the right transfer pricing data, there would be no way for a multinational to avoid penalties imposed by tax authorities. It is very important for MNCs to note that transfer pricing tax rules in France, Mexico, Netherlands, and the United Kingdom may impose penalties up to 100 percent of the amount of tax determined to be underpaid by tax authorities as a result of a tax audit examination or if taxpayers acted fraudulently or negligently. However, for any related-party transfer pricing fraud or substantial valuation misstatement, Canada imposes

TABLE 10.1 Transfer Pricing Tax Issues of Selected Countries

Transfer Pricing Tax Issues/Countries	Follow OECD Guidelines	Arm's-Length Standard	Formal Documentation	Transfer Pricing Penalties
Canada	Yes	Yes	Yes	10%
France	Yes	No	No	40% to 80%
Germany	Yes	No	Yes	5% to 10% for a minimum of 5000 Euro
Japan	Yes	No	No	10%, +5% for >500,000 yen, 35% for fraud
Mexico	Yes	No	Yes	30% to 40%, 50% to 100% after audit examination
Netherlands	Yes	Yes with ranges	No	0% to 100%
United Kingdom	Yes	Yes	Yes	Up to 100%
United States	No	Yes	Yes	20% to 40%

penalties of 10 percent, Japan up to 35 percent, and the United States between 20 and 40 percent. Germany is the only one of the eight countries that does not specify the penalty rates for violations of transfer pricing tax rules.

At the international level, the United States and the Pacific Association of Tax Administrators (PATA), including Australia, Canada, and Japan as its members, issued a proposal to harmonize transfer pricing documentation requirements. PATA members have agreed on principles under which taxpayers can create uniform transfer pricing documentation so that one set of documentation can meet their respective transfer pricing documentation provisions (PATA documentation package) and thus eliminate the need to prepare different documentation for each country. The PATA documentation package is a voluntary procedure that, if satisfied, will protect taxpayers in each of the four PATA jurisdictions from otherwise applicable transfer pricing documentation penalties. The objectives of the proposal are to reduce transfer pricing compliance costs and burdens; to promote the efficient and equitable operation of the tax systems; to facilitate the efficient preparation and maintenance of transfer pricing documentation, thereby enabling the timely production of such information upon request by tax auditors; to develop a uniform, multilateral guidance for taxpayers and tax administrators; and to create and maintain a single package of transfer pricing records and documentation in order to satisfy the transfer pricing documentation of all PATA members.

In general, specific areas in the PATA documentation package should be addressed here, including the inability of MNCs to comply with all the principles discussed in the package, the open-ended list of documentation required, and the difficulty of subsidiaries' producing a worldwide group structure. First of all, the PATA should coordinate its proposal with the OECD guidelines related to uniform and consistent multilateral guidance in respect to transfer pricing rules, documentation requirements, and penalty standards. Second, the development of cost-effective standards that MNCs can comply with will, as with the OECD's efforts, require a careful balance among the needs of MNCs and tax administrators, especially because MNCs would be reluctant to support more burdensome multilateral requirements than those imposed by the countries with which they are required to comply.

Finally, the scope and amount of information required, under the PATA documentation package, to be produced and maintained is more detailed and extensive than that required under either section 6662 of the U.S. or section 247 of the Canadian transfer pricing tax rules. Thus, in resolving a transfer pricing tax issue involving controlled third-party transactions between a U.S. and a Canadian subsidiary of an MNC, the PATA documentation package guidelines may be irrelevant or not applicable in establishing that the taxpayer has undertaken reasonable steps to comply with the arm's-length price, maintained adequate documentation in support of the arm's-length price of its controlled third-party transactions, or whether a documentation penalty should be imposed.

REFERENCES

Abdallah, Wagdy M. 2002. Global transfer pricing of multinationals and e-commerce in the twenty-first century. *Multinational Business Review* 10, no. 2 (fall): 62–71.

Anonymous. 2003. Tightening rules on transfer pricing. *Asian Today International* 21, no. 5 (October/November). 69–70.

Benson, David, Peg O'Connor, and Lilo Hester. 2002. Inside Washington. *International Tax Review* 13, no. 8 (September): 55–60.

Birkholz, Christian, Christian Brodersen, Ulrich Ransch, Sonja Klein, et al. 2003. German tax act. *Journal of International Taxation* 4, no. 8 (August): 24.

Burns, Paul. 2002. US outbound: IRS issues study of documentation practices. *International Tax Review* 13, no. 6 (June): 60.

Durst, Michael C. 1999. United States. *International Tax Review* (London) (February): 56–62.

Ernst & Young. 2003. Newsletter—German Business Center (GBC) Singapore-transfer Pricing Alert. June: www.ey.com/global/download/Singapore.

Felgran, Steven D., and Mito Yamada. 2001. Transfer pricing: A truly global concern. *Financial Executive* (Morristown, N.J.) (November): 21–27.

Levey, Marc M. 2001. Transfer pricing—What's next? *International Tax Review* (London) (June): 91–92.

Levey, Marc M., Lawrence W. Shapiro, Robert J. Cunningham, Gregg D. Lemein, and William S. Garofalo. 2002. DHL: Ninth Circuit sheds very little light on bright-line test. *Journal of International Taxation* 13, no. 10 (October): 10–19.

Li, Jinyan. 2002. Global profit split: An evolutionary approach to international income allocation. *Canadian Tax Journal* 50 (3): 823–27.

Lyons, John, and Albertina M. Fernandez. 2002. Why the PATA proposal increases the compliance burden. *International Tax Review* 13, no. 9 (October): 26–29.

Miesel, Victor H., Harlow H. Higinbotham, and Chun W. Yi. 2002. International transfer pricing: Practical solutions for intercompany pricing. *The International Tax Journal* 28, no. 4 (fall): 1–22.

Narvaez-Hasfura, Jorge, and Eric Torrey. 2002. Mexican transfer pricing under the microscope. *International Tax Review* 13, no. 7 (July/August): 37–38.

Organization for Economic Cooperation and Development Committee (OECD). 1995. *Transfer pricing guidelines for multinational enterprises and tax administrations.* Paris: OECD.

Pacific association of tax administrators' transfer pricing documentation package. 2002. *Tax Executive* 54, no. 5 (September/October): 464–69.

Purcell, Thomas J., III. 2002. TEC initiatives. *The Tax Adviser* 33, no. 11 (November): 732–33.

Rutges, Dave, Eduard Sporken, and Barry Larking. 2002. The arm's-length principle—when the burden of proof shifts. *International Tax Review* 13, no. 8 (September): 51–53.

Schmitz, Annette E., and Gesa Korner. 2000. Recent developments in transfer pricing. *Corporate Finance* Supplement to Germany Meets the Challenges (May): 41–43.

Sporken, Eduard, Alexander Vogele, William Bader, and Pascal Luquete. 2001. Transfer pricing in Europe: OECD versus local practice. *International Tax Review* 12, no. 9 (October): 46–53.

Stanley, Georgina. 2001. Transfer pricing takes center stage. *International Tax Review* 12, no. 9 (October): 25–31.

Swaneveld, Hendrik, Martin Przysuski, Venkat Nagaraian, and Sam Krishna. 2002. Canada targets transfer pricing transgressions. *International Tax Review* 13, no. 3 (March): 27–30.

Valdes, Miguel, William Hahn, and Nicolas Muniz. 1999. Mexico builds on promising start. *International Tax Review* 10, no. 7 (July/August): 53–57.

Vogele, Alexander. 2001. Germany. *International Tax Review,* Supplement, Transfer Pricing Forum 2001, pp. 52–65.

Voegele, Alexander, and Markus Brem. 2003. How to comply with German transfer pricing rules. *International Tax Review* (November): 1–5.

Wrappe, Steven C., Ken Milani, and Julie Joy. 1999. The transfer price is right . . . or is it? *Strategic Finance* (July): 38–43.

Zorzi, Alfred. 1999. No more "wait and see." *CA Magazine* 132, no. 9 (November): 45–46.

Looking Ahead

The Future Global Trend of Transfer Pricing

The purpose of this chapter is twofold: to present a summary of the key factors in transfer pricing tax regulations of different tax authorities and practices of multinational companies to help corporate executive officers design their transfer pricing strategies and defend them when they get hit with transfer pricing tax audits from different tax authorities; and to state general conclusions and guidelines of the future global trends of transfer pricing tax regulations and its effect on multinational companies in designing, planning, and managing their cross-border business transactions, including issues related to e-commerce and intangible assets.

In chapter 1, it was noted that the primary purpose of this book was to provide multinational companies with strategies and ideas to understand and use in designing their transfer pricing systems and to deal with challenging and complicating issues of transfer pricing when their own products or services transferred across the border from one subsidiary located in a country to another subsidiary located in another country. The transfer pricing crisis facing MNCs and tax authorities around the world was covered in chapter 2. Nine different corporate goals of transfer pricing policies were discussed in chapter 3. Transfer pricing methods that are appropriate and acceptable to achieve certain goals of MNCs in managing their foreign operations were reviewed in chapter 4.

Management accounting, including performance evaluation, and transfer pricing strategies were discussed in chapters 5 and 6. E-commerce activities of MNCs and its impact on designing transfer pricing techniques and strategies were discussed in chapter 7. The most related and recent issues of international transfer pricing of intangible assets were covered in chapter 8. Recent international developments and changes in transfer pricing tax regulations and practices with respect to four different pricing issues—arm's-length standard, advance pricing agreement programs, documentation, and penalties—were covered in chapters 9 and 10.

In this last chapter, we take a global approach of designing transfer pricing policies and avoiding the transfer pricing crisis for MNCs in the twenty-first century to summarize the major findings from research on the following issues:

- Corporate goals of international transfer pricing policies
- E-commerce activities and its impact on designing transfer pricing techniques and strategies
- Transfer pricing of intangible assets and the best method rule
- Arm's-length standard
- Advance pricing agreement programs
- Documentation and penalties of transfer pricing systems
- Global trend of transfer pricing in the twenty-first century

MAJOR FINDINGS OF THE RESEARCH

Corporate Goals of International Transfer Pricing Policies

Chapter 3 identified and discussed nine different goals of designing international transfer pricing systems for MNCs' activities. Unfortunately, business literature, especially accounting, does not provide MNCs with any unique technique or model to help them arrive at the appropriate transfer price. Therefore, MNCs are in urgent need for a practical and objective technique or model that can avoid conflicts between different objectives of the system, and at the same time achieve the global goals of MNCs to continue doing their foreign business activities under different economic, political, and social environmental conditions. The nine corporate goals of designing transfer pricing systems can be summarized as follows.

- Reduction of global income tax liability of MNCs is considered as one of the most important goals of establishing transfer pricing systems. International transfer pricing policies are generally set to maximize the after-tax profitability of worldwide business transactions. However, the IRS and tax authorities of other countries are concerned that MNCs could use these transfer prices to shift profits between related parties through cost of goods sold. MNCs often have at their disposal several alternative methods of structuring and financing their foreign investments, arranging transactions between related parties located in different countries, and returning profits to investors in the home country. These alternatives have important tax implications, and there is considerable evidence that tax considerations strongly influence the choices that firms make. International tax avoidance typically entails reallocating taxable income from countries with high tax rates to countries with low tax rates, and may also include changing the timing of income recognition for tax purposes. Many of these methods are quite legal (Hines 1999).

- Tariffs on imports are used as a way of reducing the volume of imports coming into the country and to protect local industries. MNCs use transfer pricing strategies as a way to reduce import or export tariffs and to avoid paying high tariffs to foreign governments, and consequently to reduce their global production costs and maximize their global profits. However, the use of transfer pricing for both reduction of income taxes and tariffs at the same time complicates the transfer pricing system.

- Transfer pricing is one of the best means to be used to minimize foreign exchange losses from currency fluctuations or to shift the losses to another subsidiary by moving assets from one country to another under the floating exchange rates system. This can be done by determining what currency is to be used for payment and whether the buying or selling subsidiary has the foreign exchange risk. If this is done, the appropriate transfer price for foreign activities will have a significant effect on the net exposure of the foreign subsidiary. In this case, funds in weak-currency countries are moved through the use of transfer pricing, especially when the foreign currency is not allowed to move out of the country.

- To avoid a conflict with the host country's government, an MNC should not charge high transfer prices for any goods and services transferred, because high prices mean more cash or fund outflows from the country than cash inflows, which will have a direct impact on the country's balance of payments and consequently on its economy. Therefore, MNCs need to determine what price to charge for their own products manufactured in one country and transferred to another country to achieve reasonable global profits.

- MNCs can control their cash flow in foreign countries through the use of transfer pricing techniques. In cash flow management, the transfer-pricing strategy of MNCs comes into play. For example, if a U.S. corporation has a subsidiary in China and through an IRS examination is required to shift $400 million of income from the

Chinese subsidiary to the U.S. Parent Corporation, there obviously would be major tax and cash flow effects.

- An MNC must help its subsidiaries in their first stages of business in foreign countries. ITP systems can be used to help them in competition against other businesses by charging a low transfer price for goods shipped into those countries to keep these foreign subsidiaries competitive with other local businesses.

- Motivation is considered as one of the objectives of setting an international transfer pricing policy for domestic and foreign subsidiaries. Foreign subsidiary managers need to be motivated to maximize (or increase) their subsidiary's profits and transfer their products or services in and out of their areas of responsibility within the MNC at appropriate transfer prices. Transfer prices, in this case, can be used to motivate foreign subsidiary managers to achieve their subsidiaries' goals (by maximizing their own local profits) and at the same time achieving their MNC's goals (by maximizing the global profits).

- In establishing the right transfer pricing policy, top management would like to motivate foreign subsidiary managers to achieve the subsidiary's goals by contributing toward the achievement of the MNC's goals. It is almost impossible to achieve perfect congruence between foreign subsidiary managers' goals and the MNC's goals. However, at least the ITP policies should not motivate foreign subsidiary managers to make decisions that may be in conflict with the MNC's goals.

Performance Evaluation and Transfer Pricing

In chapter 6, performance evaluation of foreign subsidiary managers and the related issues of transfer pricing systems of MNCs were examined. A model for performance evaluation of foreign subsidiary managers was included. The major issues can be summarized as follows.

- With the fluctuations in foreign exchange rates, assets in weak currencies can be moved through the use of higher transfer prices. However, host-government intervention with or without price controls will certainly limit the MNC's use of this technique. When performance evaluation systems combine with fluctuations in foreign exchange rates, transfer pricing policies will lead to misleading and imperfect financial measures of performance. A transfer pricing system (dollar-indexing technique) was suggested, and it is believed to help in evaluating foreign subsidiary managers' performance and avoid any distorted financial results for performance evaluation.

- It was noted that traditional management accounting techniques are inadequate to appropriately solve these problems, and MNCs are unable to achieve satisfactory and desired levels of performance evaluation. A suggested performance evaluation system for foreign countries was presented to estimate foreign subsidiary managers' relative performance after considering the effects of noncontrollable foreign environmental factors on the measured performance of foreign subsidiaries.
- There are many implications of this proposed model for performance evaluation for foreign subsidiary managers and decision making in allocating the limited resources of MNCs. Certainly, the proposed foreign environmental model is useful for MNCs in designing a system of performance evaluation of subsidiary managers combined with transfer pricing system. The proposed system incorporates the distinction of each foreign environmental factor into its design. Definitely, this new system will lead to improved systems, improved planning, and improved decision-making processes and outcomes.

E-Commerce and Transfer Pricing Systems

In chapter 7, the e-commerce activities of multinational companies and their impact on designing transfer pricing techniques and strategies were examined. The major issues of e-commerce activities and some guidelines for MNCs can be summarized as follows.

- One of the most important issues of e-commerce is whether a traditional permanent establishment concept retains its vitality when business is conducted in cyberspace. To impose tax on e-commerce tangible and intangible transactions, it is important to know whether or not an MNC has created a taxable presence in a country.
- In deciding which one will be an indicator of the permanent establishment (PE) and determining the taxability of the income generated by e-commerce transactions, three important issues were discussed: the Web server (hardware), the Web site (software), and the Internet service provider (ISP). A Web site should be distinguished from the server that hosts the site. A Web-hosting arrangement with an ISP will not create a PE for the Web site owner because an ISP will not be considered an agent of the Web site owner (Merrill 2001). The Web server that is located for a sufficient period of time within a country and is used to carry on part or all of a business may constitute a PE even if no personnel are at that location.

- Given a lack of clear understanding and agreement of tax authorities on taxation of electronic transfer pricing activities, it is not surprising that MNCs will continue facilitating the use of transfer pricing for business-to-business e-commerce transactions, and make them increasingly difficult for governments to detect. Moreover, executive financial officers of MNCs need to deal with the growing trend of formal documentation requirements, the new world of e-commerce will create fresh challenges.
- Given the uncertainty involved in transacting in this virtual economy from a tax perspective, the potential for an Advance Pricing Agreement to resolve taxpayer uncertainty arising from electronic transfer pricing issues in such a rapidly evolving environment may be the best choice for MNCs.
- Two important steps should be taken: Consider the degree of comparability between controlled and uncontrolled e-commerce transactions; and test the arm's-length standard of e-commerce under different transfer pricing methods to determine whether there are significant differences among them and then decide which one will be the most convincing and most acceptable for most tax authorities that are involved.
- There are two keys for MNCs to win the game. The first is to go for an advanced pricing agreement program with the tax authorities of the countries in which they have income tax liability. The second is to make a successful and conceptually coherent presentation of your transfer pricing method of e-commerce to prove compliance with the arm's-length standard. However, MNCs should be aware of the confidentiality issue. In most countries, all information disclosed to tax authorities under the advance pricing agreement program might be available to the public.
- Accountants and CFOs need to prepare an effective TPS supported by documents and need to be ready to meet the IRS or go to the court, if necessary, to successfully present, defend, and win the game of transfer pricing against tax authorities. There are seven strategic steps that accountants and CFOs should consider in winning the game of transfer pricing audit.
    1. Design an effective transfer pricing system of e-commerce by
        a. ensuring technically perfect results by applying the appropriate TPM of e-commerce that satisfy the arm's-length standard.
        b. determining the right goals of the system.
        c. seeking an APA with tax authorities.
        d. having sufficient data of profitability of all joint ventures to use in supporting the system with facts and documents.
    2. Use a global transfer pricing method of e-commerce by

a. deciding to use one of the three methods prescribed by the IRS in Section 482 or any other alternative that may be the best fitted for their e-commerce.
b. considering the degree of comparability between controlled and uncontrolled e-commerce transactions.
c. testing the arm's-length standard under different TPMs of e-commerce.
d. determining whether there are significant differences among them, to specify the expected range resulting from applying different TPMs.
e. deciding which one will be more likely acceptable and most convincing for tax authorities.

3. Allocate income and management fees of e-commerce equally between related and unrelated parties. Most court cases, regulations, and administrative rulings often focus less on close legal analysis and more on reaching equitable results of allocations among related parties.

4. Have sufficient global transfer pricing documentation of e-commerce to support and prove compliance with the arm's-length standard.

5. Make a successful and well-communicated coherent presentation of e-commerce for an audit of the TPS before the IRS and foreign tax authorities, and a clearly understood story to explain the facts that support and prove the MNC's compliance with the arm's-length standard.

6. Ensure the confidentiality of e-commerce and that tax authorities would not disclose confidential information of e-commerce acquired in the course of tax examination to outsiders, except when authorized.

7. Review the transfer pricing system of e-commerce and supporting documentation on a continuous basis to be ready for a transfer-pricing audit by tax authorities. Check what assumptions your company used last time for an acceptable and convincing TPM, and whether the same assumptions are still valid. If there are any changes in the assumptions, the consequences for the company's tax liability should be considered and integrated into the TPS.

Transfer Pricing of Intangible Assets

Chapter 8 introduced, discussed, and analyzed the issues most related to international transfer pricing of intangible assets and e-commerce, including general understanding of the nature of intangible assets of MNCs and the related transfer pricing issues; the new trends in transfer pricing of intangible assets; MNCs' strategies of intangible assets ownership, transfer pricing methods for intangible assets; and designing the right transfer pricing system for intangible assets. The most important issues of transfer pricing of intangible assets and some guidelines for MNCs can be summarized as follows.

- In the strategic planning stage, an MNC's transfer pricing system should be based on certain strategies to manage global earnings appearances throughout the entire value chain of the MNC and the relevant management accounting needs. Rather than use tax to drive the design of a business, this approach ensures that any change to the structure or process of a business is made with the full knowledge of the tax prospects and any administrative risks that they expect. Management can then design strategies based on the true effect on earnings per share (Emmer and Henshall 2002).
- The driving motivation behind developing an effective transfer pricing system is to reinforce the integrated MNC's goal of maximizing total after-tax net income in order to focus on increasing the global value chain profit, rather than dividing the profit among foreign subsidiary units (Miesel, Higinbotham, and Yi 2002).
- Strategic planning for intangibles requires a strong understanding of the environmental conditions in which they will operate. Transfer pricing most often is concerned with the appropriate charge for the right to use an intangible rather than the intangible's absolute value (Emmer and Henshall 2003).
- Incorporate short-run active features within the system for adjusting transfer prices as a function of marketplace environmental variables consistent with the MNC's allocation of resources for managing these variances or risks (Miesel et al. 2003). Rules for adjusting transfer prices in response to external marketplace variables (risk factors) are as critical to a successful transfer pricing system as the initial budget price levels themselves particularly when performance incentives and other management strategies for responding to external risks are interrelated with the transfer pricing system (Ibid.).
- When using intangible assets to reduce taxes, MNCs frequently assign income to special purpose subsidiaries in tax-haven countries. However, most tax regulations require that profit follows the underlying economic value drivers. Tax-induced special purpose subsidiaries are either risky (if they lack economic substance) or complicated to implement (if they require operational change). In a number of cases, moving conventional intangibles across the border does require prohibited high buy-in (transfer pricing) payments. Knowledge intangibles, on the other hand, derive their value from the pooling of fragmented preeminent intangibles that

have little stand-alone value and thus require minimal transfer pricing payments. Therefore, financial executive officers or tax planners of MNCs should identify and pool fragmented knowledge assets tax efficiently (Collardin and Vogele 2002).

- Another important issue is the potential income tax consequences of their operations in high tax rate market countries. The income tax consequences of local operations are usually discussed in terms of whether operation of the intangible or ownership of the computer equipment—server—will create a taxable presence. Where the Web site owner is fiscally resident in a country with a broad income tax treaty network, the issues are usually resolved with reference to the permanent establishment (PE) articles of applicable income tax treaties. Where an income tax treaty does not apply, the issues are resolved with reference to the domestic law of the host country, for example, the less favorable U.S. business standard (Ibid.).

- Another important issue is how to select the best method. Under Section 482 of the U.S. IRC, the selection is based on application of the "best method rule." The transfer pricing method that provides the most reliable and acceptable application of an arm's-length result, taking into account not only the comparability factors but also the availability of reliable information from comparable uncontrolled business transactions and parties, should be used (Warner 2002). In practice, application of the best method rule requires a careful balance in which an MNC selects the appropriate pricing methods, taking into account the business and economic circumstances, the availability and quality of potential comparable business transactions under each method, and the measures of comparable performance (Miesel et al. 2003).

- Under the OECD guidelines, the selection of the best method generally follows the same approach articulated in the U.S. Treasury regulations. In general, there will be one method that is suitable to provide the best estimates of arm's-length price. When no one method is conclusive, the method with "higher degrees of comparability and a more direct, closer relationship to the transaction" (OECD 1995) is preferable. Thus, the comparability and functional analysis are emphasized in the OECD guidelines.

- MNCs might encounter several difficulties in maintaining the effectiveness of their transfer pricing. One major difficulty is due to the fact that the arm's-length principle is based on the separate-entity approach, whereas MNCs are often globally integrated firms. Often, it is through integration that the MNC achieves economies of scale and scope in transaction costs, risk management, technological and other intangible assets, and other functions or risks (Miesel et al. 2003).

- Another difficulty that may obstruct the effective application of the arm's-length principle arises from situations in which MNCs engage in transactions that independent firms would not carry out, such as maintaining a new affiliate at a loss to create a bigger market share; transferring a valuable, closely held technology to a related party foreign subsidiary; or entering into specialized business contracts (Ibid.).
- The effect of financial accounting standards 141 and 142 on the identification and usefulness of comparables in selecting the best transfer pricing method should be considered. These standards introduced major accounting changes and also raise significant direct and indirect income tax issues for MNCs. One consequence of the accounting rule change includes a counterintuitive effective tax rate result under FAS 141 for cross-border acquisitions. U.S. acquirers of foreign objectives may experience higher effective tax rates in their U.S. GAAP financial statements if the objective of the acquisition is to minimize foreign income taxes (Hicks, Benson, and O'Connor 2001). Intercompany transfer prices may need to be reviewed and updated to ensure that they appropriately reflect impairments of indefinite lived intangible assets and that they reflect the carve-out of separately identifiable intangible assets from prior acquisitions, which were previously included in goodwill for financial reporting purposes (Ibid.).
- MNCs should evaluate their transfer pricing policies and base international transfer prices more consistently on competitive and marketplace realities, thereby supporting profit as a meaningful, constructive objective for foreign subsidiaries and affiliates.
- To assist MNCs in expanding their global international business; reducing their global tax liabilities; determining how the functions, risks, and intangible assets of MNCs' global business impact profitability; identifying operational efficiencies and inefficiencies; avoiding transfer pricing tax audits; avoiding serious conflicts and problems with home and/or foreign tax authorities; and improving the structure of management accounting and costing systems, any of the following strategic objective and practical actions would be a wise action to be used.

    1. Perform a diagnostic transfer pricing audit to discover any problematic areas in MNCs' transfer pricing systems and to minimize the risk that the examination will identify unexpected transfer pricing problems.

    2. Analyze current and planned cross-border business transactions of both tangible and intangible assets to identify transfer pricing issues and risks.

3. Develop and document the steps you follow to determine your transfer prices and contemporaneous documentation to assure compliance with government requirements and to identify ways to reduce taxes.

4. Identify all key areas of advance transfer pricing agreements with both parties to establish all the facts and circumstances regarding the activities, risks, and intangibles involved in the transaction and to select the best transfer pricing methodology.

5. Identify arm's-length comparable companies to determine the appropriate price for similar circumstances and similar transactions.

6. Prepare an Advance Pricing Agreement framework for MNCs that anticipate transfer pricing problems with home and foreign tax authorities.

Arm's-Length Standards and Advance Pricing Agreement Programs

Chapter 9 discussed and analyzed recent international developments and changes in tax regulations and practices of transfer pricing legislation with respect to arm's-length standards and advance pricing agreement programs in selected countries. The major issues and some guidelines for MNCs are summarized here.

- Tax authorities around the world require that prices charged for goods and services between related parties be consistent with the amount that would have been charged if the uncontrolled taxpayers had engaged in the same transaction under the same conditions or circumstances. Many foreign tax authorities, especially in most industrialized countries, have followed the lead of the IRS-U.S. as a model, adopting and enforcing similar arm's-length standards for transfer pricing by means of documentation requirements with penalties for noncompliance (Felgran and Yamada 2001). It should be noted that although all foreign tax authorities of the countries covered seek to adhere to the OECD guidelines in implementing these, major differences in transfer pricing policies and regulations arise.
- MNCs may have difficulties proving that the transfer price was equal to the market price; therefore, they often find themselves in disputes with tax authorities. The Advance Pricing Agreement (APA) program gives MNCs an opportunity to avoid costly audits and litigation by allowing them to negotiate in advance with tax authorities regarding the facts, the transfer pricing methodology, and an acceptable range of results. The United States was the first

country to adopt substantial penalties relating to transfer pricing and to require that companies maintain detailed documentation of their transfer pricing systems.

- Canada, France, Germany, Japan, Mexico, Netherlands, and the United Kingdom seek to adhere to the OECD guidelines. Until recently, these countries had worked largely within the existing statutory framework. However, in 1998, Canada tried to blend its transfer pricing legislation with the 1995 OECD guidelines.
- France strengthened its tax authorities' powers in 1996 and imposed new obligations on taxpayers. The United Kingdom implemented specific transfer pricing legislation in 1998/99 and fully incorporated OECD guidelines into the U.K. legislation. Netherlands issued a transfer pricing decree in March 2001 based on the arm's-length principle and OECD guidelines. In Germany many transfer pricing regulations have and will be introduced. Whereas the U.K. legislation makes a specific reference to the OECD, and so will the Dutch legislation in the near future, France and Germany, do not. France, Germany, and the United Kingdom in particular have chosen to make their own specific transfer pricing tax rules. Netherlands at present still has the least in terms of transfer pricing rules, but this will change in the near future. The Dutch ministry would like to keep the transfer pricing system open and flexible, but it is still to be seen as to whether this will be the case in practice (Sporken et al. 2001).
- The tax authorities in France, Germany, Japan, Netherlands, Mexico, and the United Kingdom are all in the process of modernizing their country's transfer pricing machinery to adhere to the OECD guidelines and better defend their share of tax revenues in both a European and global economy. This process will not necessarily be for the benefit of MNCs, as they will face ever-increasing transfer pricing compliance burdens and difficulties to prove that the transfer price was equal to the market price; therefore, they often find themselves in disputes with several tax authorities.
- In the near future, the number of transfer pricing disputes and court cases will be significantly increased. However, the APA programs with tax authorities will give MNCs an opportunity to avoid costly tax audits and litigation by allowing them to negotiate in advance with tax authorities regarding the facts, the transfer pricing methodology, and the acceptance range of results, and, then, the number of APAs will further increase significantly.

Documentation and Penalties of Transfer Pricing Systems

In chapter 10, documentation of transfer pricing and penalties imposed by tax authorities of selected countries for noncompliance with tax rules were examined. The major issues can be summarized as follows.

- Documentation of transfer pricing has become an important issue, as MNCs need to justify that their transfer pricing methods are consistent with the arm's-length standard. For MNCs, documentation of transfer pricing is often considered as just an annoying aspect of tax compliance to be accomplished with as little effort and attention as possible. Tax authorities' requirements that taxpayers maintain documentation of their transfer pricing methods appear to be spreading fast.
- Transfer pricing tax rules of most countries require MNCs to use the arm's-length principle, document all transfer pricing related-party transactions in compliance with tax authorities rules, and supply information with the documentation that is sufficient to explain completely the reported transfer prices on the tax returns. Otherwise, penalties can be imposed for tax underpayment or a substantial valuation misstatement.
- If intercompany transfer prices are not according to the arm's-length principle, the taxable income of an MNC is to be adjusted by tax authorities to what it would have been had the parties of interest not been related. In adjusting the transfer prices and other related issues to be according to the arm's-length standard, there are no specific regulations of any tax authority on what transfer pricing method(s) should be used for tax assessment.
- The United States and the Pacific Association of Tax Administrators (PATA), including Australia, Canada, and Japan as its members, issued a proposal to harmonize transfer pricing documentation requirements. The objectives of the proposal are to reduce transfer pricing compliance costs and burdens; to promote the efficient and equitable operation of the tax systems; to facilitate the efficient preparation and maintenance of transfer pricing documentation, thereby enabling the timely production of such information upon request by tax auditors; to develop a uniform, multilateral guidance for taxpayers and tax administrators; and to create and maintain a single package of transfer pricing records and documentation in order to satisfy the transfer pricing documentation of all PATA members.
- Specific areas in the PATA documentation package were addressed, including the inability of MNCs to comply with all the principles discussed in the package, the open-ended list of documentation required, and the difficulty of subsidiaries producing a worldwide group structure. First of all, the PATA should coordinate its proposal with the OECD guidelines related to uniform and

consistent multilateral guidance in respect of transfer pricing rules, documentation requirements, and penalty standards. Second, the development of cost-effective standards that MNCs can comply with will, as with the OECD's efforts, require a careful balance among the needs of MNCs and tax administrators, especially because MNCs would be reluctant to support more burdensome multilateral requirements than those imposed by the countries with which they are required to comply.

- The scope and amount of information required, under the PATA documentation package, to be produced and maintained are more detailed and extensive than that required under either section 6662 of the U.S. or section 247 of the Canadian transfer pricing tax rules.

Global Trend of Transfer Pricing in the Twenty-first Century

In the twenty-first century, fast technological innovation, including e-commerce, is having a considerable effect on the way MNCs conduct their cross-border business transactions. Consequently, MNCs have changed their ways of conducting global business from the traditional country-by-country basis to the implementation of new global business models, such as e-commerce and shared services or intangible assets. To be successful in managing their global business operations, MNCs should implement the following recommendations in updating and reviewing their transfer pricing systems in the twenty-first century.

- MNCs need to make fundamental changes in their transfer pricing business model to meet the new challenges in the global competitive market. This will provide MNCs an ideal opportunity to review and update the transfer pricing system and the tax strategy of the group.
- MNCs need to engage in transfer pricing strategy by integrating their business with their suppliers and customers, regardless of the geographic locations concerned with the activity to reduce their global tax liability and simplify their transfer pricing system.
- Several potential advantages may be gained by MNCs by combining changes in their operating environment with tax-efficient strategies.
- An Advance Pricing Agreement program may be the best and the only open option for MNCs to reduce their uncertainty arising from transfer pricing disputes with several tax authorities in such a rapidly evolving global environment.
- A global transfer pricing system should be based on certain strategies to manage global earnings appearances throughout the entire

value chain of the MNC and the relevant management accounting needs to ensure that any change to the process of a business is made with the full knowledge of the tax consequences and any administrative risks that they report.

- In developing an effective transfer pricing system for intangible assets, the driving motivation should be reinforcement of the integrated MNC's objective of maximizing global after-tax net income in order to focus on increasing the global value chain profit.
- Short-run active features should be incorporated within the system for updating and adjusting transfer prices as a function of marketplace environmental factors consistent with the MNC's allocation of resources for managing these variances.
- To select the best transfer pricing method, MNCs should analyze transfer prices in accordance with the most reliable estimate of the arm's-length standard under the facts and circumstances of the case.

REFERENCES

Collardin, Marcus, and Alexander Vogele. 2002. Knowledge intangibles—leveraging the tax advantages. *International Tax Review* 13, no. 7 (July/August): 59–61.

Emmer, Maurice, and John Henshall. 2002. Building and maintaining brand value. *International Tax Review,* Supplement, Industry Guide: Financial Services (July): 41–46.

Felgran, Steven D., and Mito Yamada. 2001. Transfer pricing: A truly global concern. *Financial Executive* (November): 21–27.

Hicks, Hall, David Benson, and Margaret O'Connor. 2001. U.S. revitalizes its treaty network. *International Journal Review* 12, no. 10 (November): 48–52.

Hines, J. R., Jr. 1999. Lessons from behavioral responses to international taxation. *National Tax Journal* (June) 305–22.

Merrill, P. R. 2001. International tax of e-commerce. *The CPA Journal* (November): 30–45.

Miesel, Victor H., Harlow H. Higinbotham, and Chun W Yi. 2002. International transfer pricing: Practical solutions for intercompany pricing. *The International Tax Journal* 28, no. 4 (fall): 1–22.

Miesel, Victor H., Harlow H. Higinbotham, and Chun W Yi. 2003. International transfer pricing: Practical solutions for intercompany pricing—part II. *The International Tax Journal* 29, no. 1 (winter): 1–40.

Organization for Economic Cooperation and Development Committee (OECD). 1995. *Transfer pricing guidelines for multinational enterprises and tax administrations.* Paris: OECD.

Sporken, Eduard, Alexander Vogele, William Bader, and Pascal Luquete. 2001. Transfer pricing in Europe: OECD versus local practice. *International Tax Review* 12, no. 9 (October): 46–53.

Warner, John P. 2002. Taxing interbranch dealings: Application of separate taxpayer arm's-length principles to inbound interbranch distribution dealings. *Tax Management International Journal* 31, no. 3 (March 8): 155–70.

Index

About the Author

WAGDY M. ABDALLAH is associate professor of accounting at Seton Hall University, where he specializes in international accounting and various aspects of doing business in the Middle East. He is the author of the Greenwood titles *International Transfer Pricing Policies* (1989) and *Managing Multinationals in the Middle East* (2000).

CPSIA information can be obtained
at www.ICGtesting.com
Printed in the USA
JSHW022322290821
18216JS00001BA/1